DYING
TO FLY

DYING TO FLY

THE HUMAN COST OF MILITARY FLYING

EAST MIDLANDS

ALASTAIR GOODRUM

First published 2010

The History Press
The Mill, Brimscombe Port
Stroud, Gloucestershire, GL5 2QG
www.thehistorypress.co.uk

British Library Cataloguing in Publication Data.
A catalogue record for this book is available from the British Library.

ISBN 978 0 7524 5302 6
Typesetting and origination by The History Press
Printed in Great Britain

CONTENTS

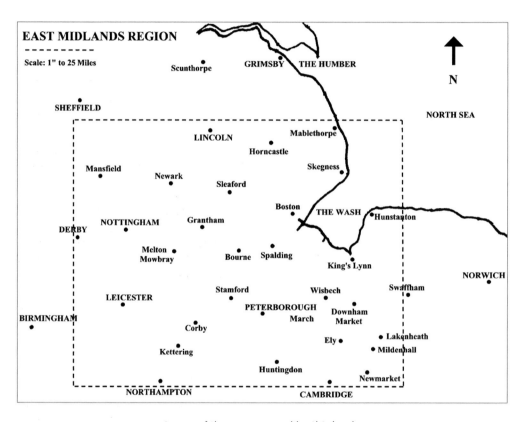

A map of the area covered by this book.

INTRODUCTION

Danger and excitement, courage and selflessness, and life and death are the heady ingredients of the lethal cocktail that is military flying. Whether in peacetime or war, the sky above the East Midlands region has an association with military flying as long as the history of flying itself.

While now it echoes daily to the roar of RAF and US fast jets, since the days of faltering flights that brought about the RFC and the RNAS in 1912 – through the *Biggles* biplane days of the First World War and the inter-war period – through dangerous operations during the Second World War – to the post-war jets that became Britain's defence from the start of the Cold War era to the era of the Falklands – it is without doubt the place where flyers of past eras have most continuously plied their trade. Even now the intensity of military flying activity in the region continues undiminished, as the RAF and its allies train for Afghanistan, Iraq and other duties in the service of their countries.

For almost a century, then, airmen of many different nationalities and from all walks of life – some fresh out of school, some men who came from the region itself and those who came to it from all corners of the world – took to the air not only to uphold the peace and practise for war, but also to begin or end hazardous operational flights in its skies. It is clear that the region has a strong connection with the very birth of the RAF and equally clear how, from the beginning, aerial mishaps became an every-day occupational hazard.

This book contains diverse, exciting and often harrowing, stories behind military aeroplane accidents in peace and war that occurred in the region. By no means all the incidents that have been traced in the region are detailed here, but these accounts will nonetheless illustrate how Fate or Luck or Providence is always on hand to decide who will walk away and who will be unfortunate enough not to live to fight another day; it does not apportion blame. In peacetime, some incidents might be reported with bare facts and perhaps a name, beneath a garish headline. In the maelstrom of war, though, it was usually an unsung passing, lamented by families and loved ones but with their exploits and individual contributions unknown to, or forgotten by, the outside world.

Nevertheless, behind every incident there are human beings and *Dying To Fly* brings their courage and human-interest stories into the light of day in a way that will appeal to a wide audience. This book ensures the airmen involved cease simply to be names carved on a cold memorial stone or stark entries in some dusty filing system. They have faces and first names; they have personal backgrounds and they have patriotic or duty reasons for being where they were when tragedy struck. Equally important is the way in which the narrative takes the reader along a clear time-line to show how the events described fit into the pattern of military flying in Britain during the past century and to illustrate the human price that was paid in order to fly along that path.

Hundreds of airmen have left their mark – literally – on the landscape and seascape of this region. *Dying To Fly* remembers them and pays tribute to their passing.

ACKNOWLEDGEMENTS

I would like to thank:

Mike Bennett for his help and information from his Ejection History Web Project
Roy Bonser
Martin W. Bowman, for his assistance with extracts and images from his book *The Wellington* for Sergeant Petts' story
Derek and Pam Brown kindly for allowing me access to material about Flight Sergeant Leslie Chapman CGM
Jonathan Falconer
Paul Garland for his help with RAF Feltwell matters
Greg Gregson, Bomber Command Wireless Operator/Air-Gunner, for his contribution on the BC website
Terry Hancock
Tony Hancock, for his particular help with sourcing images
Mike Hodgson
Leslie Holland
Chris Howard
Chris Howlett
Martin Jeffery
Gary Jucha for his help with the Tinwell tragedy story
G. Stuart Leslie
Ian MacLachlan for his generous help with the Prickwillow collision story
Brian Martin
Michael T. Melnick (RCAF)
Rick Miller
Gary Moncur and the 303BG (USAAF) Association
Simon Parry
Pascal (Pat) Powell (deceased) and Syd Solomon (USA) for their *Inside Curve* memories
Bob Reid and members of the Aircrew Association (South Lincolnshire Branch)
Millie Seitz (Canada)
Clive Semple for assistance with photographs and permission to quote from his father's diary
Rod Smith, a Canadian pilot with 412 Squadron in the Second World War, for his recollections of the Magee and Charlesworth collisions
Dave Stubley, Ian Blackamore and the Lincolnshire Aviation Recovery Group
Pavel Vancata for his help and permission to use extracts from his article *The Last Flight of Anson R9649*, published in the Czech language aviation magazine *REVI* No.68 in 2007
Bill Welbourne and the Fenland & West Norfolk Aircraft Preservation Society
Ray Wilson (deceased)

Norman Wright for permission to use material from the reprinted biography of W. E. Johns

452nd AMW Public Affairs, March Air Reserve Base for information from articles by Senior Master Sergeant Matt Proietti about the 452BG

Air Mobility Command Museum for information about Tactical Carrier groups in the Second World War

My thanks also to editor Amy Rigg and the team at The History Press. And I apologise in advance to anyone else I have overlooked. I thank you all.

Chapter 1

FIRST WORLD WAR & INTER-WAR
RFC, RNAS & RAF Accidents

FIRST WORLD WAR: FROM FLEDGLINGS TO HAWKS

Lieutenant Leonard Dawes, Middlesex Regiment and Royal Flying Corps, was a native of Long Sutton in Lincolnshire and in 1913 caused quite a stir when, at the controls of his BE2a biplane, he dropped in unexpectedly one day for tea and a hot bath! Regarded locally as something akin to a superman, Leonard was in fact one of the very first intrepid birdmen of the Royal Flying Corps and his 'visit', being the result of an engine failure, introduces the fragility of flying that will unfold in this story during the remainder of the twentieth century.

Being in its infancy, initially all of the pilots joining the recently created RFC were products of civilian flying schools and in Dawes' case, he learned to fly at his own expense at the Bristol Aeroplane Company's school at Larkhill on Salisbury Plain while still serving in the army. Leonard Dawes, therefore, is a prime example of the approach to military flying being taken at that time in the history of British aviation and in his own way, played a small but valuable part in the foundation of military flying in Great Britain.

Having completed a few hours' training on Bristol Boxkite No.55 (Bristol's own number), Leonard was awarded his Royal Aero Club aviator's certificate, number 228, in June 1912, which entitled him to fly solo after a series of flying tests in the process known as 'receiving his brevet' or 'getting one's ticket'. Little is known about his early days in the Flying Corps, but there is photographic evidence to show he was one of the first airmen to receive 'service flying training' at the Central Flying School. It is therefore reasonable to assume that Leonard formally transferred from the army to the RFC in June. CFS No.1 course, of which he was a member, ended on 5 December 1912. Leonard must have

Lieutenant Leonard Dawes, Middlesex Regiment and Royal Flying Corps. Born in Long Sutton, Lincs. An original member of No.2 Squadron and first Officer Commanding No.29 Squadron.

completed it satisfactorily because he came to prominence, in the context of this story, not only as a native of the East Midlands, but also as a result of his participation in the formative years of No.2 Squadron, which he appears to have reached before the end of December 1912 and which now acts as a starting point for the rest of this story.

Just to the north of the Tay Estuary, Montrose Airfield in Scotland was, in 1913, home to No.2 Squadron having having moved from Farnborough, where it originally formed in 1912, in the RFC's first major redeployment exercise. Due to a high rate of attrition while operating from Montrose, four pilots were ordered to collect a replacement aeroplane each from the Royal Aircraft Factory at Farnborough and make their way back to Montrose. Lieutenant Dawes picked up aeroplane BE2a, service number 267, on Thursday 20 October 1913 and headed northwards. Aeroplane 267 was previously on charge to No.3 Squadron in March 1913, but had been wrecked a month later. Now, having been repaired by the Royal Aircraft Factory, it was reallocated to No.2 Squadron.

First port of call for Lieutenant Dawes was Tydd St Mary landing ground on the Lincolnshire/Cambridgeshire border near Sutton Bridge, where he landed to replenish his petrol and oil. The actual field was near the North Level Drain and belonged to Mr T.W. Maxey. Insufficient petrol was available so Lieutenant Dawes stayed near the field overnight while further supplies were brought to him. Word spread like wildfire and despite this being a sparsely populated area, a large crowd gathered to see him set off for Montrose at 9.00a.m., aiming, he said, to reach Berwick-on-Tweed by nightfall. It was not to be, though, as a fog had come down and delayed his departure until noon. When the fog cleared, Dawes swung the prop, climbed aboard and took off. In recognition of the crowd and indeed his own parents, Mr and Mrs Edwin Dawes, who had motored over from Long Sutton just to see his departure, he made a circuit of the field at 600ft before climbing away to about 2,000ft.

No.2 Squadron pilots in 1913. Back row from left: Lieutenants Harvey Kelly; Empson; Corballis; Noel; Rodwell; Mastyn. Front row from left: Captain Todd; Captain G. Dawes; Major Burke (CO); Captain Waldron; Lieutenant Leonard Dawes.

By 12.45p.m. he was nearing his home town of Long Sutton, and less than five minutes after the clatter of his engine was heard and the aeroplane seen to be descending near the railway station, the town market place was empty. Everyone – townsfolk, traders, shop assistants and solicitors alike – rushed headlong to see their hero. '[They] joined in the human stream until it gave one the impression of a cinematograph chase rather than real, live Long Sutton!' reported the local paper. Lieutenant Dawes had landed in Mr H.M. Proctor's field, where the machine was quickly surrounded by a couple of hundred people. He called upon the services of the local constabulary to rope off and guard this wonder of the age, while he was driven to his old home by the churchyard to indulge in a bath and a spot of lunch.

Just before 3.00p.m., suitably refreshed, he returned to his aircraft to find the crowd not only swelled by the arrival of many more people but with excited schoolchildren lined up in rows – no doubt absolutely delighted to see this flying machine and to have escaped a dreary classroom in equal measure! As the *Spalding Free Press* put it:

> As the man of the moment wrapped himself in thick warm waterproofs, nothing could repress a cheer, led by an elderly lady who waved her umbrella from her carriage. He then started his 70hp Renault engine himself and climbed into his seat.

As the adoring crowd watched its brave Lieutenant flying northwards, someone cried out, 'He's down again!' Just a couple of miles from his departure point, the Renault engine clattered to an abrupt stop and Leonard Dawes was forced to land at Mr Arthur Holborne's Manor House Farm, near Gedney railway station. Diagnosing the problem as a faulty magneto, Dawes left the aeroplane in the charge of the village bobby while he sent a telegram to Army HQ for a mechanic to come and carry out repairs. In the meantime, what better place to stay than at his parent's home just down the road in Long Sutton, where he was again entertained to a meal, a bath and a comfortable bed.

BE2a, 267 at Long Sutton, Lincs, en route to Montrose, 1913.

In his absence, almost the entire population took this rare opportunity to admire his aerial steed. Several contemporary photographs of this event exist and one of the inquisitive lads was able to identify himself. Then a fourteen-year-old ironmonger's errand boy, Mr Ben Gee vividly remembered the day he 'sneaked off to gawp at Lt Dawes' wonderful machine.' Lieutenant Dawes' sojourn in the Fens came to an end on the Saturday morning when, after a quick local air test, he took to the sky at 11.00a.m., heading for Scotland. Reported as making overnight stops in north Yorkshire – due to another engine failure – and Berwick, he eventually reached Montrose, a distance of about 450 miles, almost a week after leaving Farnborough.

Posted to France on outbreak of the First World War, Leonard Dawes continued to fly BE2s – but not 267, which was relegated to a training role in England – with No.2 Squadron. He distinguished himself in August 1914, at least in the eyes of the French Army. On a reconnaissance flight, during which he exchanged rifle shots with a German *Taube* aeroplane, he was one of a number of aeroplanes that spotted von Kluck's German 1st Army as it made its unexpected advance in the vicinity of Le Cateau. 'For gallantry during the operations between 21st and 30th August, 1914' the French government awarded Dawes a *Croix de Chevalier de la Légion d'Honneur* medal (*London Gazette,* 3 November 1914).

Leonard had more adventures on the Western Front, before returning to England to form a new squadron: No.29. He survived the war and eventually found his way back to rural Long Sutton around 1930 to take over management of the family wines and spirits business. In the twenty-first century, No.29 Squadron – equipped now with the Typhoon jet – still exists as a fighter squadron within that Royal Air Force which Leonard Dawes helped to establish nearly a century ago, and as a man with roots in the East Midlands, his story provides us with a starting point for more tales of the fragility of flight and the daring and bravery, fortitude and tragedy of the men who came after him.

In what was to become one of the acts precipitating the First World War, Archduke Franz Ferdinand of Austria was assassinated at Sarajevo on 28 June 1914. During those final, tense, weeks between that apocryphal event and 4 August, when Britain declared war on Germany, the RFC and RNAS – the RFC's Naval Wing was reorganised as a separate entity, the Royal Naval Air Service, on 1 July 1914 – were making preparations for war.

Aeroplanes from the principal RNAS base at Eastchurch on the Isle of Sheppey, having flown air defence exercises that month and a fly-past for the *Naval Fleet Review* of 22 July, were ordered to disperse around the UK coast, thus combining further training with a prestige tour. With the European situation deteriorating, however, these aircraft were recalled to Eastchurch at the end of the month.

One of their number, a Bristol TB8, service number 43, met with a mishap on its outward cross-country flight from Eastchurch to RNAS station Immingham, on the Humber. Lieutenant E.T.N. Clare RN, with Chief Mechanic Roberts as passenger, were obliged to make a forced landing at Kirton Skeldyke near Boston on 28 July due to engine failure. In a rather bumpy landing in Mr Bowser's grass field close to the sea bank, damage was caused to some wing strut wires but both airmen emerged unscathed. It was not long before that desolate spot, in time-honoured fashion, was crowded with curious farm workers gaping at what, for probably all of them, would be their first sight of one of these new-fangled flying machines. On inspection, Roberts found a broken cylinder ring had caused the motor to seize up. A new engine was sent for, arrived and was fitted the next day, allowing the aeroplane to finish its journey north early the next morning, 30 July. Yet another naval airman caused much excitement on 1 August, when he landed near Willow Hall, Thorney near Peterborough, his aeroplane having suffered magneto trouble en route to Eastchurch from the north. A few days after this feverish activity, the RFC and RNAS went to war.

Bristol TB8, RNAS No.43, force-landed, Kirton Skeldyke, August 1914. (Care of Chris Howard)

The first evidence of the impact of war to be noticed by the local population was the passage of aeroplanes over south Lincolnshire during the first week of hostilities. All this flying activity was part of the deployment of an RNAS 'mobile force' that patrolled the North Sea coast on anti-Zeppelin duties.

On 9 August, five aeroplanes flying north caused quite a stir near Long Sutton at various times during the day. One of these, BE2a No.50, a naval machine piloted by Lieutenant Merricks with a mechanic on board, landed in Mr Bates' field in Hospital Drove due to shortage of petrol. As might be expected, a large crowd soon gathered and full courtesy was extended to these knights of the sky. A local man drove his car into Long Sutton to fetch a supply of petrol and with lusty cheers from the throng ringing in their ears, the two airmen were soon able to resume their journey to Immingham and Newcastle.

Engine failure was an all too common occurrence in those days, and caused the demise of Sopwith Admiralty Type 880 seaplane, No.898, on 27 October 1914. On patrol from RNAS station Great Yarmouth, its Monosoupape rotary engine failed over The Wash and the aeroplane force landed on its uninviting waters. The pilot, Flight Sub-Lieutenant J.P. Wilson was unhurt, and having been rescued by the crew of the Hunstanton lifeboat, spent a night in the town as the guest of its coxswain, Mr Riches. The seaplane survived being towed to shore, but overnight broke adrift from its moorings and was completely wrecked. During the remainder of 1914, routine air patrol activity across the region continued along these lines but there was little by way of action.

In January 1915, however, the German Kaiser, Wilhelm II, authorised his Imperial Navy – responsible for operating part of the German airship (*Luftschiff*) force – to mount air raids on Britain. The RFC and RNAS lost several aeroplanes and some aircrew lives carrying out abortive anti-Zeppelin patrols in bad weather and in the wrong places. It was a fiasco

BE2a, RFC No.50, force-landed at Long Sutton, Lincs, due to shortage of petrol, 1914.

for the defenders, precipitating a major reorganisation of the Home Air Defences (HD) in forthcoming months. Progress was, however, painfully slow and not without its share of mishaps, too.

By 1916, as part of this reorganisation, 51 (HD) Squadron was formed with its HQ flight at Thetford and other flights, including Tydd St Mary (Lincolnshire), Mattishall, Harling Road/Norwich and Marham/Narborough (Norfolk). Most of the Home Defence squadrons created were initially (under!)-equipped, with BE2s of the type flown by Lieutenant Dawes, mentioned at the beginning of this story. However, in mid-1916 the single-seat BE12 and two-seat 'pusher' FE2b were being introduced. No.51 Squadron began with a mix of BE2, BE12 and both single- and two-seater FE2b aeroplanes, eventually standardising around the latter type.

No.38 Squadron had its HQ in Melton Mowbray (Leics) and dispersed its Flights at Stamford/Wittering, Buckminster and Leadenham. A night landing ground was also established at Gosberton Fen, primarily for the use of 38 (HD) Squadron during that unit's period of operations in the region between October 1916 and May 1918, when the landing ground passed into the control of 90 (HD) Squadron headquarters at Buckminster until the end of the war. No.90 Squadron also took over operations at Leadenham. Forming the northern segment of the ring of RFC airfields around The Wash was 33 Squadron, with its HQ initially at Gainsborough and Flights based at Scampton, Kirton-in-Lindsey (later HQ) and Elsham – all names that were to become permanently etched in the history of the RAF.

With the onset of shorter nights as the summer of 1916 wore on, Zeppelin raids decreased in frequency. The as yet untried defending fighters were busy practising to ready themselves for a renewed onslaught, and aeroplane accidents thus began to increase accordingly. Reports of accidents began appearing in the columns of newspapers right across the region around this time, such reports signalling the beginning of what was to become a sad litany on one of the more unhappy aspects of aviation.

New aeroplanes in the hands of new pilots could of course be a recipe for disaster. For example, 16 June 1916 was the date stamped on the maker's plate of one that came to grief on 23 June, near Shippea Hill railway station – coincidentally the scene of an horrific US aeroplane crash in the Second World War. Telling his rescuers that it was only his third flight, the pilot – an unknown Australian – managed to escape severe injury or even death. By sheer good fortune, his seat strap parted on impact, catapulting him from the aircraft and depositing him shaken but unhurt, some yards away on Messrs Chives and Sons farm. The aeroplane was severely damaged but, after recovering his composure, the pilot returned to his base more sedately, this time by motor car. Impact with Mother Earth was in a wheat field where the machine presented a strange sight, with its propeller partially buried in the ground and the tail pointing to the sky. The aircraft is believed to be from 51 Squadron.

Further indication of the increase in the level of air activity is provided by the *Cambridgeshire Times*, which was moved to comment on this phenomenon. 'Aeroplanes,' it said, 'are becoming such a common sight … now, that few people take but little note of their flight. On Saturday last, for instance, in the afternoon as many as nine machines flew over.' The public was not yet quite as blasé as that newspaper would have its readership believe, since shortly afterwards it reported:

Mind your heads! A BE2c of No.51 Sqn, Tydd St Mary.

On June 26, unusual excitement was caused when an aeroplane alighted in a hayfield at Upwell. It appears that the pilot, meeting with a thunderstorm, lost his bearings and made a landing to establish his whereabouts.

This was eminently sensible of the airman, but he made a botch of his take-off. Possibly due to the field being of small dimensions, the aeroplane, as it seemed to stagger into the air, struck the raised bank of a drain that skirted the field. Performing a neat somersault, ejecting the pilot in the process, it collapsed into a heap. Once again the pilot, unhurt except perhaps for a dent in his pride, was conveyed to nearby Needham Hall from where he telephoned for a recovery party. Word of the mishap spread rapidly and a crowd quickly gathered to survey the wreck. Such was the size of the throng that, coupled with a constant stream of motor vehicles cruising slowly by, local police had to be called out to control the hordes of sightseers! It was all over the next day, when the aeroplane had been dismantled and removed by lorry.

For several months, the region was spared any incursion by the Zeppelin force. Practice sorties, by 51 Squadron, covering the region from the east, supported now by 38 Squadron at Buckminster (Leics), Stamford/Wittering and Leadenham/Sleaford (Lincs) to the west, continued unabated. The latter unit was equipped initially with BE2s, but had been re-equipped with the FE2b by October 1916. Finally, to the north of the region was RNAS Cranwell, which opened for business in April 1916.

Germany had quickly recognised the military potential of lighter-than-air craft, originally as long-range reconnaissance vehicles for its fleet then later as strategic bombers. The British Government, on the other hand, subscribed to the view that heavier-than-air aeroplanes were of more military value in a reconnaissance role than for bombing on the limited scale then envisaged. Aside from the British Army's use of kite, barrage and spherical observation balloons, it was the Admiralty that was eventually to utilise airships, primarily in an anti-submarine role. Early in the First World War, British lighter-than-air craft were of the non-rigid type, although, later, some rigid examples were constructed for the Royal Navy. Examples of such British operations can be found in the history of RNAS Cranwell in Lincolnshire. Construction work was largely completed in 1916 and the site near Cranwell village was opened as a Royal Naval Air Service establishment named HMS *Daedalus*.

Cranwell's primary task was to train service personnel in all types of airmanship, including flying and handling balloons and airships for the Royal Navy. During the second half of 1916, Cranwell became home to examples of the main lighter-than-air type used by the Admiralty in the First World War. These were Submarine Scout (SS) non-rigid airships. Compared to the mighty Zeppelins, examples of which reached over 650ft in length and contained up to 2 million cubic feet of hydrogen gas, these SS types were mere 'tiddlers' at 145ft and 70,000ft^3. The crew were usually carried aloft in a converted aeroplane fuselage, such as BE2c, Maurice Farman or Armstrong Whitworth FK3 types, suspended beneath the envelope, the whole thing being powered by a single 75hp or 100hp Renault, Rolls-Royce or Green engine driving a propeller. One of the first of six SS models to serve at Cranwell was SS39, and it is this particular airship that managed to gain for itself considerable notoriety.

The erection of a portable hangar, in November 1916, to house such airships was the signal for SS39 to make the journey north from London. Its passage across the Fens brought it to the vicinity of Thurlby, near Bourne, on 15 November 1916. First seen hovering over Thurlby Fen, it flew slowly towards the village, getting ever lower until it only just cleared trees and telegraph poles. This alarming situation was caused by a pronounced loss of gas escaping through a broken valve. With its crew unable to check this descent, the sagging airship became uncontrollable, circling roof and chimney tops in the main street until it finally staggered to a halt, firmly locked against a chimney pot near the village school. Bricks, dislodged by the collision, fell into the control gondola, with one actually hitting the head of a crewman. These unfortunates were, however, able to clamber from their precarious perch to *terra firma* whereupon a local doctor tended the injured airman.

Thurlby's main street remained blocked for several hours, during which a strong smell of gas and petrol fumes pervaded the air. Next problem was to fully deflate and recover the craft, a task requiring drastic action in the form of slitting the fabric with knives. Petrol from fuel tanks was allowed to run away down the nearest drain – no environmental issues in those days!

SS39 must have been fated to be a maverick. Having been rebuilt after the Thurlby accident, it came to grief once more when its rigging fouled a tree and caused it to make a forced landing in May 1917. But on 20 July 1917, SS39 finally turned on its masters with dire consequences.

Following an instructional flight, the airship was being 'walked' back into its shed at Cranwell, when a violent up-current of wind pulled SS39 from the hands of her handling party. Nearly all of these men let go. All, that is, except the Officer Commanding, Lieutenant Colonel Clive Waterlow of the Royal Engineers (attached to the RNAS as Wing Commander), Petty Officer Mechanic Maurice Collins, and Airman 2nd Class Simon Lightstone. These three clung to the rope and were swiftly carried aloft to a great height until their arms could no longer stand the strain and they fell to their deaths. SS39 floated back to earth a mile and a half away. Lieutenant Colonel Waterlow is buried in Leasingham village

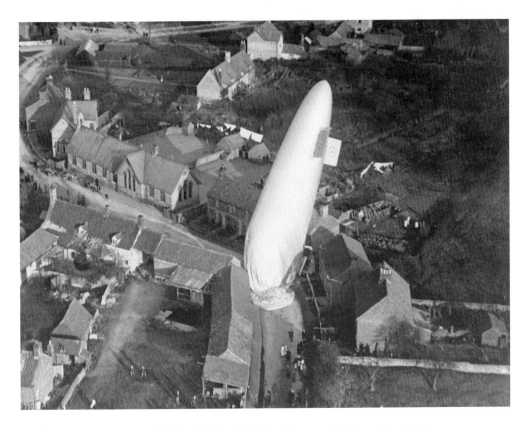

Airship SS39 comes to grief in the middle of Thurlby village on 15 November 1916.

churchyard, a few miles from Cranwell, and the other two victims rest in Cranwell village churchyard. The Admiralty still persisted with this wayward craft as SS39 was later rebuilt as SS39a, but from here on it seems to have led a trouble-free existence – at least until 1919, when it was finally scrapped.

As outlined above, Cranwell's purpose was to train naval officers to fly and operate not only airships and balloons but also aircraft. Officer aircrew destined for aeroplanes were generally posted in from preliminary flying training schools at Chingford, Redcar, Eastbourne and Eastchurch. The final two weeks of Cranwell's advanced aeroplane course was taken at its satellite airfield at Freiston Shore before aircrew were posted to operational squadrons or for other specialist duties.

Soon after HMS *Daedalus* had opened it was decided that it would need a live gunnery and bombing facility for training purposes. An aerial survey of the south Lincolnshire coast was carried out and from this it was decided that the mud flats to the south of the village of Freiston, near Boston was the most suitable site. Thus began an association between air gunnery and The Wash that has lasted to the present day. As the war progressed, there was a need for a growing number of aircrew to be trained in the art of fighting in the air and it was therefore decided to purchase grass fields on the landward side of the bombing range so that a fully functioning aerodrome could be established, thus saving the forty minutes it took to fly to and from Cranwell to the range.

Initially ninety acres (forty hectares) were requisitioned near Freiston Shore at OS map reference TF388408, but this was later extended twice to allow for hangars and accommodation to be built. Being close by The Wash sea bank, the grass airfield was just ten feet above sea level with a take-off and landing area measuring 500yd². Initially it was known as the RNAS Gunnery School, operating as a sub-station to RNAS Cranwell. In September 1917, the airfield began functioning as a joint facility for the RNAS and RFC (later RAF) until its closure in 1920. On the formation of the RAF on 1 April 1918, the resident flying unit became the School of Aerial Fighting & Bomb Dropping, only to be redesignated on 6 May as No.4 School of Aerial Fighting & Gunnery and again on 29 May to No.4 Fighting School. As we shall see later, aircrew officer cadets undertook their final fourteen days' flying training at Freiston, after which, if considered proficient, they could, for example, find themselves pitched into combat on the Western Front. Between August 1918 and June 1919 the airfield had a secondary role as a Home Defence Night Landing Ground (HD NLG) for 90 (HD) Squadron RAF. At the end of hostilities in 1918, No.4 School of Aerial Fighting remained open until March 1919.

In some respects Freiston, near the mouth of the River Witham, can be seen as the First World War forerunner of No.6 Operational Training Unit (6 OTU) located, twenty-five years later, only a stone's throw away across The Wash, at RAF Sutton Bridge. Bombing targets were laid out on the sand and mud flats, together with a few dilapidated surplus aircraft dotted around to be used as targets for air to ground gunnery practice.

As of 31 December 1917, the Officer Commanding Freiston was Squadron Commander J.I. Harrison, ably assisted by Flight Commander Noel Keeble DSC DFC, a fighter ace credited with six air victories, and Lieutenants C.K. Jupp RNVR and E.A.B. Tooth RNVR. Thirty-seven Flight Sub-Lieutenants were listed as receiving instruction at the airfield on that date. Records also show that during the eight months from January to August 1917, of the 485 officers that graduated from Cranwell, 227 went on to fly seaplanes and 258 to fly land-based aeroplanes.

Perhaps the most notable of Freiston's Officers Commanding was the Canadian, Harold Kerby DSC, AFC. Kerby joined the RNAS in 1915 and learned to fly at the Grahame-White School in Hendon. While flying on the Western Front with 'Naval 9' then 'Naval 3' he was credited with shooting down or sharing in the destruction of seven enemy aircraft

(Left) Officer Commanding No.4 SAFG Freiston, Squadron Commander Harold Kerby DSC AFC and (right) Capt E.D.G. Galley, ex-56 Sqn RFC. Pictured in front of a Sopwith Camel at Freiston, 1918.

between 24 March and 27 May 1917. Posted back to England, he became CO of a Home Defence squadron based at Walmer in Kent and, while there, he destroyed two German Gotha bombers during daylight air raids in August. He was awarded a DSC and in 1918 took command of No.4 SAF & G at Freiston with the rank of Major, where he was awarded an AFC in the New Year Honours list of 1919 (in which there was also an AFC for Captain J.S.T. Fall, mentioned later in this story).

Over the course of the war, in addition to a mixed bag of aeroplanes for training purposes, such as Avro 504, BE2, Bristol F2B Fighter, Sopwith 1½ Strutter, Pup, Triplane, Camel, Snipe and Dolphin, in the early days Freiston also maintained a flight of Bristol Scouts for anti-Zeppelin patrols, as well as normal training. The 'finishing school' programme was rudimentary to say the least and completing it was frequently affected by the weather. It is thanks to the diary of Flight Sub-Lieutenant Leslie Semple RN that a lasting memory of what the daily routine of life at the airfield was like has been recorded:

Feb 12 1918. Leave King's Cross by 4.00pm train to Freiston. Arrive at Boston at 7.00pm. Catch tender up to Freiston camp. Very small place on the shore. Four hangars – Bessonneau tents [canvas-clad demountable hangars] and one hut for officers accommodating twenty-four. Gun room adjoins mess room which is also small. A range is situated on the far side of the 'drome where silhouette, moving target, moving gun, Aldis and ring sights and jam clearing on Vickers and Lewis guns are taught. Have some supper and then go down in the tender to Marine Hotel [now demolished], being billeted there since the camp is full. Have a nice little room with Sinclair. They charge us three shillings per night.

Having settled in, Leslie Semple found little time for quiet contemplation:

> February 13. The routine at Freiston is:
> Called at 6.45a.m.
> Tender to camp
> Breakfast 7.30a.m.
> Firing on the range or flying
> Lunch 12.00p.m.
> Parade 1.00p.m.
> Firing on the range or flying
> Make up log books 5.00p.m.
> Lecture 5.45p.m.
> Dinner 7.30p.m.
> Tender to Marine Hotel 8.30p.m.

But there was still time to think wistfully about some of the more pleasurable things in a young man's life:

> February 15. Up in the camp firing all day but the place is covered in mud. I should very much like to hear from a little girl called Mabel that I met at Finsbury Park. She promised to write to me.

Saturday afternoon brought some respite:

> Saturday Feb 16. Leave the camp about 1.00p.m. and walk along the sea wall and out across the marsh to the sea. Two miles of marshland before reaching the sea when the tide is out. It is covered in deep channels like rivers running out to the sea. Then back to Marine Hotel for tea and dinner. Stay in chatting. Air raid on London.

> February 17. Stand by for flying in morning and afternoon. Calibrate a gun on a BE today by adjusting sights and barrel of gun to the same object at a definite distance. Another air raid on London.

> February 18. Stand by for flying. Calibrate another gun. Firing on the range in the afternoon. Order some photographs. Must buy a camera – very useful indeed. Lecture in the evening by Lt Tooth on bomb sights – very humorous. New fellows arrive. One of them phoned up to enquire about transport from station to camp. I answered pretending to be the CO and asked why they had not reported earlier etc. Quite put the wind up them!

> February 19. On the range again today. Make some very good shots. We have one shilling stakes [about £2.40 today] on the results. Four of us. I won twice – eight shillings. With luck and good weather I may be fortunate enough to leave this station on Monday. Then most probably report to Manston near Margate and then to France. Lecture from the CO in the evening on organisation. Bed about 9.30p.m.

Manston was the location of the pool to which RNAS pilots were sent before being posted to squadrons and that is why Leslie expected to be sent there. It was, however, also a training base for the new Handley Page bomber squadrons that were being formed.

Flight Sub Lieutenant E.A.B. Tooth RNVR (on right) at Freiston with Petty Officers Porter, Street, Moseley and Thomas.

February 20. Finish firing on the range. Now have bomb dropping and firing in the air to do. Waiting for good weather. Lecture in evening by Lt Jupp on 'The trajectory of a bullet.' Wire received from Billy Vidler [Leslie's future brother-in-law] saying that he is marked AIII fit for active service and that he is coming on embarkation leave on Friday. I ask for leave, too.

February 22. Get leave at 11.00a.m. Rush down to Marine Hotel to change and get back at 12.15p.m. but the tender has gone. But at 12.50p.m. a lorry leaves for Boston. Get on this and just catch train for London. Stop a train as it leaves the station for some ratings to get in. Arrive home at about 4.45p.m. Spend a pleasant evening with the gramophone. Nice weekend with Billy and other relatives.

February 25. Arrive Freiston 12.45p.m. Fly in evening as passenger to Flt Sub-Lt Binckes and fire Very lights over Batchelor's Moor.

Familiarity with Very pistols and lights was important for pilots and navigators because flares were an essential part of the primitive air traffic control and recognition procedures then in use.

February 27. Go up again with Binckes as passenger. He also takes me up again to drop bombs. Flying all the morning. Nothing doing in the afternoon and still have 150 rounds to fire in the air. Shall do this tomorrow and leave for Manston on Friday.

February 28. Up in the air all morning with Flt Sub-Lt Allen. Firing in the air. Finish at Freiston today. Make up log book.

Friday March 1. Pack up at Marine Hotel. Pay bill, twenty-six shillings. Paid [received] £23 today. Report back to Cranwell. Told to report to Stonehenge on Monday afternoon. Catch train from Caythorpe and arrive home about 7.00p.m.

Leslie Semple's posting to Stonehenge came as a surprise to him. He thought he was going to the RNAS pilot pool at Manston for immediate posting to France or to learn to fly Handley Page 0/400 bombers. However, by the time he had finished at Freiston, a school of navigation, bomb dropping and night flying had been established at Stonehenge, equipped with FE2b, DH4, DH9, HP 0/100 and HP 0/400 aircraft. Manston had ceased to be the training station for 0/400s and HP training for both RNAS and RFC aircrew was now combined at Stonehenge. And thus did Leslie Semple join – and survive – the shooting war. Sadly many trainee pilots from Freiston were ill prepared to be pitched into operational flying, as the following small sample shows.

In November 1916, Flight Sub-Lieutenant A. Kay noted in his logbook that he had accumulated twenty-eight flying hours when he was posted to Freiston. He was sent off in the morning of the 15th for a seventy-eight-minute solo cross-country flight in BE2c No.8404 to Bourne, Spalding, Sutton Bridge and back to Freiston. That afternoon he was sent off again, this time in 8303, to find his way to Grantham, Newark and back for another seventy-five minutes in the air, then up again for a two-hour cross country in 8303, taking in Peterborough, Wisbech, Sutton Bridge, Boston and back to Freiston. Then they let him loose on a Sopwith One-and-a-half Strutter and after a few circuits in No.9893 he wrote rather proudly: 'Flew the Sopwith, very good machine. A little bumpy but good flying.'

Flight Sub-Lieutenant Mosley Gordon Woodhouse was posted to Cranwell from Redcar (Yorks) initial training station on 31 March 1917 with twenty hours in his logbook. Between 23 May and 8 June, his total flying for the fortnight during which he was 'finishing' at Freiston amounted to just four and a quarter hours. He wrote: 'Ascended for firing in air [in Avro 504B, N6156]. Gun wouldn't fire owing to [ammunition] pan not being properly put on.' He landed and had the fault rectified, then took off again, noting: 'Fired in the air. Started firing too soon.' These twenty-five minutes were his sole gunnery practice. The rest of the time was spent on bomb dropping practice in various BE2c aircraft.

At the tender age of eighteen years, Sub-Lieutenant Woodhouse was posted to France as a fighter pilot with No.9 (Naval) Squadron on 4 August, where he had his first flight in a Sopwith Camel. Two days later, on his first operational patrol, he managed to lose contact with the formation and two days later, on his second patrol, the same thing happened again. Next day he was shot down in flames while flying as part of an escort to RE8s of No.52 Squadron RFC. The sad thing was that his brother, Captain L.M. Woodhouse, was in one of those RE8s and saw the Camel go down in flames.

Flight Sub-Lieutenant H.H. Costain arrived in June 1917, after six weeks at Eastbourne initial training school. He noted in his logbook that two hours and forty-five minutes was flown on bomb dropping sorties using BE2e aircraft A8694 and A8698 at Freiston, first using a mirror device then with dummy and live bombs. He, too, had just twenty-five minutes on three gunnery practice flights in Avro 504s N5253 and N5250, during which he fired the magnificent total of 173 rounds. On 14 August he was classed by Lieutenant Jupp as 'a second-class bomb dropper' and posted to the RNAS Handley Page bomber training squadron at Manston; he seems to have gone on to survive the war.

Flight Sub-Lieutenant Geoffrey Bowman had a similar training profile, arriving at Cranwell from Chingford training station on 13 February 1917. By the time he reached Freiston he had thirty-two flying hours to his name and less than a month later he was considered ready for active service with a grand total of twelve minutes air gunnery firing and one hour and forty minutes bomb dropping practice – all in BE2c aircraft, e.g. 8433 – to his name. Sub-Lieutenant Bowman was posted to 'Naval 10', a front-line fighter squadron equipped with the Sopwith Triplane. He was allowed over the lines on 1 April in a Nieuport 12 and noted in his logbook that he was 'hit four times over Dixmude.' He got his first flight in a Triplane on 4 April and managed to survive a month before being posted away to 'Naval 1' on 1 May. Sub-Lieutenant Bowman was shot down in flames while on patrol in Triplane N5461 on 19 May 1917, believed to have been one of Hauptmann Adolf Count von Tutschek's twenty-seven air victories. Bowman was nineteen years old.

It is interesting to note that both of the above pilots only came into contact with the aircraft they were to fly operationally when they reached their squadrons. There were just not enough of the latest front-line fighter types to spare for the training units. But as officialdom eventually realised the foolishness of this situation, so – as aircraft production gradually increased – Freiston records show the arrival of Sopwith Pups, Camels and a small number of Triplanes and Dolphins from mid-1917 onwards. This is also indicative of the influence of the 'Gosport system', mentioned below, one of the cornerstones of which was to ensure that by the time a pilot was deemed ready for posting to the Front, he would have spent something like thirty hours on the type of aircraft he would use on operations.

In a quiet, tree-shaded corner of Freiston village churchyard lie three CWGC headstones marking the last resting place of a trio of Canadian pilots. Like thousands of their countrymen, these young men turned their backs on promising careers at home to volunteer for a war raging far from their native land, only to lose their lives in the most tragic of circumstances.

The first of these young Canadians was twenty-one-year-old Second Lieutenant John William Dowling. He was the son of Francis William and Dorothy Dowling of Vancouver, British Columbia, Canada. Little detail can be found of this young man's background, but it appears he had trained to be a lawyer prior to the outbreak of war. Records indicate that he was posted to Cranwell on 27 April 1918, and by the time he reached the gunnery school at Freiston, he had accumulated forty hours' flying experience. He lost his life when the aircraft

Sopwith Camel, E7234 at Freiston. The type in which Second Lieutenant Edward Bach died on 30 August 1918.

in which he was flying, Sopwith Camel C25, was seen to spin into the ground while making a turn at low altitude on 26 June 1918.

Second Lieutenant John Freele Meek was the next of the trio to die, not long after Dowling. He was born in Southwold, Ontario, Canada and his parents were James and Sarah Meek who, at the time of their son's death, lived in Port Stanley, Ontario. Second Lieutenant Meek was educated at Southwold public school then at St Thomas Collegiate. From there he entered the University of Toronto, where he gained a BA in political science. In the autumn of 1915 he was appointed to the 70th Battalion and in April 1916 joined the Canadian Expeditionary Force when it went overseas to France, where he served with the 24th Battalion on the Ypres St Eloi sector of the Western Front. He was severely wounded in one arm at Courcelette on 28 September and was repatriated to Canada at the end of that year. While recuperating, Meek returned to his studies for a time but it appears he became restless for a return to the action in France. He applied to the Canadian Forces to allow him to return, but was turned down due to the permanent injury to his arm. This did not deter John, however, who then volunteered for service with the Royal Flying Corps, was accepted and underwent flying training in Canada. On completion of this training, he returned to France in May 1918 for flying duties as a pilot. After a month of flying in France he was posted back to England in July for a course in gunnery at No.4 School of Aerial Gunnery and Fighting at Freiston, after which he was scheduled to leave for service on the Italian front.

Lieutenant Meek's final flight came on 14 August 1918, when he took off in Sopwith Camel B7263 to carry out gunnery practice over The Wash firing range. What happened during that fateful flight is recorded in an eyewitness account given by Captain J.S.T. Fall at the subsequent inquest into Lieutenant Meek's death. The account states that Meek had been at the air station for about three weeks and that he was considered a very capable pilot. This was to be his last qualifying flight in his course of instruction, during which he had accumulated more than one hundred hours' flying experience. Captain Fall said he saw Lieutenant Meek fly over the range and watched him fire at a ground target in a dive from about 1,000ft. Meek pulled out of the dive to climb away to seaward. A few minutes later Captain Fall saw the Camel diving vertically and it disappeared from his view behind the sea bank, half a mile from the water's edge and one-and-a-half miles out from the bank itself. Captain Fall ran out to the water's edge and then swam out to the wreckage of the aeroplane, which he found to be upside down in about four feet of water. He was able to turn the tail of the aeroplane over and found Lieutenant Meek strapped into his seat, dead.

Second Lieutenant Edward Lambert Bach is the final member of this unfortunate Canadian trio to lose their lives in flying accidents at Freiston Airfield. He was just twenty years old when he died flying Sopwith Camel E1429 on 30 August 1918. The son of James and Ellen Bach of Toronto, Canada, at the time of his death Edward Bach had accumulated eighty flying hours and must have been coming to the end of his course at No.4 Fighting School when he fell victim to a spinning accident near the airfield. The following is taken from an obituary that appeared in the *Toronto Star* of 3 September 1918:

Mr and Mrs J.E. Bach received a cable on Sunday stating that their elder son, Lt E.L. Bach RAF was killed in an aeroplane accident in England on 30 August 1918. He was a Toronto boy and had attended Brown Public School and North Toronto High School. In March 1916 he enlisted with the 64th Battery and three weeks afterwards he became ill with spinal meningitis. Later he received his discharge and in November 1917 he joined the Royal Flying Corps and went to England last May. Before joining the colours he was employed with Gordon, Mackay & Co. Edward was a member of St Clements church. His brother Harry, also of the Royal Air Force, is at present home and resting from the effects of a broken hand sustained in injuries he received at Camp Borden.

While each of these accidents was a tragedy for the young men who lost their lives, it must also have been heartbreaking for the families they left behind in Canada. Those families were not able to grieve for their loved ones at a funeral in their own country, which must have made it more difficult to come to terms with the loss.

What is evident from these examples, where the men had sustained injury or illness with the infantry, is the 'medical casualness' that existed in the RFC selection system. The proverbial 'blind eye' became more apparent at times of manpower shortages, for example in late 1916 and early 1917, following the high pilot and aircrew attrition rate of 1916. Aircraft wastage in France, for example, between April and June 1916, amounted to 198 machines, of which 134 were lost due to accidents, thirty-three due to disrepair and just thirty-one through enemy action. Then came the first Battle of the Somme, which really brought home the intensity of the air fighting and the need for new pilots:

RFC aeroplane losses: 780, destroyed or damaged
RFC pilots killed, wounded or missing: 308 (from an estimated 430 available)
Enemy losses: 165 claimed as destroyed and 205 claimed as 'driven down'

When the RFC deployed to France in 1914, it took with it about sixty aeroplanes. By September 1915 there were 160 aircraft; by July 1916, there were 420 in operation and 216 in store. The plan for 1916 was to take frontline strength to 600 aeroplanes. The RFC intended to keep expanding and pursue an aggressive strategy, and for that it needed all the pilots it could lay its hands on. This, though, was costly. During the second Battle of the Somme in the spring of 1918, the RFC lost almost a thousand aeroplanes in one month, against 650 German aircraft lost, while in August 1918 the RFC lost 850 aircraft, peaking at one hundred lost to all causes on 8 August alone.

Back home, training was expanding to keep pace with these losses, and with it came its own heavy price. It is no coincidence that the three Canadian airmen, mentioned above, died while flying the Sopwith Camel, a lively fighter aeroplane that was unforgiving if not handled very carefully. There were many other accidents taking place at Freiston, among them some fairly experienced pilots, as well as novices learning their trade.

In contrast to the airmen mentioned earlier, Flight Sub-Lieutenant James Sims had already seen a good deal of service as an RNAS air observer flying on the Western Front in France. In fact, his efforts had been recognised by the French military authorities from whom he received a Croix de Guerre medal with Silver Star when he was mentioned in a French Divisional Despatch. Aspiring to become a pilot, he was posted to Cranwell and eventually he, too, took his turn at the Freiston 'finishing' school. By 26 May 1917, Sims had accumulated a mere thirty-five hours' solo, and on that date he took up Avro 504E No.9285 for more practice. Shortly after take-off on his second flight of the day, the engine choked and spluttered badly. It faltered, picked up and then cut out completely while the aeroplane was in a turn. The Avro stalled and spun into the ground, killing Sub-Lieutenant Sims outright. Sims is buried in Freiston churchyard alongside the three Canadians, but his grave is marked by a private granite memorial stone rather than the Commonwealth War Graves Commission headstone.

A month later, on 16 June 1917, it was an Avro 504 that spun in near Waddington. Lieutenant Drom was flying the aeroplane from the front seat, with an Australian, Second Lieutenant Geoffrey Sulman, a more experienced pilot from 51 Training Squadron, taking the rear cockpit. Shortly after take-off, an eyewitness saw the aeroplane make a vertically banked turn at no more than 150ft with, in his opinion, too much rudder applied, from which it developed a spin and crashed to earth. Sulman died later from his injuries but Drom, although seriously injured, survived the crash.

On and on the carnage went. Reflecting the pressure on UK training units to turn out more and more aircrew for the front, hardly a week passed by without an accident being reported somewhere in the region. One interesting factor emerging from analysis of the fatalities, those at least which are recorded in any detail, is that a relatively high proportion seem to have been Canadian airmen.

Nineteen-year-old Second Lieutenant Ralph Phillips RFC of First Avenue, Ottawa, for example, had qualified for his 'wings' in June 1917, and with twenty-nine hours in his logbook, was undergoing final fighting instruction with 11 Training Squadron at Grantham/Spittlegate during August. After a session of dual practice of loops and spins under the watchful eye of an instructor on the morning of the 14th, he was sent up to do solo aerobatics in Avro 504A, B937. Gilbert Fisher, who farmed at Welby a few miles east of the airfield, glanced up from his labours to watch the by now commonplace sight of a biplane cavorting high in the sky. It was the rise and fall of the engine note that occasionally, as on this day, prompted him to glance upwards. Catching sight of the aeroplane, at perhaps 4,000ft, the farmer saw the craft complete two loops and two spins. After the second spin, the pilot seemed to right the aeroplane, but Mr Fisher's attention was caught by a flicker of flame under the fuselage. With the flame growing ever larger in the slipstream, the aeroplane started to break up before his eyes and crashed to the ground. Running frantically to the burning wreckage, he was beaten back by intense heat and flames and Second Lieutenant Phillips died in that awful pyre. Listening to the opinion of a senior flying officer from the airfield, the inquest jury concluded that, having been choked with fuel during the aerobatics, the engine caught fire when the pilot failed to cut off the petrol flow before first switching off the engine. It was believed he then lost control when the fire took hold of the aircraft structure.

Wreckage of Avro 504 in which Second Lieutenant D.A. Robertson met his death at Crowland, Lincs on 16 November 1917. (Derek Elphee)

Another Canadian airman, believed to be Second Lieutenant D.A. Robertson, met his death in an accident while on a cross-country flight from either Cranwell or Freiston on 16 November 1917. His Avro 504 aeroplane was seen circling the Crowland area, sometimes flying just above rooftop height. The pilot seemed to be searching for a suitable landing site and eventually set the machine down in Snowden Field, adjacent to the abbey. Shortly afterwards, the aeroplane took off but had gained little height before it lurched sideways and dived into the ground at the side of the churchyard. Onlookers found the aeroplane badly damaged, but managed to gently remove the still-breathing Lieutenant Robertson from the wreckage; he sadly died just a few minutes later.

In the final year of the war, Freiston reached its peak of activity and fatalities. In 1918, Second Lieutenant Charles Frederick Mossman was killed at Freiston on 14 May when the starboard wing folded up on Sopwith Camel B3910 as he pulled out of a dive while firing at a ground target out on the marshes. The aeroplane broke up and dived into the ground. Operational with 'Naval 10' B3910 was an aeroplane with a good combat record. Flying this particular aircraft, Acting Flight Commander W.M. Alexander shot down one Albatros DV near Houlhulst Forest, and Flight Sub-Lieutenant W.H. Wilmot claimed another near Lille before it was relegated to training duties.

When one considers what all these young men were doing, not only were they learning to fly – a science that was still in its infancy and hazardous enough in itself – but they were also training for war. As we have seen, that training was often woefully inadequate and pilots were posted into battle with very few hours' experience, often with their logbook endorsements covering the real truth. This made flying even more dangerous, and serves to demonstrate just what remarkable and brave young men they were.

The basic problem with flying training in the RFC up to 1917 was that it was not standardised across the training units. Moreover, individual units were always under constant pressure to provide manpower to both fill operational losses (Trenchard's mantra was 'No empty chairs') and increase the quantity of operational squadrons. This issue was recognised during 1916 and addressed by a Major Smith-Barry, who convinced the RFC that he could create a system of standardised flying training that would improve pilot skill and reduce accidents. It is not the intention here to go into detail but, in short, his idea was based around creating a school for flying instructors who would have their flying skills brought up to the high standards necessary to instruct trainee pilots with both confidence and ease. Smith-Barry was allowed to put his ideas into practice and developed his system at Gosport Airfield. In conjunction with his recommendation for the introduction of dual controls in training aircraft and later an intercom system called the Gosport tube, a balanced combination of academic classroom training, a standard set of flying training exercises and controlled progression and assessment through both, was laid down and rolled out to training stations. This teaching method became known as the 'Gosport system' and is generally credited with making pilot training quicker and more efficient, not only during the remainder of the First World War, but after the war too.

As an illustration of these latter points, and on a slightly lighter note, perhaps it will come as no surprise to discover that Freiston's most famous 'old-boy' is none other than the fictional Second Lieutenant James Bigglesworth – better known to millions of fans as 'Biggles'. His creator, William Earl (Captain W. E.) Johns, saw much active service with the infantry during the First World War and, on recovering from wounds, in common with many soldiers, sought a transfer to the RFC for pilot training. Actually, acting Second Lieutenant Johns' training progress itself provides an excellent example of the process a typical 'transferee' went through. He received extensive ground classroom subject training at No.1 School of Aeronautics in Reading and received his initial flying instruction to solo stage on a Maurice Farman MF11 Shorthorn, affectionately known as a 'Rumpity', at the School's aerodrome at Coley Park. Johns progressed to No.25 Training Squadron, Thetford, for advanced flying training between January and April 1918, and by the end of April, he was posted to No.2 School of Aerial Fighting & Gunnery at Marske-by-the-Sea on the north Yorkshire coast, as an instructor. Johns had a short spell as an instructor at Cranwell where he would have been aware of (and most probably visited) the similar School at Freiston on Lincolnshire's Wash coast – and so, where better for his young hero to be trained?

In the first chapter of the book *Biggles Learns To Fly*, our young tyro finds himself posted to No.4 School of Fighting based at a place called 'Frensham'. It is without doubt a pseudonym for Freiston, since we later read that 'Frensham', located on the Lincolnshire coast, is home to many aircraft, including Avro, FE, BE and Sopwith types:

> Most of them were circling at the far side of the aerodrome and diving at something on the ground. The distant rattle of machine guns came to his ears. Later on he heard that the far side of the aerodrome ran straight down into the sea, a long deserted foreshore, on which old obsolete aeroplanes were placed as targets.
>
> A Pup taxied out to take off and he watched it with interest. An FE was just coming in to land and he stiffened with horror, knowing that a collision was inevitable. For a moment the machines clung together motionless in mid air; then they broke apart, each spinning into the ground with a terrible noise. [There was a mid-air collision involving a Pup on 26 April 1918.] A flight-sergeant was watching him grimly: 'A nasty one sir, you'll soon get used to that, though … we killed seven here last week.' Biggles turned away. Flying no longer seemed just a thrilling game.
>
> An instructor landed, turned out his passenger and beckoned him to take his place. Biggles took his seat in the cockpit, noting with a thrill that it was fitted with machine guns. 'We're going to do a little gunnery practice', said the instructor.
>
> Three days later, Biggles was called to the orderly room. 'Heavy casualties in France,' said the orderly, 'they're shoving everybody out as fast as they can.' The adjutant gave him his movement order and rail warrant. 'But I haven't finished my tests yet, sir!' exclaimed Biggles. The adjutant entered the tests in his logbook, signed it and said with a queer smile: 'You've passed them now, you may put up your *wings.*' He had done less than fifteen hours flying, dual and solo and he was going to France.

Lieutenant W.E. Johns himself was posted to No.55 Squadron for active service in France in July 1918 – but that is another story.

Freiston by no means suffered all the casualties in the region. As we have seen above, airmen from Scampton, Waddington, Cranwell, Stamford/Wittering, Grantham/Spittlegate (sometimes spelt Spitalgate), Tydd, and Narborough have all contributed in one way or another. Aeroplanes on cross-country training flights from airfields outside the Fens were regular users of the wide, open skies of that district. Some were pleased to have so many flat fields to choose from when their engines failed – an all too common problem then and in the decades that followed.

On 17 March 1918, twenty-year-old Canadian Lieutenant Colin Douglas Sinclair, a pupil at No.1 Training Depot Station, Wittering died when his aeroplane crashed and caught fire at Bicker Fen, near Donington. Alfred Bettinson, who farmed in Bicker Fen, said he watched the aeroplane flying round for five minutes, then saw it sideslip from about 150ft into the ground where it burst into flames. He and his brother were first to reach the wreckage, but there was nothing they could do to save the pilot.

Scampton, or more correctly Brattleby in those days, was (in 1917) the home of No.81 Squadron. It formed originally as a fighter unit but never mobilised as an operational squadron before disbandment and thus remained as a training squadron until it was absorbed into No.34 Training Depot Station the following year. One of the squadron's pupils, Second Lieutenant F.E. Davis (or Davies), after accumulating the meagre total of twenty-six hours from forty flights, had been awarded his wings on 6 July and was finishing off his training a few days later with a dusk cross-country flight, probably to Tydd St Mary and back. There was still just a little daylight left on that summer's night of 10 July when, at 10p.m., Davis very nearly 'finished off' himself. Flying Sopwith 1½ Strutter A5242, his aeroplane suffered engine failure near Spalding and he glided slap bang into a willow tree at Jobsons Bridge, Mill Green while attempting to force land in the gathering gloom. The willow tree made short work of the Sopwith and the machine collapsed into a heap in a ditch. Picking over the wreckage, rescuers found Lieutenant Davis bleeding profusely, hanging upside down, unconscious and still strapped into his seat. He woke up in Spalding Hospital with a thumping headache and cuts about the face, but he had survived where others might have perished.

In contrast, an inquest report in the *Wisbech Standard*, for example, told in considerable detail the sad tale of a fatal accident over at Tydd St Mary Airfield, near the Long Sutton to Wisbech road, on 12 February 1918. Joining the army in 1914, Second Lieutenant Herbert Donaldson transferred from the 20th Battalion of the London Regiment to the RFC in September 1917 for training as an air observer. On the day of the accident, Donaldson, now posted to No.51 Squadron, carried out several training flights with the same pilot, Lieutenant Taylor. That afternoon, as their FE2b aeroplane returned to Tydd, its engine was heard to splutter and then cut out. It seems probable that, in trying to coax the aeroplane over some trees to an emergency landing, it stalled and crashed. Hitting the ground left wing down, it turned somersault and burst into flames. Somehow Taylor managed to scramble clear but Donaldson was left pinned beneath the wreckage. Both the pilot and farm labourers who rushed to the scene bravely tried to extricate the trapped airman and, despite being beaten back by the ferocity of the flames, they eventually succeeded, but not before he had been badly burned and his rescuers scorched too. Conveyed gently to Wisbech hospital, Second Lieutenant Donaldson died four days later from his injuries. On that day there were no less than four aeroplane crashes in south Lincolnshire alone, but fortunately the other three had less serious consequences for the crews.

Guy Reid was born in Puerto Orotava, Tenerife in the Canary Islands. Commissioned into the Seaforth Highlanders, he transferred to the RFC and was posted to France as a pilot with No.20 Squadron towards the end of 1915. Quickly proving his ability Reid, together with several different observer/air gunners, was credited with five air victories between February and September 1916 while flying the FE2b. It was in recognition of their fighting aggression during that summer, when he flew regularly with observer Captain Gerald Dixon-Spain – coincidentally another native of Long Sutton, Lincolnshire – that each was awarded a Military Cross. The citation, gazetted on 26 September 1916 read:

> For conspicuous skill and gallantry on many occasions. Capt Dixon-Spain with 2/Lt Reid as pilot, attacked and drove back a hostile machine. A few minutes later four hostile machines were seen, three of which were attacked one after another and driven back, the fourth being accounted for by another patrol. Another time they attacked two hostile machines, shot one down and drove the other back. Two days later they attacked two more machines, of which one is believed to have been destroyed, the other being pursued back to its aerodrome.

Having acquired considerable experience in their respective fields, during 1917 Reid, now a Captain, and Dixon-Spain were posted back to England to pass on their skills. Reid is believed to have been posted to No.51 Squadron based at Tydd St Mary as a flight commander, while Dixon-Spain became Chief Instructor, with the rank of temporary major, at the School of Aerial Gunnery in Hythe, where he remained until the end of hostilities, being awarded an OBE in June 1919 'in recognition of distinguished services rendered during the War.' He was a member of a prominent farming family in the region. Sadly on 16 October 1917, Captain Reid fell victim to an air accident in an FE2b while on a routine flight with observer Second Lieutenant George Cameron, who also died when their aeroplane inexplicably dived into the ground in south Lincolnshire.

British and Commonwealth airmen feature prominently in this narrative so far, but it would be remiss not to mention the involvement of American airmen who came to this country when the USA declared war in 1917. The reason that American potential aircrew and ground crew began to turn up at British flying training units is largely due to the parlous state of the US Army's fleet of aeroplanes at that time.

Considering the length of time the Wright brothers – and others – had been trying to convince the US Army of the value of aviation, it was not until 18 July 1914 that the US government actually passed legislation to give the Army's small aviation section recognition and status as a permanent unit of the US Army Signal Corps. Even so, this was only a part of the problem since, compared to the aviation fever that existed in Europe, it was proving equally difficult to get momentum into the development and manufacture of aeroplanes in the USA. This meant that when America entered the First World War in April 1917, its government only then realised the extent to which its aviation industry had fallen behind that of Europe. At that date the US Army Signal Corps Aviation section had just 131 officers and 1,087 enlisted men, and 250 obsolete aeroplanes that were unfit for war combat duty.

In order to address this deficiency, flying training, its organisation and aircraft production in the USA were subjected to a rapid civilian and military expansion programme. However, since it would naturally take time before the products of the expansion could work their way through to the Western Front, it was agreed with the RFC/RNAS that American personnel could be sent to British and Canadian establishments to begin flying and ground training immediately. The US and Canada then reached a reciprocal training agreement which allowed pilots to be trained for the RFC at US airfields (e.g. in Texas) in return for the US having had many of its pilots trained in Canada in the months immediately after America entered the war. Just how quickly Uncle Sam could get his act together can be seen in the statistics for training operations run in Texas between 17 November 1917 and 12 April 1918 when 67,000 flying hours produced 1,960 pilots trained for the US and RFC.

The first batch of 150 American potential pilots arrived in England during the summer of 1917 and they were the forerunners of almost 2,500 US pilots to be trained by the Allies in Britain and France. In addition, the British and French aircraft industries built a large proportion of the combat aeroplanes taken on charge by the expanding American Flying Corps.

The presence of American airmen at East Midlands airfields is evidenced from a short item in the *Lincolnshire Free Press* of 5 February 1918, that also drives home the message that losses due to air accidents touch the lives of all manner of people – no one is spared, no matter what their station in life.

An inquest was held at Lincoln on Monday night, on two young officers attached to an RFC station in the county. They were 2/Lt Evander Barkley Garnett (20) of Washington [USA], a grandson [sic; godson?] of General Pershing, and Lt Allan Johnson (24) of Toronto. Evidence was given that on Sunday afternoon [27 January] an aeroplane went up in the district with Lt Garnett as pilot and Lt Johnson as observer. At a height of fifty to a hundred feet, the pilot turned down the wind, instead of against it, with the result that he lost flying speed. One tail drooped and the machine came down. Immediately the aeroplane touched the ground it burst into flames. Garnett crawled from the machine with his clothing on fire but the other unfortunate officer remained in the machine. Garnett died the same day.

Garnett was attached to No.61 Training Squadron and Johnson to No.45 Training Squadron, both located at South Carlton, but it is not known what type of aeroplane they were flying at the time of the accident. Lieutenant Garnett's ashes were returned to the USA and Johnson is buried in Lincoln's Newport cemetery.

Several months elapsed before another American lost his life, and this time it was a pupil from No.1 Training Depot Station at Stamford/Wittering. The *Leicester, Rutland & Stamford Mercury* of 16 August reported that incident:

Flt Cadet Frank Gardner (21) and Private Ronald McNeill (21) USA Aerial Sqn [*sic*] died in an accident on 10 August 1918. An eyewitness, Private Malcolm Sibbey (USA), saw the aeroplane dive at a ground target, saw a shot fired at the target and then the aircraft climbed to 350 feet. As it did so the right wing collapsed and the aeroplane crashed. The opinion was expressed that the aeroplane was dived too quickly and with too much power. It was pulled out too hard and possibly over-stressed.

Among the last incidents in which the death of an American airman in the region was reported, there appeared a brief item in the *Boston Guardian*:

Two RAF [*sic*] men were killed in an accident near a south Lincolnshire town. They were Flight Cadet J.W. MacLawrie aged eighteen, from Ireland and Private W. Christopherson aged twenty-seven of the US Army.

It is believed these trainees were from Cranwell. There is also a grave in Cranwell cemetery for Second Lieutenant H. Higgins who, according to the station news magazine, *The Piloteer,* was a native of New York and died in a flying accident on 13 July 1918 while serving with 91st Canadian Training Squadron. Another grave commemorates Private First Class John J. Hill, who died on 3 November 1918 and who, in view of the style of his rank, is also believed to be an American airman.

In addition to the above incidents, there are also reports of American personnel being trained as aircrew and ground mechanics while serving at Bircham Newton and Sedgeford Airfields with No.3 Fighting School during 1918. Similarly, American Army airmen are also known to have served at Kirton-In-Lindsey with No.33 Training Squadron from the beginning of 1918.

Unambiguous statistics for First World War training losses have proved difficult to find. However, an analysis of personnel at Cranwell and Freiston, made by Peter Dye in 1997, found that between September 1916 and November 1918, fifty-eight pilots died in flying accidents related to activity at those two stations. Elsewhere, other purely anecdotal evidence suggests 'on average one trainee pilot died and several others injured, to varying degrees, each day in the UK before the Gosport system was introduced in the autumn of 1917.' Other sources state that in the First World War, the RFC/RAF sustained 14,000 casualties, of which 8,000 related to training incidents; the distinction between fatalities and injuries is not made clear.

By November 1918, though, the face of the now-unified Royal Air Force had changed beyond the expectations of the most forward thinkers of 1912. Although he, too, does not quantify the training losses in detail, air historian Harald Penrose summed it up thus:

The RAF had become the largest Air Force in the world, with 27,333 officers and 263,410 other ranks. The 103 aeroplanes and six airships possessed by the RFC and RNAS at the beginning of the war had increased to 22,647 aeroplanes and 103 airships and operations were based on nearly 700 aerodromes and 184 front-line squadrons and 203 others. Loss [of machines] by combat, crashes [non-combat] and obsolescence was sixty per cent, since 55,093 airframes had been manufactured in Great Britain during the war to which can be added a further 3,000 airframes purchased abroad.

In four years of bitter warfare, 6,166 men of the British air services were known to have been killed on active service on all fronts, with a further 3,200 becoming prisoners or being posted as missing.

INTER-WAR: SILVER WINGS AND BLACK CLOUDS

Over the next year, the vast majority of the airfields and landing grounds that had sprung up in wartime were closed down as the RAF rapidly contracted and thousands of airmen went home. During the immediate post-war period, some RAF squadrons were, however, committed to maintain a presence on German soil, and this aspect provides a poignant peacetime story.

Second Lieutenant William Coulson flew Bristol F2B Fighters operationally with No.62 Squadron during the summer of 1918, but had the misfortune to be shot down with his observer, Second Lieutenant W.H.E. Labatt, on 22 July. They did, however, have the good fortune to survive the crash landing, and were made Prisoners of War by the Germans. Both airmen were repatriated on 13 December 1918, when Lieutenant Coulson found himself posted to No.11 Squadron, at that time based at Spich Airfield near Cologne as part of the Army of Occupation.

In September 1919, No.11 Squadron returned to the UK prior to its run down and disbandment at the end of that December. It was to this end that, on 5 September in company with another machine, William Coulson flew a *Brisfit* back to England with AC1 James Taylor in the rear cockpit. They left France heading for Digby aerodrome, probably as a prelude to their own demobilisation and return to 'civvy street'. It was not to be, though. Resuming

Bristol F2B Fighter. The type in which Second Lieutenant William Coulson from No.11 Squadron, crashed near Billingborough on 5 September 1919. (Cliff Clover)

Bristol F2B Fighter, F4420, crashed near Chettisham, Cambs on 8 April 1922.

their flight after a refuelling stop, darkness was falling as they reached Lincolnshire, so the pilots agreed by hand signals to land and complete their journey next day. Selecting a field on Tomlinson's Farm, Beacon Hill near Billingborough, Lieutenant Coulson followed the other aircraft in to land but inexplicably lost control of the fighter while still sixty feet above the ground. The *Brisfit* dived in with such force that both airmen were killed. His luck had clearly run out.

A flurry of fatal and non-fatal crashes involving *Brisfits* and DH 9s occurred across the region throughout the 1920s. Flying Officer C.W. Bragg and LAC Wren from No.39 Squadron died in a take-off accident at Grantham in DH 9A E967 on 28 March 1922. Bristol Fighter F4420 crashed on 8 April into a field at Chettisham alongside the Ely to Littleport road, killing the pilot, while another, J6673, from No.2 Squadron crashed at RAF Digby, killing Flying Officer Green and his air gunner Sergeant J.W. Stacey. RAF Grantham lost another pilot when Flying Officer Robin Jacques from No.100 Squadron died while flying solo in an Avro 504K, H2002 that spun in near the airfield on 8 August 1923. Seven weeks later, No.39 Squadron lost another DH 9A and crew when E8695 stalled in a steeply banked turn after take-off on 29 September 1923. It crashed and caught fire, killing Pilot Officer Edward Coventry and air gunner Corporal William Wardle.

Central Flying School (CFS) moved from RAF Upavon at the beginning of October 1926, taking with it an eclectic mix of twelve Avro 504K, a dual DH 9A, a single- and a dual-seat Sopwith Snipe, and one each of Gloster Gamecock, Armstrong-Whitworth Siskin and Gloster Grebe to RAF Wittering, where it remained for the next ten years as the main training school for flying instructors.

It was not long before the first incident occurred. Flying Officer Clarence Crowden was attached to CFS from No.19 Squadron Duxford for an instructor's course when he was killed in a crash at Collyweston near Easton on the Hill on 30 November. Pilot Officer Edward Steedman was acting as pupil in Avro 504K, D883, and he suffered injuries in the incident. Steedman was unable to attend the inquest due to his injuries, but instead made a statement that was read out to the court:

I went up on a practice flight with Fg Off Crowden, who was in the front seat. We both made two practice forced landings; I made the last one myself. After climbing to a height of 500 feet, Crowden took the controls and at about 1,000 feet he put the machine into a right-hand spin. We lost a considerable height before he attempted to pull out of the spin [and] I shouted 'look out, old chap we are very near the ground.' The next thing I remember was trying to get out of the spin. I do not remember the crash.

The newspaper commented that this was the fiftieth fatal accident in the RAF that year (1926), involving a total of eighty-one deaths.

CFS lost Sopwith Snipe Two-seater E6656 on 16 June 1927, together with its pilots, Flight Lieutenant Humphrey Baggs and Flying Officer Sydney Bell. Their fighter trainer was seen apparently in trouble at 3,000ft with the engine stopped. It fell into a spiral dive and skimmed over a greenhouse in which the eyewitness was working, partially flattening out before diving into the ground near Mr C.F. Ingrey's garden in Wothorpe near Stamford.

Low flying got the better of the pilot of CFS Avro 504N, J8728, on 26 May 1930. The starboard wingtip hit the ground during a turn and caused a crash at Barholm, near Stamford, in which Flying Officer V.H. Nicholay died, and Flying Officer P. F. Luxton was severely injured. Another Avro 504N, J8568, from CFS got into difficulty on 17 March 1932. The engine was heard to be 'racing' and the machine lost height rapidly. It just cleared a stone wall then flew parallel to the Stamford to Barnack road before crashing heavily in Pilsgate. Sergeants Noah Nicholls and Joseph Richardson died when they were thrown out of the aircraft, which was completely destroyed after bursting into flames.

Many were the crashes that occurred from which the pilots and crew involved emerged relatively unscathed, but some of them still ran a close race with the 'grim reaper'. Just such an accident befell an instructor and pupil from RAF College Cranwell and brought into the public eye conduct in the highest traditions of the Service, as a subsequent entry in the *London Gazette* now shows:

The ubiquitous Avro 504 – here a 'K' model, D7580 – mainstay of the RAF training schools for two decades.

His Majesty The King has approved the award of the Medal of the Military Division of the Most Excellent Order of The British Empire to Plt Off Sidney Noel Wiltshire for conspicuous gallantry displayed at Temple Bruer landing ground, Sleaford on 21 October 1929. This officer, who is a pilot under instruction, was flying with his instructor, Fg Off H.E. Power in an aeroplane that crashed on landing and at once caught fire. Having extricated himself from the wrecked machine, he found that his companion's foot was caught in the wreckage and that he could not get out. Although fully realizing the risk he was running, Plt Off Wiltshire re-entered the flames and helped Fg Off Power to get clear. During which process he sustained burns on his neck and face. Powers' clothing was by this time alight and he would undoubtedly have lost his life but for the prompt and courageous action taken by his pupil. As it was, he was badly burned. Both injured officers were shortly afterwards taken by air to Cranwell hospital. The aeroplane was completely burned out.

Flying training had been conducted at RAF Digby (formerly known as Scopwick) since 1918 but when No.3 FTS was disbanded in 1922 the station was placed on care and maintenance until it re-opened with the arrival of No.2 FTS from Duxford in 1924. No.2 FTS had its share of air accidents with close shaves, but none quite as close as when Pilot Officer James Martin crashed his Armstrong Whitworth Atlas, K1466 into a wall alongside the Sleaford to Lincoln road. Pilot Officer Martin, flying solo, was attempting to land in a designated forced landing field when he stalled and spun in. Fortunately for him, Mr J. A. Carr, a commercial traveller, was passing by in his car, which was almost struck by the falling aeroplane. Mr Carr said:

I was driving from Lincoln to Sleaford when the aeroplane crashed into the stone wall, narrowly missing my car. Fearing the 'plane would ignite, I drove about twenty yards and parked then rushed to the wreckage to find the pilot. A few seconds later I heard a gurgling sound beneath the 'plane and clearing a way through, I found Mr Martin beneath the wreckage. His clothing was choking him so I immediately loosened his collar and shirt, releasing his neck and probably saving his life.

By this time, two more cars had stopped, then an aeroplane landed in the field and its pilot ran to assist. Between them, they lifted up the tail of the crashed aircraft so that Pilot Officer Martin could be extricated, which was found difficult because of the tangle of wreckage and wires. Eventually he was removed, his broken limbs splinted, and conveyed by ambulance to Cranwell hospital.

With fifty dual flying hours under his belt, Pilot Officer Adrian Warford-Mein, an Australian pilot trainee at No.2 FTS, set out on Thursday 14 April 1932 from Digby in perfect weather for his first solo cross-country to RAF Bircham Newton via King's Lynn. A couple of hours later, his Avro 504N, K2352, was spotted by farm workers near East Winch railway station, looking as if its pilot was trying to find somewhere to land. The aeroplane circled the station three times then headed towards Ashwicken. As the aircraft came round into wind at about 300ft up, the engine suddenly stopped and the machine promptly nose-dived into a field and burst into flames. Fire consumed the machine and its pilot in minutes, driving back would-be rescuers with the intense heat.

The same fate befell Flight Cadet John Gard from Cranwell on 16 June 1933. The Atlas in which he was flying solo crashed on approach at the forced landing ground at Ruskington and burst into flames. The local newspaper reported that Flight Cadet Gard's death brought the number of fatal accidents so far that year to twenty-three, resulting in thirty deaths. The previous year (1932) there were thirty-five accidents involving fifty-three fatalities.

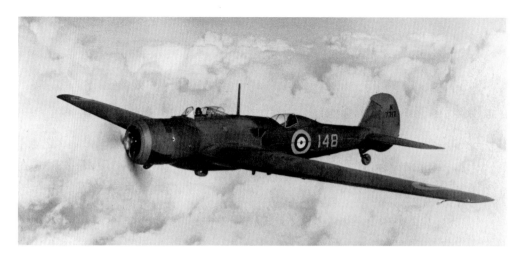

Vickers Wellesley, K7717 of No.148 Sqn.

During the mid-1930s, expansion of the RAF – one of the main objectives approved by the government in 1936 – was to increase the UK-based air force to 124 squadrons, and in particular to increase the striking power of the bomber squadrons within a newly created Bomber Command. This added striking power was to be achieved by re-equipping a number of squadrons with aircraft of increased speed, range and payload capacity, such as the Fairey Battle, Bristol Blenheim, Handley Page Harrow and Hampden, Armstrong Whitworth Whitley and the Vickers Wellesley and Wellington.

The Wellesley was one of the earliest of this 'new breed', being introduced in six squadrons from April 1937, among which was No.35 Squadron based at RAF Worthy Down. Anxious to get to grips with its new mount, a programme of familiarisation flights was drawn up, and it was one of these that brought Wellesley K7738 to Lincolnshire and an untimely end on 20 October 1937. Sergeant Tom Moon was briefed to fly K7738 from Worthy Down to RAF North Coates and back, to build up flying hours on the type, practise long distance navigation skills and to check out fuel consumption rates. His crew for this flight was observer Sergeant Vic Headley and Wireless Operator/Air Gunner, AC1 George 'Lofty' Nunn. All went well on the outward leg, but turning for home they ran into thick fog. What happened next remains unclear, but it is believed Sergeant Moon descended through the fog to try to pinpoint his position. An eyewitness said he saw the aeroplane at just sixteen feet or thereabouts above the ground. He heard a roar as its engine was revved hard and the machine started to bank and climb. As it did so, one wing tip scraped the ground, causing the aircraft to cartwheel and crash on Rowland's Farm, New Leake near Boston. All three airmen died.

> The King has been graciously pleased to approve the award of the Air Force Medal to 511912 Corporal Thomas Edward Barnes in recognition of exceptional courage and devotion to duty displayed on the occasion of the forced landing of an aircraft near Hinckley on 3rd December 1937.

Thus ran a citation in the *London Gazette* of 1 March 1938 marking the outcome of a quite unusual incident during No.114 Squadron's efforts to become the first unit to bring the Blenheim Mk 1 into service. Representing a great stride forward over its previous Hawker Hinds, part of the conversion to type routine involved long distance flights in all weather

All that remained of Wellesley K7738 after its crash on 20 October 1937.

conditions. The Met forecast for 3 December 1937 was pretty awful but good enough to fly, so a crew was briefed to fly brand new Blenheim K7110 on a round trip from RAF Wyton to RAF Aldergrove, Northern Ireland and back. Over the Midlands, the weather took a distinct turn for the worse and the Blenheim flew into a snowstorm. Much to the alarm and discomfort of the three-man crew, it was very badly thrown around inside the storm area and emerged upside down with one engine stopped and seemingly out of control. At this point, the pilot allegedly decided that recovery was impossible and crashing was inevitable, so he called to his two companions to bale out and then made a rapid exit through the cockpit roof hatch. His observer, Corporal Thomas Barnes, and wireless operator, AC1 Alfred Dearnes, struggled against the g-forces in a vain attempt to grab their chest parachute packs.

Rummaging through the wreckage later, calmly looking for his personal belongings, Cpl Barnes told a reporter from the *Hinkley Times* what happened next:

> When the pilot said 'jump for it' I had not got my parachute on. It was somewhere behind and I found that it had slipped into a well. I saw it was too late to look for it and that I should not have had time to get the thing on. The plane continued to lose height so I went to the controls and took over and tried to wake up the engines. I got her right way up but she was falling all the time. Then came the bumps. We were lucky all right.

The Blenheim crash-landed near Barwell, Leicestershire, and was badly broken up but, due to Barnes' actions, it slithered right way up along the ground and the wreckage did not catch fire. Thus both airmen were able to step from the twisted fuselage virtually unscathed. When the full story emerged the award of an AFM followed, presented to Cpl Barnes by ACM Sir Edgar Ludlow-Hewitt in front of the whole station personnel at RAF Wyton.

But this is not the last we hear of the intrepid Corporal Thomas Barnes. It would seem that Corporal Barnes had always harboured the desire to be a pilot, and when the dust had settled over the incident, this determined man actually applied successfully for pilot training and went to war as a fully-fledged pilot with No.114 Squadron. There is no happy ending to this story, though. Having been severely mauled during the Battle of France, No.114 Squadron became part of the bomber force attacking German invasion shipping in the Channel ports. Now operating from RAF Oulton, Suffolk, on 15 February 1941, Barnes and his crew took

Corporal Thomas Barnes receives his AFM.

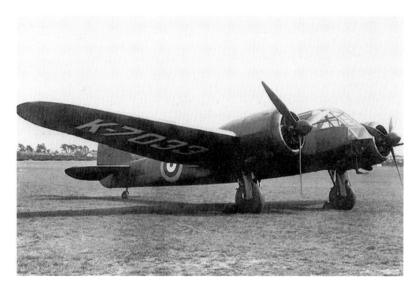

Bristol Blenheim Mk 1, K7033.

off at 8.35a.m. for an armed reconnaissance sortie along the Dutch coast. Two hours later their aircraft, Blenheim IV, T2125, was intercepted by a German fighter and shot down. Barnes and his crew died in the engagement and they are all buried in Flushing (Vlissingen) cemetery. Sergeant pilot Thomas Barnes AFM is remembered on the war memorial in his home village of Yaxley, near Peterborough.

By January 1938 the Bristol Blenheim was rolling out more rapidly to Bomber Command squadrons including, for example, No.110 Squadron at RAF Waddington, where crews worked hard to cope with the big leap to this new level of technology. As usual, the familiarisation programme of the new units included long cross-country navigation exercises that often brought this new bomber over the east of England. On 22 April, Pilot Officer Harry Green was briefed to fly a round trip from Waddington to RAF Honington, with Corporal Charles Badger and AC2 Frank Howard in Blenheim K7146.

Working on his land at Empson's Farm – now known as Boor's Farm – in the Dowsdale area of Crowland, smallholder James Andrew had stood just eighty yards from where K7146 made its final plunge to earth. He told a coroner's inquest:

> It was about 11.15am when I saw the aeroplane for the first time as it was going into the clouds in a northerly direction. I heard the aeroplane sound for about a minute then I saw it again, flying south and gradually coming down towards me from a good height at forty-five degrees with the engines full on. When it was about a quarter of a mile away I saw what I thought was a square of glass fall from the machine [later found to be the sliding cockpit roof hatch]. I didn't take my eyes off the plane as I thought it had got me, the team of horses and David Roughton who was in charge of them. It was so near that the left wing came between me and the horses. I thought it would have time to flatten out but instead the left wing touched the ground and swung it over and it seemed to explode in a huge cloud of dust. It fell in thousands of pieces over about four acres, with the two propellers sticking out of a big crater.

David Roughton said he was harrowing with a team of horses when he saw the aeroplane coming towards him from over the top of some farm buildings 'at a terrible speed', passing within thirty yards of him before crashing, left wing down, eighty-five yards away. Alf Beeken was outside his farm buildings at Vine Lodge when he, too, saw the bomber first fly north then turn left to go southward. He told the coroner:

> When it had completed the turn it seemed to come down pretty steeply with the engines full on. If I had had a ten-foot hoe I could have touched it. It seemed to go into a grass field and then rose again to a height of several hundred feet. There was a terrible row and it went towards the ground at a terrific pace. The left wing touched first and there was a terrific explosion and pieces of plane were sent flying in all directions.

An official enquiry into the incident, based mainly on an inspection of the site and information emerging at the inquest, was unable to determine definitely the cause of the accident. It was noted that the pilot was inexperienced with the Blenheim – borne out by his RAF record of ten hours on the type, of which eight were solo – and although he had flown through cloud the previous day, he had not officially carried out instrument flying on the type. It was also claimed that he had been ordered not to fly in cloud during this flight. The conclusion was that he had lost control in a cloud, and emerged from it at 2,000ft in a dive from which he was unable to level out before hitting the ground. In returning a verdict of misadventure, the coroner said: 'They are some poor people's sons. These men died in the service of their country and they might have been called upon to make some other sacrifice.'

The late 1930s also saw civilian flying schools contributing to the general upsurge in flying training now that the black clouds of war were looming. One example was No.4 Elementary & Reserve Flying Training School based at Blackburn Aircraft Company's Brough Airfield in south Yorkshire, one of whose most famous pupils came very close to writing off what turned out to be a glittering flying career.

Eighteen-year-old Acting Pilot Officer Harold 'Birdie' Bird-Wilson was flying with Acting Pilot Officer Dennis Baker in a British Aircraft Manufacturing Co (BA) Swallow, G-AFIG, a Cirrus-engined light civilian aircraft, one of fifteen operated by the School. The airmen were returning to Brough after visiting Hanworth Airfield near London on 19 September 1938 when the accident occurred. Harold Bird-Wilson later claimed to have been flying the aeroplane at the time of the crash. Nearing Cranwell, they encountered a heavy thunderstorm that forced them down to low level in an effort to get under it. As the aircraft flew beneath a large black cloud it suddenly nose-dived into the ground in Dorrington Fen, just north of Sleaford. Baker was killed outright and Bird-Wilson was seriously injured and badly burned about the face. His burns were treated in Queen Victoria Hospital, East Grinstead where he was among the earliest aircrew 'guinea pig' patients of the surgeon Sir Archibald McIndoe. Harold Bird-Wilson recovered to fight in the Battles of France and Britain and his leadership qualities in the air and on the ground took him to the rank of Air Vice Marshal CBE, DSO, DFC★, AFC★, before his death in 2000.

RAF Hemswell, north of Lincoln, opened in December 1936 as part of 3 Group in the newly created Bomber Command. It had an establishment of two bomber squadrons, with No.144 Squadron moving in during February 1937 followed by No.61 Squadron in March of the same year. Effective from 1 September, the station changed to No.5 Group and re-equipment with the Blenheim began immediately. The programme of re-equipment was completed by No.144 in December 1937 and by No.61 in January 1938, by which time the construction of the station was still in progress and not fully completed until late that year. Spurred on by the political events of the period now referred to as the 'Munich Crisis', all bomber squadrons continued to practice long distance navigation and it was during one of these vital practice trips that No.61 Squadron lost Blenheim L1160 on 7 November 1938.

Pilot Officer Arthur Steele-Perkins, with observer Corporal John Bentley and Wireless Operator/Air Gunner AC2 Alfred Laurens, took off from RAF Hemswell for a navigational exercise to Felixstowe, Bournemouth and back to Hemswell. The Blenheim I, L1160, left at 1.45p.m. and by 2.25p.m. was approaching The Wash on the first leg of the triangular course. Arthur Everitt and his father, from Spalding, were enjoying a day's fishing from their boat *Mavis* out by Gat Sand when they saw an aeroplane about 1,000ft up, heading towards Holbeach Main.

> It was on fire and coming down – but not steeply. It appeared to be attempting to land on a sandbank and then it fell a little. At about one hundred feet it slewed round and then fell on top of Shelridge Run on the Holbeach Main, just inside the bombing range beacon. Immediately there was a terrific explosion and a mass of flames shot up. We were about three-quarters of a mile away and all that could be seen was a burning wreck. A King's Lynn fishing smack and Mr W. Lineham's boat from Fosdyke, went up near it and Mr Lineham, who knows the area well, went in to see if he could help. It is in a very difficult spot to reach because it is surrounded by creeks which are too deep to wade and it is awkward even for a boat to get in.

One of the Blenheim's engines had caught fire as it reached The Wash. Pilot Officer Steele-Perkins descended through cloud, but the aircraft fell into an uncontrolled dive after the cowling of the failed engine broke away. At this point he ordered the crew to bale out and then, with some difficulty, escaped through the roof hatch himself. His parachute opened with little time to spare and he injured an ankle in a heavy landing on the mud flats. Mr Lineham's boat went to his assistance and conveyed the airman back to Fosdyke, from where he was eventually taken to RAF Sutton Bridge in a state of shock.

Corporal Bentley was not so lucky. His body was recovered from the wreck the next day and an RAF investigation found that as he exited the aircraft his parachute had caught on some part of the aeroplane, possibly due to the 'chute deploying prematurely, and he had been unable to separate from the aircraft. Of AC2 Laurens, however, there was no sign. Then, two weeks later, under the headline: 'Sea Gives Up Its Dead', the *Spalding Guardian* reported a grim discovery:

While out exercising a horse on the beach, riding master Len Wright came upon a body lying below high water mark in the vicinity of Gibraltar Point, three miles south of Skegness. The body was dressed in airman's clothing, wearing an inflated lifebelt [*sic*] and parts of some wireless headphones, on which were the words: 'Laurens of Hemswell', were attached to the tunic.

It was the missing wireless operator Alfred Laurens. No mention was made of a parachute being attached, so it seems possible that Laurens may have been able to release it while he was in the water, but was subsequently overcome by either the cold or the waves, or both.

Pilot Officer Steele-Perkins, still limping with a walking stick, recovered sufficiently to attend the inquest on AC2 Laurens. About the flight, he said he was not satisfied with the way one engine was running and he decided to return to Hemswell. As he was turning over Holbeach Marshes the aircraft became uncontrollable and he gave the order to bale out. Corporal Bentley and AC2 Laurens both acknowledged the order. Steele-Perkins was unaware of what happened to Bentley after the latter went out through the roof hatch first and he thought Laurens went out of the gunner's escape hatch alright but was carried out over the sea. He himself landed close to the water's edge but was able to reach the aeroplane, which he found completely burned out with a body lying amongst the wreckage. The official investigation recommended modifications 'for WTO [wireless telegraphy operator] escape hatches to be enlarged and for downwards exit in nose for pilot and observer.'

The action of the cowling on one engine coming off seems to be the point at which the Blenheim became uncontrollable. If the cowling panels peeled back they would act as an asymmetric airbrake and perhaps account for the dive and uncontrollability mentioned above. Although a couple of years later, a report has come to light about a similar incident involving a Blenheim I from No.23 Squadron that lends weight to this theory, and its explanation will be of interest. Following the crash of a Blenheim near Middle Wallop, No.23 Squadron adjutant, Pilot Officer Alan Garwith DFC made these observations:

Our engineering officer and I were detailed to investigate the cause of the [Blenheim] accident that killed Plt Off Orgias and an air gunner on 25/9/1940. From the trail of evidence on the ground – namely a battered engine cylinder, then a frayed steel cable and nearer the crashed aircraft, a twisted and buckled engine cowling and finally the crashed engine with these parts missing, we came to the conclusion that for some reason, the bolts holding the top cylinder of the radial Mercury motor had come loose. The pounding of the piston in the loose cylinder eventually broke the steel cable at the front of the motor, allowing the hinged top and bottom cowlings to open out, suddenly forming an overpowering air brake on one side of the aircraft, beyond the control of the pilot. The cowling is held on by steel cables clamped tightly round at the forward and rear of the motor. The cable strapping the engine cowling came off and the cowling acted as a severe air brake and was found later some distance from the crash site. The pilot, Sgt Laurence Karasek, baled out safely.

After an extremely difficult logistical project, both Bristol Mercury engines were recovered from this site in 1977 by the Lincolnshire Aircraft Preservation Society.

Although the Munich crisis was a particular milestone in the slide into the Second World War, in reality the RAF had been actively preparing itself for war for at least a year before Neville Chamberlain confronted Adolf Hitler. History shows the RAF, while naturally optimistic, was poorly equipped for a shooting war with Germany at that time, but this never stopped it striving to improve its organisational efficiency and the ability and competence of its personnel. It was this scenario that underpinned the biggest air and ground exercise ever held in the UK over the weekend of 3–4 August 1938, when the public was informed that 'over 900 aircraft would be involved' in the exercise area. It is interesting to note that one renowned author, Denis Richards, reveals the front-line strength of the RAF at the time of Munich as 1,982 aeroplanes, while another, Dr R.J. Overy, states only 1,642 aeroplanes could be classed as serviceable at that time. In addition, 15,000 air and ground staff, 17,000 Territorial anti-aircraft personnel and 4,000 members of the Observer Corps would also take part across the whole of south-east England.

The defensive force, known as 'Westland', encompassed the area between the Humber, Dover, the south coast, Andover, Evesham, Leamington and Rotherham. Targets, known only to its commanders, were to be attacked from Friday morning by the bombers of 'Eastland', a territory assumed to be located in the North Sea. This required bombers from Eastland Airfields to fly out over the North Sea then turn back to make for their various secret objectives. During the weekend, civilian authorities, householders and motorists were required to add to the realism by 'blacking-out' the whole of an area encompassing the East Riding and part of West Riding of Yorkshire together with the shires of Lincoln, Nottingham, Derby, Leicester, Rutland, Northampton, Huntingdon, Cambridge, Norfolk, Suffolk, Bedford and part of Buckingham, between 1.00a.m. and 3.00a.m. on the Sunday morning. It was some blackout! The Observer Corps had good practice but searchlight batteries were hampered by low cloud and to make matters worse, a thick fog was descending across East Anglia, while elsewhere there were scattered thunderstorms.

RAF Honington supplied twelve Harrow bombers to the exercise and these operated in pairs, but their first 'attacking' sorties could not be launched until 3.00p.m. on Friday afternoon due to a low cloudbase. The sun eventually came out and air raid sirens wailed at 4.00p.m. as RAF Honington was attacked by two 'enemy' bombers that dived in and made off at such speed that none of the airfield defences had any chance to react! After a break over Friday night, the exercise was due to restart at 10.30a.m. on Saturday but low cloud and fog again delayed this until 2.00p.m. Shortly after this time, RAF Feltwell was 'bombed' by sixteen aircraft followed by a further sixteen attacking RAF Honington. RAF stations Hornchurch, Debden and Northolt were also 'hit' with, of course, many claims for buildings 'destroyed', counter-balanced by fighter claims for 'kills'. As darkness fell, more bombers began attacks over a wide area. Between Saturday midnight and 2.00a.m., twenty-four Avro Ansons crossed the south coast making for targets around London, in some cases being intercepted by the brand new Hawker Hurricane. Twenty-two other bombers went for an assortment of objectives in East Anglia. In the final phase of the exercise 'Eastland' sent off a small raid at 2.00a.m. on Sunday morning, but due to bad weather, heavy rain and poor visibility over most of the region, the aircraft were recalled. It was generally agreed that the bad weather had made the air exercise inconclusive, as neither attackers nor defenders had had a real chance to test each other robustly. The human and equipment price of this exercise was the loss of one HP Harrow and its crew, one Fairey Battle of No.88 Squadron with one of its crew and four Hawker Demon fighters without fatalities.

Villagers in Conyers Green, near Bury St Edmunds were wakened from their slumbers at 12.45a.m. on Sunday 4 August by the noise of a terrific explosion. HP Harrow, K6961, of No.37 Squadron from RAF Feltwell was returning to base following a recall due to the worsening weather situation and had crashed in thick fog. Wreckage, containing the bodies of all five members of the crew, was found on land belonging to Vicarage Farm at the side of the road from Barton to Fornham. The crew comprised: Flying Officer John Adam, pilot; Pilot Officer Edward White, navigator; Pilot Officer Albert Gillespie, second navigator; AC1 Patrick McGovern, radio operator; and AC1 Charles Suthers, air gunner.

As part of the big exercise, this bomber took off from Feltwell at 7.10p.m. on Saturday 3 August on a sortie that was due to last until 12.30a.m. A radio message from K6961 to Feltwell said the aircraft was crossing the coast at North Foreland at 7.58p.m., heading out to sea for its first attack. At 9.10p.m. another message indicated it was re-crossing the coast inbound for its first target, which it reported reaching at 9.47p.m. Having 'attacked' one target, K6961 turned and re-crossed the coast at 10.19p.m. outbound to begin a second 'attack'. At 10.25p.m., however, a general re-call signal was transmitted to all aircraft instructing them to return to their bases by midnight because of bad weather. The crew of K6961 acknowledged this message. At 11.05p.m. the bomber sent a signal that the coast was being crossed inbound for the second objective and the crew reported reaching the second objective at 11.55p.m. No further messages were received.

After reaching the second objective, the Harrow and its crew were due to return directly to Feltwell Airfield at an altitude of between 1,000–2,000ft, which should have taken them about forty minutes. By now, though, thick fog enveloped East Anglia and from notes on a message pad found later in the wreckage, it seems the crew was unsure of its whereabouts and had obtained some DF bearings. Several eyewitnesses told a coroner's court they had fleeting glimpses of the aircraft through the fog, flying very low – one said only 35ft – before hearing the sound of its engines revving hard. This surge of noise was followed by yet more tearing and crashing sounds as the machine tore through the tops of trees. These dragged it ever lower until finally it struck a large oak tree and fell to the ground engulfed in flames. The crash site was roughly on track but about eighteen miles from Feltwell Airfield.

It was clear that when 'the balloon went up', components of the RAF would be sent to France, if only to minimise the flying time to German homeland targets. It was quite usual, therefore, for navigational training exercises to include round trips to France. Working up a sweat scything grass near the village of Corby Glen, George Bish straightened his back to sharpen his blade when he was startled by two large aeroplanes flying low overhead.

Handley Page Hampden, L4088, KM-D of No.44 Squadron RAF Waddington, from the same unit as L4046 which crashed at Corby Glen on 21 July 1939.

It was drizzling with rain and it seemed as if they were lost because they turned round and flew back the way they had come, then they came back over me again a few minutes later. They were still flying low – one was a bit lower than the other. They had just passed over me for the second time when the lower aeroplane dived steeply with its engines full on and crashed two fields away from where I stood. There was a big explosion and the machine burst into flames. My mates and I ran over to the crash but it was almost burned out by the time we got there.

The aeroplane that crashed was Handley Page Hampden, L4046, of No.44 Squadron based at RAF Waddington. It came down in a grass field belonging to Irby Estates near a stream that divides the parishes of Corby Glen and Irnham, Lincolnshire. The explosion gouged a crater six feet deep and several yards across and the blast, which rattled windows in nearby Corby Glen, hurled a cylinder block 200yds from the impact point. The crew that fateful day included: Flying Officer D.I. Jobson, a pilot from New Zealand; Sergeant J.A. Hawes, navigator and a qualified pilot; Acting Sergeant E.W. Jones, observer; and AC2 R.J. Andrews, a wireless operator/air gunner. There were no survivors.

This Hampden was one of twelve aircraft that set off from RAF Waddington on 21 July 1939 to fly to an airfield in France via RAF Tangmere, and it was during the first leg to Tangmere that the accident occurred. Encountering low cloud and rain, Flying Officer Jobson veered upwards and away from the aircraft flying in company with him, and shortly after this, L4046 was seen by the eyewitnesses to dive into the ground.

Two weeks later, the RAF went to war.

Chapter 2

SECOND WORLD WAR
RAF Accidents

Part One: Running On Fumes

On 3 September 1939 the RAF went to war. The practising was over – now it was for real! But, for Bomber Command, this was certainly no 'phoney war', as evidenced by the decimation of daylight raids against the German fleet right from the first days of hostilities. Bomber Command had come a long way over the past three or four years, but though the bravery of its airmen was never in doubt, its initial tactics were found wanting.

The first raid, on 4 September, met with relatively light casualties, but even then it was three weeks before another raid was mounted. Casualties sustained on 29 September would be a sad but more realistic portent of what was to come. On this day, too, the little south Lincolnshire town of Holbeach came to mourn the death of one of its sons, a pilot lost on that second raid of the war. That day, eleven Handley Page Hampdens in two separate formations were despatched to seek German naval targets in the Heligoland Bight. In one group were five aircraft from No.144 Squadron based at RAF Hemswell, L4121, L4126, L4127, L4132 and L4134, led by Wing Commander James Cunningham in L4134. In addition to Sergeant Albert Povey and AC1 Harry Liggett, the squadron commander's crew included Sergeant Ronald Herd, a native of Holbeach and the crew's usual pilot who, on this occasion, had given up his cockpit to his CO and was acting as navigator for the trip, a role in which – because pre-war pilots like him were schooled in navigation as well – he would have found quite comfortable.

Finding two destroyers, the first formation dropped its bombs and returned unscathed. But the five aircraft from No.144 Squadron disappeared without trace. No radio messages; no enemy propaganda. They had been wiped from the face of the earth. An official RAF communiqué later describing the loss was somewhat terse:

> Five aircraft led by Wg Cdr Cunningham took off at 06.50 to search the German coast between 5 and 8 degrees East. Nothing further was heard of the raid and it is presumed the aircraft were shot down while carrying out an attack on the German fleet.

Indeed the Hampdens had been wiped out. Post-war research shows them to have been shot down by Bf109 fighters of 1/ZG26, from whose pilots Oblt Specht claimed two, Hptmn Dickore one and Uffz's Pollack and Pirsch one each. In addition to Sergeant Herd, Wing Commander Cunningham and sixteen other airmen died. Just seven airmen survived to spend the entire war, bar a mere twenty-six days, as Prisoners of War. Sergeant Herd was buried in Sage War Cemetery, Oldenburg, Germany, but he is also commemorated in his home town of Holbeach by a fine copper beech tree that his mother arranged to have planted in the churchyard, beneath which is a plaque bearing the inscription:

> Sergeant Ronald E. Herd,
> Killed in action,
> 29 September 1939.

When Sergeant Frank Petts brought his crippled, bullet-riddled Wellington to a halt on the welcoming green pastures of RAF Sutton Bridge, he would have been the first to agree that he was damn lucky to be alive.

At 9.00a.m. on 18 December 1939, nine Vickers Wellington Mk IA bombers of No.9 Squadron, including N2873 flown by Frank Petts, climbed away north from RAF Honington for a rendezvous point over King's Lynn. Here they were to meet up with another nine Wellingtons from No.149 Squadron based at RAF Newmarket Heath. Together, these eighteen aircraft would be joined by six more from No.37 Squadron, RAF Feltwell, as they all headed out over The Wash and across the North Sea to attack shipping targets in the German port of Wilhelmshaven.

One of a series of similar raids by the RAF, this latest would prove equally ineffective, but it actually achieved far greater significance by heralding the end of unescorted daylight attacks by Bomber Command in Europe – at least for the next four years or so. Nevertheless, it underlined the bravery and tenacity of RAF bomber crews right from the very outset of the air war – bravery that cost them dearly in lost aircrews, a pre-war resource which the RAF could ill afford to fritter away before an effective training system for replacements was in place. But that ending also marked a beginning, too, for out of the tragic lessons of those ill-conceived early daylight raids came the rationale for the RAF's night bombing campaign.

In the meantime, on that crisp, clear, December morning, one of the key factors in RAF daylight raid planning was singularly absent. There was not a cloud in the sky. Concealment – considered in those days more important even than defensive fire – was going to be out of the question on this trip. If enemy fighters found them … As the formation approached the enemy coast near Cuxhaven, that's precisely what happened. No.149 Squadron's Wellingtons rendezvoused on time over King's Lynn with those of No.9 Squadron, and as Wing Commander Richard Kellett AFC led the group out over the North Sea, the other six Wellingtons from No.37 Squadron slotted in at the rear of the formation making twenty-four in total, each of them carrying three 500lb semi-armour piercing bombs. As the flight progressed, two bombers turned back with engine trouble, while the rest headed for landfall off the island of Sylt. The approach of the formation had, however, already been detected by experimental radar units located on the islands of Wangerooge and Heligoland, and the Luftwaffe, although slow to react, began to home in on the bombers. Frank Petts now takes up the story.

> Leaving Sylt to port, in clear skies we turned south to fly over the Schillig Roads at 15,000 feet, where our briefing stated enemy warships might be anchored, but none were to be seen. Coming abreast of Cuxhaven Sgt Robertson, my rear gunner, spotted Me109 and Me110 fighters diving on others in our formation. These attacks seemed to be beaten off though and we continued southwards along the coast past Bremerhaven, before the whole formation made a sweeping turn across Jade Bay and headed directly for Wilhelmshaven.

Intense flak, some of it from capital ships, greeted them over the port area. Frantically juggling throttles and revs, Sergeant Petts was having great difficulty holding his position on the outside of this unwieldy formation and began to lag behind. At least the fighters, having downed two bombers already, left them alone while the flak had a go.

The bomb doors were soon open, but just as their targets hove into view, there came a rapid change of plan. Formation leader Wing Commander Kellett, having seen that his targets were berthed alongside quays and harbour walls, radioed the order not to bomb, believing it impossible to attack without risk to German civilians. As the formation roared impotent across the target – not once, but twice – it became even more loose and strung out. The hail of flak stopped; now it was the German fighters' turn to attack. With 109s and 110s coming at them from the beam and above, vulnerable points where front, rear and ventral 'dustbin' guns could not cover well, the Wellingtons were sitting ducks. As Frank Petts' Wellington emerged from the barrage, he dumped his bombs, not even worrying where they might fall now but just hoping to gain some extra speed. He continues:

> About this time LAC Balch on the front guns got his first fighter. I saw tracer from Balch's first burst hit a 109 in the cockpit area. The canopy, or part of it, flew off and his second burst sent it into a dive with white smoke pouring out. I think he got a 110, too.
>
> In spite of full throttle and full revs, I could not keep up with my section. Plt Off Ginger Heathcote [observer] pointed out six 37 Squadron aircraft behind us and suggested we drop back and tag on to them. It's just as well that I didn't take his advice. Enemy fighters tore into that group and shot down five of those six Wellingtons! Since I couldn't catch up with my own section, I turned to starboard, put the nose down, screaming from 15,000 feet to sea level. I cannot remember just how many fighter attacks there were but the first came before we dived and there were more on the way down and I remember my astonishment at seeing the ASI flickering on 300mph while we were going down!

Left to right: Sergeant Lawson, Sergeant Frank Petts, LAC Whitham and LAC Balch. Air Gunner LAC Balch claimed two enemy fighters during the 18 December 1939 raid. (Jeremy Petts via Martin Bowman)

Sergeant Petts and his crew played cat and mouse in a running battle with 110s right down at sea level. Working as a team, tracking each enemy attack as it came in, at the last moment Petts would slam throttles shut and pitch levers to coarse while the gunners poured machine-gun fire at the fleeing enemy as their guns bore. Then full throttle and revs again to make more headway towards home. The crew heard a whoop of delight from Sergeant Robertson in the rear turret as he put a burst into another 110 and saw it dive away, apparently out of control. In the heat of the engagement, however, first ventral gunner AC1 Kemp was seriously wounded, and LAC Balch was shot in the foot. Fortunately Balch was not badly hurt, but Kemp was losing a lot of blood from a bad thigh wound and needed attention quickly. Ginger Heathcote went back to extricate Kemp from his 'dustbin' turret; a difficult task due to the gunner's bulky clothing in the confined space and the effects of his wound. By this time both Robinson and Kemp had expended all their ammunition, the centre section of the fuselage had sustained innumerable hits and both beam guns were out of action. With Kemp laid out on the rest bunk, Heathcote then went forward to help Balch out of his turret, taking his place to keep up a measure of defensive fire. Meanwhile in the cockpit, Frank Petts had enough problems of his own to contend with:

> When the fighters left us, I eased back to normal cruising throttle and propeller settings and checking round was shaken to find the starboard engine oil gauge reading zero. The propellers on the Wellington IA did not feather so I had to be content with pulling the starboard engine right back. With that setting it would give less drag than if I switched it off. If it did not seize I thought it might be of some use if I needed it later. Opening up the port engine to climbing power I found I was able to climb gently to 1,000 feet. During this time I turned onto a course of 270 degrees which was bound to bring us up somewhere in England.

In the event, Sergeant Petts' course brought him back to The Wash and within a few more minutes, the airfield at RAF Sutton Bridge hove into view. Safely back on *terra firma* it was time to view the damage. No doubt it would be a sobering sight, not only to Petts and his crew, but also to the aspiring fighter pilots on whose grass runway he had just landed.

From starboard wingtip to the middle of the wing fuel tanks was badly shot up and had at one stage been on fire. It was pure luck that most of the attacks had come from that side, as armour plate, which prevented fire from reaching the fuel, had for some reason only been installed in that wing. The fuselage aft of the wings resembled a colander. Petts and his crew were lucky. No.9 Squadron had lost five out of nine aircraft despatched. It was said that forty-four enemy fighters harried the Wellingtons for half an hour, breaking off their attacks only eighty miles from the English coast. Out of the twenty-two bombers actually reaching the target, seven were shot down, two were forced to ditch and three crash-landed back in England. Despite our air gunner claims, the Germans actually lost only two fighters.

This operational fiasco prompted an enquiry by Bomber Command, but there was much 'buck-passing'. Most of the Wellingtons were lost to fighters making beam attacks, catching fire easily as petrol poured from unprotected fuel tanks. As a result of these and earlier hard lessons, extra armour and self-sealing fuel tanks were fitted. But this did not overcome the fundamental issue that poorly planned, unescorted daylight raids against fighter opposition – although even the enemy was somewhat disorganised and less than thorough on this occasion – were doomed to failure.

In an effort to maintain its quest to seek out and destroy the German fleet – while painfully aware of the price of being caught by day – the RAF mounted one particular anti-shipping raid on 20/21 February 1940, illustrating an interesting change of tactics. Two Wellingtons of No.99 Squadron (RAF Newmarket Heath) were detailed for a night reconnaissance patrol over the Heligoland Bight; they were to act as eyes for a separate bombing force. Eighteen Wellingtons, standing off over the North Sea under cover of darkness would, if definite targets were spotted, be directed straight to them, to pounce quickly and to get out fast. Although the Wellingtons played their part, fog and dense cloud made it impossible to find anything, let alone ships, and so the strike force had to be recalled. For one of the *Wimpeys*, though, the night was far from over.

Having left Newmarket at 9.30p.m., Flight Lieutenant J.F. Brough in P9219 set course for the Dutch coast, making landfall at Ameland island some two hours later. Cruising at 8,000ft to a dead reckoning position of 54.00 N by 06.20 E in the Heligoland Bight, he found the whole area covered by ten-tenths cloud up to his own altitude. Circling for a while and descending gingerly a few thousand feet into the murk, there was no sign of a break. After consulting with Lieutenant Commander Phillimore, a Royal Navy observer carried specially for the trip, Brough radioed an adverse weather report that resulted in the aforementioned recall.

Setting course for home himself, Flight Lieutenant Brough was unable to locate RAF Newmarket due to a real pea-souper of a fog. Circling round until his fuel was exhausted, after seven and a half hours in the air he elected to crash-land his Wellington. Fortunately P9219 came down relatively safely at Walsoken, near Wisbech with the only casualty being the unfortunate naval gentleman, who was slightly injured. This novel attempt to avoid enemy dayfighters, while admirable in theory, in practice fell victim to the weather and does not appear to have been repeated.

While current British war policy prevented air attacks on German soil, Bomber Command war diaries tell of night leaflet raids to Germany and the occupied countries, known as '*Nickel* raids' – plus minelaying and anti-shipping patrols – continuing over the following months. Dropping leaflets may seem innocuous enough, but these operations, although providing crews with much needed long-range navigation experience at night, were still subject to the weather and to technical problems, as well as the usual malicious attention of the enemy. An example of such technical problems occurred on the night of 1/2 March 1940.

Poor flying conditions, encountered all over Europe since December 1939, continued into March of the following year, seriously interfering with night operations by the RAF and the enemy alike. Flying Officer Leo Field of No.149 Squadron was briefed for a *Nickel* raid to Bremen, and at 12.30p.m. lined up Wellington IA, N2984, for take-off from RAF Mildenhall. Shortly after leaving the runway, the bomber entered clouds and the port engine failed. It was not clear what happened next, but it is believed the Wellington went into a dive, stalled near the ground during an attempted recovery and crashed at Burnt Fen south of Downham Market ten minutes after take-off. All six airmen on board were killed: Flying Officer Field, pilot; Sergeants Maurice Wiffen, second pilot and James Murdoch, observer; LAC Ernest Prior and AC2s Laurence Hughson, wireless operator/air gunner and Thomas Smith, AG. The ranks of these latter three are typical among aircrew of the time. Murdoch, Hughson and Smith were all Scottish, and are believed to have crewed up together for that reason. LAC Prior was a native of Waterbeach and, like all the others, was buried in his home village.

Flying at altitude in winter was debilitating too. Recording his experience for the Bomber Command web site, Wireless Operator/Air Gunner Greg Gregson recalled:

It was freezing! The aircraft used to ice up. We had leaflets to drop and if you cut the pack and touched the knife to your skin it would stick. You tried to put as much clothing on as you could because you couldn't get a lot of movement in the aircraft; you can't jump up and down to keep warm. One of the things I remember about the winter of 1939/40 was the absolute cold. If I could get a pair of silk stockings I'd wear these, then woollen socks and then flying boots, which were fur lined, then an inner jacket like a teddy bear with a canvas coating, then a leather jacket with fur, three pairs of gloves – a silk pair, wool then leather gauntlets. Sheer cold is one of the worst things. You had to sit there and try to think warm.

It was not until the opening of the Norwegian campaign in April 1940, however, that Wellington and Hampden bombers again ventured forth, unescorted, in any strength in daylight. When enemy fighters shot down nine of these during a daylight attack on shipping targets in the Stavanger area on 12 April, it seemed to be the Wilhelmshaven situation all over again. After this point, Bomber Command, unable to accept such a rate of attrition any longer, diverted its Wellington and Hampden squadrons to join the Whitley force in the night bombing role. A further significant event occurred during the period that became known as the Battle of France. On 15 May 1940 the severe bombing of Rotterdam by German aircraft brought about a decision to implement the RAF's strategic bombing plan – with real bombs now instead of leaflets – and such raids could be made on Germany itself.

Throughout that fateful summer of 1940, while by day the fighter boys held the Luftwaffe at bay, RAF bombers went out night after night carrying the fight into enemy territory. It was not until October 1940 though, mainly due to steady deterioration in weather conditions as summer gave way to autumn, that Fenland night skies began now to reverberate with sounds of wayward and weary bombers. We should not forget, either, that airmen from the occupied countries played a vital role and that many of them paid a high price in their struggle for freedom. Equipped with the Wellington bomber, No.311 (Czech) Squadron, for example, began night operations in July 1940 from RAF Honington. These were the days before the bomber OTU organisation got into its stride and final crew training was carried out in Avro Anson aircraft held on charge by the squadrons themselves. A curious and poignant story emerged relating to this unit, illustrating that even the most innocuous training sortie could become fraught with danger. That immortal phrase, 'In some foreign field', applies equally well to these European allied airmen.

Four CWGC headstones in Peterborough's Eastfield cemetery mark the end of a training sortie that went horribly wrong for a 'rookie' Czech bomber crew on a training exercise on 1 October 1940. Six of the seven airmen on board Avro Anson I, R9649 that day were members of a new Wellington crew, while the seventh was a British radio instructor, Sergeant George Powis, a wireless operator/air gunner by trade. Only two would return alive.

The crowded Anson took off from Honington for a cross-country navigational exercise across the Midlands, but ran into bad weather and somewhere in the vicinity of Leicester, a decision was made to turn back to base. Shortly afterwards, R9649 crashed at Elton, a small village near Peterborough. The strange circumstances leading up to the accident emerged when Wing Commander J.M. Griffiths, No.311 Squadron CO, carried out his own investigation, during which he examined the site, questioned the two survivors and produced the written report which follows:

I examined the scene of the crash within a few hours of the accident. The burned out wreckage covered an area approx. fifteen yards square. The position of the engines indicated that the aircraft had dived vertically into the ground. This was subsequently confirmed by a witness who stated that the aircraft approached at low altitude emitting large quantities of smoke, before suddenly bursting into flames and diving into the ground.

Prior to examining the wreckage, it was ascertained from one of the survivors that the fire had broken out very suddenly somewhere on the floor in the vicinity of the navigator's table. This indicated the likelihood of someone having fired the Very pistol. The pistol

N5331, an Avro Anson from a Polish unit and similar to the aircraft of No.311 Squadron lost in the accident on 1 Oct 1940. Note the Polish Air Force badge behind the '5' on the nose. (John Rennison)

[a large-bore, single-shot, hand-held pistol, used to fire coloured flare cartridge e.g. in times of distress or danger] was discovered amongst the wreckage and found to contain a cartridge that had been fired.

The Anson was being flown by Sgt Oskar Valosek. When it turned back to base, navigator Plt Off Jaroslav Kula, seated at his table on the port side behind the pilot, asked for the wireless op to get him a bearing. Meanwhile, Plt Off Josef Slovak, who was sitting next to the pilot on the starboard side of the cockpit and Plt Off Ludvik Nemec, the captain of this new Wellington crew sitting on the main spar behind him, attempted to work out the aircraft's position by means of map reading. [The pilot appears, therefore, to have let down through the cloud to obtain visual contact with the ground.] About thirty minutes before the crash, WOp/AG Sgt George Powis came forward to hand a bearing to Plt Off Kula then, ten minutes later, Czech WOp Sgt Frantisek Koukol came forward from his seat at the W/T desk with a second bearing, which he handed to Plt Off Kula.

At this point Plt Off Kula apparently had difficulty in laying down the bearing and some sort of argument ensued between himself and Sgt Koukol, who stood next to Plt Off Kula's seat. Sgt Powis had moved slightly further forward and positioned himself as a spectator at the end of the navigator's table, standing directly beside the Very pistol stowage [believed to be an open pouch secured to the end of the table]. With Plt Off Jaroslav Skutil sitting at the back of the fuselage in the dorsal gun turret, these were the positions of all the airmen when the fire broke out.

Plt Off Nemec was peering out of the starboard cockpit side window when he heard a loud detonation and turning suddenly, he saw a fire on the floor under the navigation table. Yelling 'Fire!' Plt Off Nemec attempted to stamp out the fire but, unable to do so, for some unaccountable reason he then commenced beating at the flames with the butt of the Very pistol. Meanwhile, with the aircraft rapidly filling with dense smoke, Nemec then leaned towards the instrument panel and attempted to turn off the flow of petrol. He was prevented from doing this by the pilot, Sgt Valosek, who knocked Nemec's arm away as he reached for the petrol cocks. Plt Off Nemec then gave the order to bale out and having clipped on his own parachute, strode down the fuselage and left the aircraft via the side door. During his passage through the fuselage he saw one WOp trying to get out through the roof exit hatch and another through the starboard side window. He had also noticed the altimeter was registering 600 to 700 feet. The ground at this point is about 200 feet above the level of Honington, which would make the absolute height of the aircraft about 400 feet. Plt Off Kula saw the fire under his table after hearing a loud bang and grabbing his parachute he, too, made a rapid exit through the side door.

I am of the opinion that this accident is attributable to some member of the crew having accidentally pulled the trigger and discharged the Very pistol through the floor of the aircraft. The facts combined with the discovery of the pistol containing a spent cartridge appears to me as a clear indication of the means by which the fire was started.

Signed W.R. Griffiths, Wg Cdr commanding 311 Squadron.

Pilot Officers Nemec and Kula escaped safely by parachute, but the other five men perished. Sergeant Powis is buried in his hometown of Derby, while the four Czech airmen are buried in Peterborough.

Although a highly unusual occurrence in the air, it was certainly not the last time a Very pistol was accidentally discharged inside an aeroplane. For example, a Very pistol was discharged in a Mosquito from No.105 Squadron as it came in to land at RAF Marham after a bombing operation on 12/13 May 1944, causing the deaths of Flight Lieutenant Norman Clayes DFC and Flying Officer Frederick Deighton in the ensuing crash. A ground incident was also recalled by an airman at a Canadian training school, coincidentally one that operated the Avro Anson.

One day an armourer was checking the Very pistol behind the second pilot's seat and without bothering to take the pistol out of its pouch, he reached in and pulled the trigger. It fired a three-star flare. He caught each star in his bare hands and threw them out the window. He wore bandages for a long time and was awarded a MID!

After their brush with death, both Pilot Officers Nemec and Kula flew operationally with No.311 Squadron. Ludvik Nemec completed eleven operations in mid-1941 before being promoted Flight Lieutenant and posted to a Czechoslovak depot unit until the end of the war. Sadly, Jaroslav Kula's name appears among those missing in action on 12/13 March 1942. He was the navigator of Wellington IC, R1802 when it was reported missing that night, believed to be the result of engine problems over the North Sea while outbound for an attack on Kiel. No trace of the aircraft or its Czech crew was ever found.

Walking on a little further through the cemetery brings one to the CWGC grave of Yugoslavian Flying Officer Nebojsa Kujundzic, who sacrificed his own life on 3 March 1943 to save his crew and civilians in the village of Yaxley. This pilot was on a training flight in Lancaster I, W4333 from No.103 Squadron at RAF Elsham Wolds when, near Peterborough, the starboard outer engine caught fire. Shutting down the engine and feathering its propeller failed to put out the blaze and with fire spreading to the mainplane, unable to maintain height and heading for a village, Flying Officer Kujundzic ordered his crew to bale out. He remained at the controls until it was too late for him to jump before the starboard wing broke off. Due to Kujundzic's efforts, his crew was saved and the bomber missed the houses and crashed into a field beyond. The people of Yaxley, realising the devastation that could have befallen their village, were so moved by Flying Officer Kujundzic's sacrifice that they collected the tidy sum of £65 and asked his squadron to hand it to his relatives. Naturally in wartime that was a nigh impossible request to fulfil so, instead, the cheque was handed over to the RAF Benevolent Fund and a letter of thanks was sent to the villagers for their kind gesture.

Bad weather, that age-old enemy of the airman, still took its toll, and will – as in most of these chapters – continue to play a leading role in this story. What will also become evident – if it hasn't already – is the spirit of endurance and fortitude of aircrew in the face of so much adversity, both man-made and natural. It is also useful to bear in mind that the maximum RAF bomber strength classed as suitable for night operations in winter conditions in 1940 and 1941 (realistically the Wellington, Hampden and Whitley component) fluctuated between only 150 and 230 aircraft. So just what special qualities did it take to keep those aeroplanes in the air for so long?

Decaying, barnacle encrusted remains of military aeroplanes are often yielded up by The Wash, and one such find in July 1990 received front page coverage in the *King's Lynn Citizen* newspaper. Fishermen, out trawling the shallow waters of The Wash off King's Lynn, brought to the surface what turned out to be a Bristol Pegasus engine and propeller. Identified as the type of engine fitted to Hampden bombers, Bob Collis, a member of the Norfolk and Suffolk Aviation Museum, was able to offer readers a possible explanation of events from material he had gleaned from MOD archives. The newspaper story that follows well illustrates the results that can be achieved with the application of effort and patience:

> Judging from its bent condition, the three-bladed De Havilland constant-speed airscrew was obviously running on impact with the water. From the location of the wreckage and the probable aircraft type it is believed this aeroplane may well be Hampden P1354, OL-Y of No.83 Squadron based at RAF Scampton.
>
> After participating in the first RAF attack on Berlin on the night of 25/26 August 1940, squadron records reported P1354 as crashing in The Wash.
>
> Three aircraft were lost over the target, while three Hampdens, operating at the maximum limit of their range, fell victim to an un-forecast strong headwind on the return leg. One of these, P1354, was coaxed to stay airborne for 10 hours and 40 minutes until, at 06.55 over The Wash, its engines finally spluttered through shortage of petrol.
>
> Spotting two ships below him, pilot Fg Off Neil Svendson DFC decided to ditch near them. Challenged by one of the vessels, the approaching aeroplane's response was not seen. This prompted the 'nervy Navy' to loose off a four-inch shell which fell perilously close to the Hampden as it hit the sea. Stalling at sixty feet the bomber hit the water tail-first, both engines being wrenched off by the impact.
>
> Despite quite a swell running at the time, very little water actually entered the fuselage. Unhurt, Svendson and his crew, Sgts Threlfall, Gear and Dale, were able to inflate their dinghy and climb in without getting their feet wet. By the time the Hampden sank ten minutes later, the airmen had been picked up by a Naval vessel and were soon on their way to Harwich. Questioned later by 'Bomber' Harris, AOC No.5 Group, Svendson was asked by the great man if he thought Berlin was too distant a target for the Hampden. With typical RAF aplomb he replied: 'Oh no sir – as long as the wind doesn't change while we are in the air!'

As a Flight Lieutenant with No.83 Squadron, Neil Svendson – not to be confused with New Zealander Pilot Officer Neil Svenson of No.77 Squadron, who went missing on operations on 16 December 1940 – ran into trouble on the night of 30 June/1 July 1941 when his Hampden, AD916, was hit by flak during a sortie to Düsseldorf and crashed at Düren.

He survived and became a Prisoner of War, so maybe Lady Luck smiled on him again that night.

The 'nervy Navy' had 'had a go' at another Hampden around dawn on 9 August. Pilot Officer L. Metcalfe's AE259 of No.61 Squadron was approaching the Lincolnshire coast at the end of a long sortie to Kiel when the bomber was hit by light flak from a British convoy. Taking hits on both engines, first the starboard engine failed followed later by the port engine, Metcalf – who had made a valiant effort to reach his base at RAF North Luffenham – finally ran out of sky and had to force land in a field at Algarkirk, just inland from the mouth of the River Welland. Pilot Officer Metcalfe naturally lodged a strong complaint along the lines that he 'had quite enough to do to cope with the enemy pooping off at him let alone the Royal Navy!' It was noted by the subsequent enquiry that 'it was a frequent occurrence for convoys to fire at our aircraft even though the letter and colours of the day have been signalled', which concluded: 'the matter is being taken up with higher authorities', although it is unlikely that either the Merchant or Royal Navies would take such complaints to heart.

They seem to have continued their 'shoot first and ask questions later' attitude regardless, as evidenced even years later by the loss of Halifax DT742, from No.51 Squadron, off the north Norfolk coast on the night of 11/12 June 1943. Flight Sergeant J. Collins and his crew had bombed Dusseldorf and, homeward bound, no doubt thought they were home and dry until a British convoy fired on them and Collins had to ditch his aircraft! Wireless Operator/Air Gunner Sergeant Phillip Spreckley died and Sergeant H. Parker was injured, but the rest of the crew survived the ditching and were rescued quite quickly.

On the night of 16/17 October 1940, attacks by seventy-three Hampden and Wellington bombers were dispersed across four targets: Bremen, Kiel, Merseburg and Bordeaux. With less than an average of twenty aeroplanes attacking each of these targets and each doing so as an individual unit rather than as part of a single force, the impact on the enemy's war effort

Hampdens, AE257 KM-X and AE252 KM-K of No.44 Squadron, RAF Waddington.

at this stage was more psychological than destructive. So bad was the weather over England for the return journey that it contributed to the loss of no less than ten Hampdens and four Wellingtons in crashes that night. Three other bombers were lost over enemy territory, giving a total loss rate of thirty per cent – almost as costly as the daylight raids!

Among the Hampdens dispatched were eight from No.44 Squadron, based at RAF Waddington and the story of just one of their number will illustrate the perils of a typical raid. Easing Hampden P2142 upwards over Ermine Street, with the splendour of Lincoln Cathedral disappearing beneath the port wing, Sergeant L.F. Kneil set course for Germany. With his crew, Sergeants Hazelden, Thorne and Yates, he was briefed to take off at 6.20p.m. on 16 October and attack Merseburg near Leipzig, with six 250lb bombs and sixty incendiaries. Unable to find his primary target (a common problem in those days), Sergeant Kneil dropped his load instead on what he later described as 'an unidentified factory with two chimneys, situated in woods about twenty miles south of the primary target area.'

Running into bad weather on the return leg, Sergeant Kneil found Waddington completely 'socked in' by fog. Already low on fuel, he was directed to head for RAF Bircham Newton, an airfield about eighty miles south, near King's Lynn. Extending across the whole of East Anglia, the same blanket of fog prevented him from landing at Bircham too and he was diverted yet again. Heading now towards RAF Mildenhall, at 3.30a.m. on 17 October, after more than nine hours in the air, the petrol tanks on P2142 finally ran dry. Now with no option but to force land, the flat arable Fens above which he had been 'stooging around' for so long offered Sergeant Kneil a pretty good chance of survival. Crash-landing the Hampden at Ramsey St Mary, the crew emerged without injury and even P2142 was assessed as only 'Cat R' (repairable). A very lucky escape indeed.

Six of No.44 Squadron's eight Hampdens claimed to have bombed Merseburg while another dropped its bombs on a railway line twenty miles west of Leipzig. Two Hampdens crash-landed back at Waddington and RAF losses for the night totalled seventeen aircraft, of which fourteen had fallen victim to weather-related mishaps in England. Four nights later, on 20/21 October, more Hampdens were lost in similar circumstances. Once again the total raiding force of 139 aircraft were despatched to several targets. Among those attacking Berlin that night were eight Hampdens of No.144 Squadron and eight from No.61 Squadron, both based at RAF Hemswell. The primary target was Lehrter railway station, Berlin's eighteen-platform main gateway to the north of the country, and the alternative was the Siemens-Halske electrical equipment works. Sergeants R.G.W. Oakley (pilot), Horn, Durtnall and Keet, in X2980 from No.61 Squadron, encountered atrocious weather en route, but claimed to have reached and hit their target. Dogged by bad weather all the way home too, buffeted by strong winds and storm clouds, X2980, its crew uncertain of their position, pressed on until the aeroplane finally ran out of fuel well south of its home airfield. Sergeant Oakley crash-landed the bomber at North Brink, near Wisbech, but once again the crew escaped with only minor injuries.

A similar fate befell X2906 and P4418. In the former, Pilot Officer I.A. Stewart (pilot) with Pilot Officer Reeve and Sergeants Brewer and Beck also bombed the primary target, with the rear gunner claiming he saw a fire break out after the bombs were released. Approaching the English coast on the return leg this aircraft, too, ran out of fuel. Coming in over The Wash, X2906's engines coughed their last just over dry land in the vicinity of Tilney St Lawrence near King's Lynn, and in the circumstances, Pilot Officer Stewart pulled off a brilliant wheels-down forced landing, saving both crew and aeroplane from serious damage. When bad weather reports for the target area eventually filtered back to base, a signal was sent diverting crews to alternate targets, but many had already battled their way through to Berlin. However, for Pilot Officer H.T. Gilbert with Sergeants Mapp, Jones and Thomas on board P4418, this order was received before they found the city. It made little difference, though, as they were equally unable to locate the alternate target in such atrocious conditions. Jettisoning his bombs into the Zuider Zee, Gilbert turned for home but he, too, ran out of fuel and crash-landed close to Guyhirne Bridge near Wisbech. That brought No.61 Squadron's tally of mishaps for the unhappy night to a close. It was noted in squadron records that this raid was Sergeant Jones' twenty-ninth operation, and no doubt he was glad to see the back of it!

Accurate navigation under such adverse flying conditions was virtually impossible that night, costing yet more aeroplanes when, hopelessly off course and short of fuel, three Hampdens of No.144 Squadron trying to find their way back to Hemswell also had to crash-land in Norfolk. In addition, No.44 Squadron at Waddington lost two Hampdens; one to the enemy over Berlin and one forced landing out of petrol near Colchester. No.49 Squadron also sent its Hampdens to Berlin, and one of these was so far off track it, too, ran out of fuel and was forced to land in Cornwall!

During the autumn and winter of 1940/41 the Blenheim contribution to the official bomber strength of the RAF amounted to about 200 aircraft, a substantial proportion of the total available for operations at that time. After the Battle of France, it was used to harry barge concentrations in the Channel ports, but with the successful outcome of the Battle of Britain, the onset of winter and the Blenheim's range and payload limitations, it was difficult to see it making a practical contribution to the mounting night bombing offensive against Germany. Nonetheless, it deserves mention at this point since No.2 Group's Blenheims did indeed participate in bomber operations as the following two incidents will testify.

Bristol Blenheim IVs of No.82 Squadron lined up at RAF Watton. The squadron used RAF Bodney for dispersal and operations in 1941.

No.235 Squadron, based at RAF Bircham Newton, was tasked to bomb Wilhelmshaven in daylight on 2 December 1940, and among those detailed was Sergeant Evans' crew in T1946. Making an unfamiliar landfall on the return leg they became lost in atrocious weather and could not get an R/T bearing to help. Following the coast into The Wash, Sergeant Evans spotted the windsock on Holbeach range landing ground and at 12.45a.m. set the Blenheim down in the small grass field. He overshot slightly then had to swing his aircraft suddenly to avoid an anti-invasion trench in its path, causing a ground-loop and the undercarriage to collapse. All emerged unhurt.

On the night of 3/4 December, Blenheims of No.82 Squadron at RAF Bodney joined Whitley bombers in small-scale raids against Duisburg, Essen and Mannheim. Squadron Leader J.H. McMichael with his crew of Sergeants Hodges and Lawrence led the Blenheims attacking the steelworks at Essen, but he ran into extremely bad weather on the return. Squadron Leader McMichael could find no gaps in the thick cloud cover that would enable him to land at Bodney. He tried without success to get in at Bircham Newton so, with fuel getting very low, he climbed to 6,000ft and ordered the aircraft to be abandoned. McMichael landed near King's Lynn while the two sergeants came down near Marham, the gunner quite conveniently dropping onto RAF Marham cookhouse! T1813 crashed to earth half a mile east of Denver Sluice, near the town of Downham Market. That night, No.82 Squadron lost three more Blenheims, with one crew becoming Prisoners of War and the two other crews being killed in weather-related crashes in England.

German synthetic oil production installations were primary targets for Bomber Command, with attacks on industrial cities, airfields and minelaying being undertaken as and when resources permitted. Tactics, though, still involved despatching small groups of aircraft against several individual targets on any given night, but the oil targets were notoriously difficult to pinpoint and the clearest of weather conditions were needed to find them with any degree of certainty. Sorties by Whitley bombers in this context – which will underline feats of endurance that ended with Fate uncharitably deciding the loss of both men and machines – can be found all through the harsh winter of 1940/41.

In the evening of 28 November 1940, for example, No.51 Squadron despatched six Whitley V aircraft against the synthetic oil works at Politz near Stettin on the Baltic coast. Pilot Officer D.J. Dunn, with his crew Pilot Officer Myers and Sergeants Gray, Cresswell and Eddowes, took off from RAF Dishforth in T4201 loaded with two 500lb bombs, four 250lb bombs and two containers of incendiaries. Although Dunn reached Politz without too much difficulty and made his run over the target at 11,000ft, results could not be seen due to the blinding effect of many searchlights and an intense flak barrage. Bad weather back at base meant a diversion, so Pilot Officer Dunn headed well to the south to try for a landing at RAF Bircham Newton. Unfortunately, cloud cover was still impenetrable over Norfolk and to make matters worse, his radio failed. 'Stooging' around to no avail only used up more precious fuel. When that reached a critical state, still without having found an airfield, Dunn headed in the general direction of The Wash with the intention of ditching.

It was at 5.00a.m. on 29 November when Pilot Officer Dunn and his crew, Dunn having pulled off a brilliant ditching in the choppy water, took to their dinghy. In the bitter cold dawn all five airmen were rescued safely, six miles off King's Lynn. T4201 finally went to a watery grave, but to her credit she had stayed airborne for no less than twelve hours before her petrol was finally exhausted.

How to hit the oil plants effectively, would continue to be a thorny issue for Bomber Command for many a long year. Middlebrook and Everitt, for instance, state:

Armstrong-Whitworth Whitley V, T4131 MH-W, a veteran of No.51 Squadron.

> In 1944, Bomber Command would judge that nearly 200 four-engine bombers carrying 1,000 tons of bombs would be a reasonable force to attack Wesselling [one of the list of synthetic oil targets].

Incapacitating such targets was clearly beyond the capacity of the 1940/41 Bomber Command. Sometimes Bomber Command was able to take advantage of a rare moonlight night, but then conditions often deteriorated by the time the bombers either approached their targets or regained English shores. Despite the rudimentary nature of long-distance weather forecasting at this time, it seems unlikely, in view of RAF philosophy of carrying the fight to the enemy, that raids would have been called off, even if bad weather was anticipated. Command said 'press on', and so the crews pressed on. But fog was a particular bane in a bomber pilot's life.

Returning from a raid against Kiel on 13/14 December, another Whitley V, this time N1485 of No.78 Squadron based at RAF Dishforth, was well off track over The Wash when both engines failed. On this occasion the pilot, New Zealander Pilot Officer Michael Stedman, chose to abandon his aircraft rather than ditch and gave the order to bale out. Sadly only two of the crew – Sergeants Waldren, navigator and Grunsell, wireless operator/ air gunner – survived, and of the remainder, only the body of the second pilot Sergeant Dennis Angell was recovered by lifeboatmen among wreckage found drifting six miles west of Hunstanton. Pilot Officer Stedman and wireless operator, Sergeant Frank Allcock, were posted as missing. Sergeant Ernest Grunsell is believed to have been killed in action on 27 March 1941 while flying with No.78 Squadron, and had been awarded a Mention In Despatches in the intervening period.

Poor weather also claimed Hampden X3007 of No.144 Squadron from RAF Hemswell, returning from a successful attack on Hannover on 11/12 February 1941. The details provided by its pilot, Sergeant Dainty, describe a typical sortie and serve to illustrate what the crews were coping with as a norm at that period of the air war:

We took off in formation with Sgt Pearman [in X3048] and Sgt Matthews in daylight at 5.30p.m. but broke formation at 6.45p.m. shortly before reaching the Dutch coast and as darkness was falling. There was almost ten-tenths cloud the whole way over Holland and Germany. We found ourselves south of the target and so flew north, picking up our bearings from Steinhuder Meer and correcting our course towards Hannover where scattered fires could be seen. Cloud cover was now about eight-tenths but we could see the town and dropped our bombs in the centre from 9,000 feet at 8.35p.m. My rear gunner saw the bombs burst and at least two fires broke out and a string of fires, probably caused by our incendiaries. We spotted two Wellingtons while we were over the target area. Our W/T went u/s so the journey home was made under some difficulty. We did manage to get a couple of QDMs from Bircham Newton and also from Hemswell but after that nothing more as the set again ceased to function. We arrived over England at 11.30p.m., by which time the weather had completely closed in on us. We tried the searchlight organisation and were actually led to a fighter station that turned out to be Kirton in Lindsey. They fired rockets but when we got to within about a mile of the station they stopped. We tried the searchlights again but owing to the clouds they were of little help.

I decided to get beneath the cloud in order to make a crash landing and succeeded in dropping down to fifty feet. On seeing a church steeple looming rather rapidly, however, I thought it advisable to climb again. At 2.45a.m. I decided to abandon the aircraft. Wireless operator, Sgt Grosvenor and rear gunner Sgt Bottomley went first followed by navigator Sgt Wilmot. I engaged the autopilot, set the aeroplane on a course for the east coast and baled out at 3.10a.m.

Ready to go. The crew of Wellington T2888 in Feb 1941, from left: J.H Parry, W/Op; J.R Goodman, First Pilot; G.A. Masters, Second Pilot; G.B. Cooper, Obs; R. Wickham, AG. (Group Captain J.R. Goodman via Bill Welbourne)

We all landed safely but X3007 flew on serenely until, fuel exhausted, it crashed just inland from Snettisham on the Norfolk coast of The Wash, seventy miles to the south. During the whole time we were cruising round over England looking for a gap in the 'clag', we never caught a glimpse of a single visual beacon.

Sergeant Dainty had kept his Hampden airborne for nearly ten hours that night. The weather played havoc with navigation for the other two aircraft as well, but Sergeant Pearman made it back safely, landing at 11.07p.m. and Sergeant Matthews, with some guidance from 'Darkie', landed safely at RAF Newmarket at 11.05p.m. Examined by FAWNAPS in 1985, the impact area was located by uncovering lumps of molten aluminium and the group recovered several radio components, parts of the control panel and a Very cartridge.

On a raid to Bremen that same night, twenty-two aircraft were lost in crashes in England due to fog on the return, and despite losing no aircraft to enemy action, this was a loss of thirty per cent of the force despatched, at the hands of the other 'Old Enemy' – bad weather. Fog, it seems, played just as effective a role in the defence of enemy installations as German AA batteries themselves. Certainly RAF losses to weather-related incidents were greater than losses to enemy AA fire at this time.

One of those casualties was a No.99 Squadron Wellington, T2888, which crashed at Stagg's Holt, Elm near Wisbech. Unable to land at RAF Newmarket Heath (due to very low cloud) at the end of the raid on Bremen on 11/12 February, the pilot, Sergeant C.T. Robinson, was not diverted to another airfield. After trying unsuccessfully to force land, fuel shortage and the unrelenting bad weather persuaded Sergeant Robinson that the aircraft should be abandoned instead. He, his second pilot, navigator and wireless operator all baled out safely,

The remains of T2888 recovered from the crash site at Stagg's Holt, Elm, near Wisbech, by FAWNAPS in 1982. From left: Bill Welbourne (FAWNAPS), Group Captain J.R. 'Benny' Goodman DFC AFC RAF ret'd (the regular pilot of T2888), Fred Cubley (FAWNAPS). (Bill Welbourne)

but the two gunners, Sergeants Alan Clough and Donald Beale, were killed. Sergeant Clough baled out but fell into a stretch of water, while Sergeant Beale's body was missing for thirteen weeks before he too was found in the marshy ground of Welney Wash.

This was the first time Sergeant Robinson had flown T2888, as he was only a stand-in due to its regular pilot, Pilot Officer Goodman, being ill at the time. In September 1982, now Group Captain (retired), 'Benny' Goodman had the unusual pleasure of seeing the remains of 'his' aircraft brought into the light of day when Fenland and West Norfolk Aircraft Preservation Society (FAWNAPS) carried out a very successful dig of the site.

During the war, Skegness lifeboats saved many an airman from a watery grave in The Wash, and these 'services' are proudly displayed in the lifeboat station along with a few relics of those far-off days, among them a wooden oar from a survival dinghy, donated by its grateful RAF crew.

Dawn on 11 October 1941 was still hidden behind angry clouds as Sergeant E.E. Jones of No.58 Squadron doggedly tried to reach home at RAF Linton-on-Ouse in Whitley Z9204. He and his crew, Sergeants A.C. MacKenzie (NZ), W.C. Fraser, R.J. Harwood and J.D. Carmichael (Can) had weathered an intense flak barrage over Essen, but were now being battered by gale-force winds over the English coast. Nearly eight hours into the sortie, blown well off course, forced down to low altitude and 'running on fumes', by 8.25a.m. Jones had no alternative but to ditch the Whitley in The Wash, eleven miles south-east of Skegness. An RAF air-sea rescue launch was sent out from Boston, but it could make no headway at all in the heavy seas and so the Skegness lifeboat *Anne Allen* was launched. After three hours being tossed around on the cold waters of The Wash, all five airmen were rescued and taken ashore to the RAF hospital in Skegness, where they quickly recovered from their ordeal. Before their departure the airmen presented the lifeboat crew with a paddle from their dinghy. This was later inscribed with their names and now resides in the present day lifeboat station as a reminder of that stormy rescue. Curiously, it seems likely that whoever painted the inscription on the oar may have done so in 1944, but had to correct a bit of a *faux pas* with the final digit since, when the light falls on the varnished blade in a certain way, it looks as if the year of the incident is 1944 rather than 1941.

Life-raft oar presented by No.58 Squadron to the crew of Skegness lifeboat after their rescue of a Whitley crew on 11 October 1941. The final '4' has been altered to a '1'.

Examples of the strategic ineffectiveness of Bomber Command operations have already been given – a situation brought into the open by the oft-quoted Butt report of August 1941. Among its revelations was that only one-third of those crews claiming to have bombed their target actually dropped their bombs within a five-mile radius of the aiming point, i.e. within an area of seventy-five square miles. After contending with all the adversities that the weather and the enemy could muster, in aeroplanes that were robust but inadequate for the demands being placed upon them, there is small wonder that the Butt report findings came as a blow to Command morale. Even the lack of aeroplane numbers, limited bomb loads and commitment to piecemeal operations was nothing, though, compared to the inherent inability to find and hit targets with precision at night and in all weathers.

Gordon Musgrove, on the opening page of his book *Pathfinder Force* summed up the situation:

> Poor equipment … was only half the story; bad navigation was the other half. Crews had not been trained for night raids, and … darkness which hid them from fighters … hid the target from them. Navigating was largely a matter of map-reading and relied on pin-points, confirmed by radio bearings, or astro-navigation … a lengthy and highly skilled operation. Astro needed cloudless sky above, pin-pointing cloudless sky below, with preferably a moon to help. There are very few nights in a year when these conditions prevail over both England and the Continent. Small wonder many aircraft got lost.

Bomber Command's 'Thousand Plan' was a proposal to mount an air raid by 1,000 RAF bombers against a single target and was the outcome of a series of events that, at the end of 1941, found Bomber Command in something of a crisis. It is not the intention here to plunge into the detail or the rights and wrongs or the politicking that led to the Plan, except to suggest that for the purposes of this story, matters such as the findings of the Butt Report into RAF operational bombing (in)accuracy, the appointment in February 1942 of AM Arthur Harris as C-in-C Bomber Command and the availability of the *Gee* navigational aid, are three key factors to bear in mind. Out of the first came Governmental misgivings about the effectiveness and value of RAF bombing operations thus far, together with further disquiet about the future value of the Air Ministry's (note: not Harris's) new Area-Bombing directive. Furthermore, under a campaign of increasing pressure from the Admiralty and the War Office, there also grew a Governmental perception that, at this critical period of the war, it was now far more likely that the war could be lost on land or at sea than in the air and thus the Army and Navy could not only employ such bomber resources more effectively but it was also in the nation's best interest – some might say not unreasonably so – to reassign that resource in support of their actions. Out of the second factor came the RAF's response and out of the third came a new means of getting such a quantity of disparate aircraft to a chosen target with maximum effect.

Amidst the clamour for reassignment of his bombers, Harris sought ways of stemming the tide. He wanted to mount a raid so spectacular that it would wipe out an important major target so completely as to cause the Government to support actively a strategic area-bombing campaign against Germany. He also recognised that the civilian population of Britain held bitter memories of the Blitz and would seize upon a successful hammer blow against Germany and bring public opinion to bear on the Government. Harris and his staff felt that a bomber force of 1,000 aircraft sent against a significant German target, within *Gee* range, would generate the desired reaction, and he was prepared to gamble all his resources on this one throw of the dice.

It was May 1942 before the magic figure of 1,000 became a reality. It would be achieved by using every medium and heavy bomber on squadron strength, plus those under repair, replacement spares at airfields and those waiting at supply pools for delivery to units. It would also utilise: two Bomber Training Groups; Flying Training Units; Bomber OTUs; Army Co-Operation units and Coastal Command. In the event, Coastal Command pulled its 250 aircraft out of the 'deal', but relentlessly the search for more aircraft and crews went on until just over 1,000 aircraft were ready to go. When weather issues had been sorted out, Harris gave the order for 1,000 bombers to attack Cologne on the night of Saturday 30/31 May 1942. It was an enormous logistical and security project that meant moving a hundred or so second- and third-line aircraft and their crews to stations where they could be brought to operational readiness. Author Eric Taylor wrote:

> At 21 OTU, RAF Moreton in the Marsh, battered old Wellingtons long since relegated to the training role were patched up and with doubtful engines, were pressed into service for the big raid. Even student aircrews – anyone with two or more solo cross-country flights – went. At 14 OTU, RAF Cottesmore, instructors who thought they had escaped the near certainty of death on ops were now faced with crewing up with 'green' crews. Tired Whitleys which had last seen active flying in 1940/41 were readied for ops once more. Even a dodgy drogue target-towing Whitley from Dumfries went along, while RAF Lichfield contributed what was probably the oldest Wellington on the raid – one of the first six from the Vickers factory. It had no guns fitted! At RAF Finningley's OTU, spare, unallocated aircrew, usually referred to as the 'Awkward Squad' formed themselves into a crew then looked around for an aircraft. Seeing an old Wellington that had been declared u/s, they pestered mechanics to get the old girl airworthy so that they could go on the big do.

Aviation historian Ralph Barker also wrote:

> All available Hampdens from the Bombing and Gunnery School at RAF Jurby on the Isle of Man were ordered to move to RAF Syerston near Nottingham. The most ambitious move was that of fourteen Wellington IC from 20 OTU at Lossiemouth to Stanton Harcourt, a satellite of RAF Abingdon – a flight of well over 400 miles.

Some fifty-three bomber airfields in England were involved and down at the bottom of the barrel, the Central Gunnery School at RAF Sutton Bridge was asked to scrape up some of its tired old Wellingtons to help reach the magic thousand. On the day of the raid, no less than forty-seven Wellingtons lined up at nearby RAF Feltwell ready to go: twenty from No.57 Squadron, twenty-three from No.75 Squadron, and four from Flying Training Command. Armed with real guns, carrying live bombs in the normally unused bomb bay and with as full a set of working instruments as possible, three of the latter were Wellington IAs from Central Gunnery School – all they could trust to stay in the air with a chance of making the long round trip. Usually the furthest a CGS Wellington had to fly was to trundle air gunners and instructors a few miles from base around The Wash while they pooped off miles of cine-camera film at friendly Spitfires, so no one worried too much if the compass was a bit dodgy.

Warning orders were issued on 25 May and CGS Operations Record Book entry for 26 May reads:

> Three Wellington aircraft flew to Feltwell on attachment for special operational co-operation with Bomber Command. Pilots, wireless operators and air gunners and complete ground crews sent by station with aircraft.

These pilots were members of CGS staff, who themselves were usually tour-expired veterans, while the air gunners were qualified and also generally experienced 'pupils' who had been posted in for turret-gunnery leader courses. Wireless operators were picked from the most experienced on those courses and second pilots and navigators were to be provided by RAF Feltwell.

Timing was of the essence since saturation bombing of the target was vital. To achieve this at Feltwell two parallel flare-paths were laid out on the grass field and on the wink of a green light from control shortly after 10.30p.m., one aircraft took off every six seconds, with the CGS aircraft leaving last, heading east towards The Wash and Cologne. Bombers equipped with *Gee*, drawn mainly from Nos 1 and 3 Groups, began to mark the target just before 1.00a.m. on 31 May to light the way for the non-*Gee* majority.

All was going well for the CGS crews, thick cloud thinned out then miraculously cleared about thirty miles from the target. They had managed to dodge the flak and night fighters and having followed the simplest of instructions – 'Find the Rhine, fly down it and you'll soon see the target lit up'– they bombed the target. Now they could head for home. Last off from Feltwell was Wellington IA, N2894, captained by Pilot Officer David Johnson, a staff pilot at CGS. In his crew that night was second pilot, Czechoslovakian Warrant Officer Oldrich Jambor and navigator Flight Lieutenant Hector Batten, both temporarily detached from No.75 Squadron. The remainder of his crew were gunnery leader course instructors on the staff of CGS, wireless operator Flight Sergeant Josiah Connor, Canadian air gunner Flight Sergeant John McLean and rear gunner Flight Sergeant George Waddington-Albright. Something went wrong though that caused the aircraft to stray from the comparative protection of the bomber stream and be caught alone among the night fighter bases in Holland. According to Ralph Barker:

> Johnson's crew bombed the target successfully, but they must have turned almost due north away from the target area, presumably due to some navigational or compass error. At some stage, though, they were almost certainly chased by a fighter. Their Wellington eventually crashed into flames in the Hessen Allee in Klarenbeek, eight miles south-east of Apeldoorn at 02.30 that Sunday morning. Only one man, rear-gunner Flt Sgt Waddington-Allbright, escaped to be taken prisoner.

With a total of 403 flying hours to its name, N2894 is believed to be the last Wellington IA to be lost on bombing operations and its demise was credited to night fighter pilot Oblt Emil Woltersdorf of III/NJG1. The other two CGS crews made it home without incident.

Many statistics have been produced for this raid but for the purposes of this book, these will be kept to the minimum. Of the 1,046 bombers despatched against Cologne, forty-one were missing and seven crashed in the UK, a loss rate of 4.6 per cent. Of the forty-one missing aircraft, twenty-four were from squadrons and seventeen from training units, and the majority of casualties were inexperienced crews. In addition to this force, a further eighty-eight aircraft were despatched on intruder or diversionary sorties from which three aircraft were lost.

From Feltwell, No.57 Squadron lost just one Wellington, in a crash landing near Lakenheath shortly after take-off, fortunately without casualties. No.26 OTU at RAF Wing near Leighton Buzzard despatched all its Wellingtons, including a few dodgy spares from its Cheddington satellite, some of which were manned by trainee crews posted in for the occasion from other OTUs up and down the country. These aircraft were flown over to RAF Graveley where they could be fuelled and armed and from where they would make the raid. No.26 OTU lost four aircraft that night, three to night fighters and one, DV709, in a crash landing near Soham, near March, at the end of the four-and-a-quarter-hour sortie. The crew had just completed its OTU course and was awaiting a posting to No.57 Squadron when the Thousand Raid intervened. Sergeant John Dixon, the pilot and Sergeant Brian Camlin, rear gunner, died in the crash, but the other three members of the crew escaped.

Apart from the collision that appears in a later chapter, the only other incident in the region involves the death of Sergeant Ernest Webb of No.78 Squadron. The Halifax in which he was rear gunner ran into cumulo-nimbus storm clouds as it crossed The Wash coast on the return leg of the Cologne raid. For the pilot and newly appointed squadron commander, Wing Commander Sam Lucas, it was his first operational sortie and he had his work cut out to hold the aircraft steady in the turbulence. As he climbed to try to get above the clouds, ice formed quickly, chunks of it flying off the props and hammering on the fuselage. Wing Commander Lucas decided to turn the Halifax around and head back out to sea, then drop down to try to get below the clouds. As he turned, the aircraft fell out of control; the instruments all went haywire and a spin started. At 3,000ft, still spinning, Lucas gave the order to bale out and all the crew abandoned the aircraft – except Lucas who, reckoning he had no chance of getting out himself, held on desperately to the belief that he might still pull the bomber out of its spiral. With just 1,000ft on the clock he got the nose up and finally stabilised the bomber, but now, of course, he had no one to help him land the machine. Spotting a set of 'Sandra' emergency searchlights in the darkness south of his position, he headed towards their glow and came to an airfield; he had no idea which one. Landing lights on, he made one low circuit to see what awaited him below then made a belly landing on the grass alongside a hard runway. Wing Commander Lucas had arrived at RAF Wittering. His crew came down near Spalding, all unhurt except for the rear gunner. He landed awkwardly in the high wind and broke his neck. Sergeant Webb died on the way to hospital.

So ended the greatest raid of the war so far. The destruction caused and effectiveness of the raid was well below that envisaged by the planners and two more 'Thousand Plan' raids, mounted during June, were no more successful in materialistic terms. However, Harris had achieved his aim of showing both the Allies and the Germans what an area bombing strategy was capable of doing. As a direct result of the Thousand Plan, German air strategy took on a defensive mindset. It caused the Germans to make rapid, huge and debilitating redeployments of their air resources from all foreign fronts to the defence of the homeland, greatly to the advantage of Allied ground campaigns. And as we have seen, even the 'minnows' of the RAF played their part in achieving this.

Whitleys, Wellingtons, and Hampdens continued to give sterling service in all weathers, manned by crews who defied the odds time and again, as well as staying in the air for prodigiously long sortie times. But the effectiveness of these bombers was definitely more psychological than destructive. It was time for a new breed of bomber to join the fight.

Part Two: Maximum Effort

'Coughing, banging, trailing smoke and sparks, it roared low across the Spalding to Weston road, before disappearing in a huge cloud of dust.' This was how the late Peter Sanderson remembered his boyhood view of L7427's flight as it crash-landed on 3 July 1941, in a potato field just short of Wykeham Abbey, near Spalding. Canadian Pilot Officer T. W. Dench and his crew, from No.97 Squadron at RAF Coningsby, however, emerged unscathed.

This incident summed up what the troubled Manchester was going through. Although classed as a medium bomber, the Avro Manchester actually represented the beginning of the age of the 'heavies'. First used operationally in small numbers from February 1941, it was not until July that this twenty-ton, twin-engine bomber began to be seen over Lincolnshire. Sadly the reason for its appearance was as a result of persistent engine-troubles, which dogged most of its service career. Charges of 'unreliable' and 'lacking in power' were directed at the

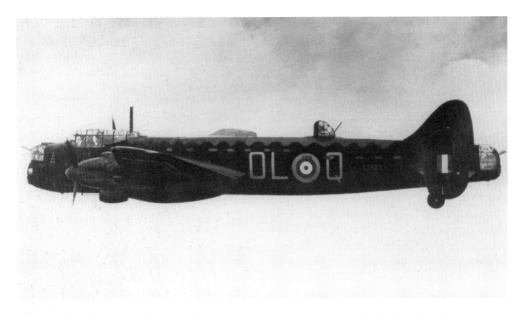

Avro Manchester I, L7427, OL-Q of No.83 Squadron RAF Scampton, had a troubled life in common with its breed.

unusual Rolls-Royce Vulture power plants. By comparison with its predecessors, though, the aeroplane itself was well designed and positively well equipped, being quite roomy and capable of hauling a five-ton bomb load into the air.

In the preceding four months, the frequency of engine-failure had reached such proportions that all Manchesters were grounded on 30 June for thorough engine overhauls. The initial plan was for five aircraft to have their engines overhauled by Rolls-Royce and to incorporate all the latest modifications. One aircraft from this batch was then allotted to each user squadron which was instructed to fly it for 250 hours as soon as possible by intensive daylight cross-country flying, followed by servicing through the night, to try to induce engine failure. Like everything else involving the Manchester, this process did not go without incident. 'A' flight of No.97 Squadron at Coningsby was assigned L7427 for the trials.

On 3 July Pilot Officer T. W. Dench drew the short straw – the poor chap had only joined the Squadron that day – and was sent off on a six-hour cross-country flight: Coningsby-Debden-Catterick-Coningsby. It all started to go wrong on the northward leg when, true to form, the starboard engine 'packed up'. Dench could not get the Manchester to maintain height with one sick motor, hence the crash-landing two miles from Spalding. Although apparently unrelated to the crash, the unfortunate Pilot Officer Dench also found himself posted out to the newly-formed No.408 (Goose) Squadron on 12 July.

And what of L7427? Well, it was dismantled, removed from the potato field, eventually repaired and then re-issued as OL-Q to No.83 Squadron at RAF Scampton. Problems or not, Manchesters had to return to service out of sheer operational necessity. On its fifteenth operation, a raid on Hamburg on the night of 8/9 April 1942, it failed to return. The sortie began at 10.15p.m. and a wireless transmission was received at 12.10a.m. when it was believed the bomber was in the vicinity of Lastrup. It was subsequently established that L7427 had crashed north-east of Cloppenburg, en route to Hamburg. Of the crew that night, Pilot Officer Jack Morphett (pilot), Flight Sergeants Geoffrey Hutchinson, the navigator from

Flight Sergeant Gordon Hartley of No.97
Squadron. (Ann & Vic Savage)

New Zealand and Albert Salter (WOp/AG),
Sergeants Reg Williams (WOp/AG), George
Fisk (AG) and American 'Canadian' Charles
Gellatly (AG) all died. Flight engineer,
Pilot Officer Peter Lovegrove managed to
bale out and was made a Prisoner of War.
According to the Commonwealth War
Graves Commission web site data, Lovegrove
died in captivity on 12 November 1942 and
is buried in Poznan Old Garrison cemetery
in Poland. Many of those buried there were
airmen held captive in Stalag Luft III at
Sagen and other camps in the vicinity, and
include some of those who were shot during
what became known as the 'Great Escape'.
Incidentally, there is still an anomaly to clear
up since MOD Air Historical Branch quotes the year of Lovegrove's death as 1944. So, events
finally caught up with L7427 – but was she shot down, or could she have been the victim of
yet another Vulture engine failure? It seems no one will ever know.

Running out of fuel did not become any less of a hazard just because aeroplanes grew in
size. Manchester R5783 V-Victor, one of eight aircraft despatched by 97 Squadron to bomb
a railway junction at Bremen, had to be crash-landed on the night of 20/21 October by
its pilot Flight Sergeant Gordon Hartley. Plagued by a jammed elevator trim wheel on the
return journey, Hartley nearly made it back to base but ran out of fuel near Boston and
had to force-land on Friskney Marshes at the edge of The Wash. His CO commented later,
perhaps rightly, even if not charitably, 'On making landfall the pilot should have made for the
nearest aerodrome and not attempted to return to base.' Hartley was a very popular member
of the squadron who, having written off two Manchesters, became known affectionately
by his ground crew as 'Crasher' Hartley. His first mishap occurred on 13 September when
Manchester L7306 suffered a burst tyre while taking off on a training flight. Piling up on the
runway, it burst into flames, but Hartley and his crew managed to scramble clear without
injury. Despite these incidents, Hartley survived the war, rising to the rank of Squadron
Leader with the DFC.

The last Manchester to crash in this region was L7495 of No.61 Squadron. Aboard one of
nine aircraft despatched from RAF Woolfox Lodge, Pilot Officer J.R. Hubbard and his crew
set off at 7.50p.m. on 13/14 March 1942 to bomb Cologne. Almost immediately after take-
off the port engine developed a coolant leak and with the temperature going off the clock it
gave every indication of being about to go up in flames. Hubbard found himself faced with
the aircraft continually stalling at around 150mph, with one 250lb and two 1,000lb bombs
hung up and his wireless and instruments all failing. Wisely, he ordered the crew to bale out
of the doomed aircraft and left L7495 to crash east of the Great North Road, one and a
half miles south of Wittering. Despite the intensive investigations of 1941 the Manchester's
Vulture engine problems never really went away and one can only speculate on how many
aeroplanes and crews were lost on operations for that reason.

Meanwhile, in July 1941, Bomber Command had refocused its attention on Germany and was still reliant on the sturdy and dependable Wellington, Whitley and Hampden. When the weather was good or on moonlight nights, Bomber Command targeted the Rühr area, but on nights when the weather was poor but still flyable, bombers were despatched to a list of widely dispersed German cities. Few aviation enthusiasts – and many other people besides – are unaware of the name of Pilot Officer John Gillespie Magee, the American-born fighter pilot who gained immortality through the lines of his evocative poem *High Flight*. While serving with the Canadian No.412 Squadron, Magee met his untimely end in a collision above the village of Ruskington, Lincolnshire on the morning of 11 December 1941, detailed in another chapter. He will be remembered forever as the man whose words encapsulate the beauty of flight. In juxtaposition, later that same day another Lincolnshire-based Canadian squadron, No.407, was to provide an accident that, though definitely part of a dangerous operational sortie, had a happier outcome. The latter was just another incident in the ebb and flow of war, unremarkable in its own right but providing stark contrast to the impact of the earlier event that day.

For two months Lockheed Hudson crews of No.407 Squadron based at RAF North Coates had been relentlessly pursuing enemy shipping in the North Sea. Weariness was becoming a daily companion on these dangerous low-level missions, but night and day in all weathers the squadron kept up the pressure, sinking or damaging 150,000 tons by the end of their three-month stay at North Coates. Canadian Pilot Officer Bill Shankland was pilot of Hudson V, AM619, RR-Q, detailed for a night anti-shipping sortie known as a 'Rover'. He was to patrol off the Dutch Friesian Islands, search for enemy ships by means of ASV (anti-surface vessel) radar and attack targets with four 250lb semi-armour piercing bombs. On this occasion, though, no targets were found and in deteriorating weather Bill set course for home. He now takes up the story:

On reaching the English coast the weather was pretty poor and I was unsure of our position. We made two runs at the coast using the very primitive ASV radar on board but still could not identify our position. Our wireless was u/s so we could not contact base. Although we were actually in the vicinity of the airfield, it transpired later that the reason we couldn't see aerodrome lights or signals was because an enemy air raid was in progress at the time.

I decided to fly further inland to try to find a 'Pundit' or 'Orbit' beacon that might lead me to another aerodrome. After a while a beacon was indeed spotted but it was not on our secret list for that time period.

Circling it, I flashed the letter-of-the-day on the under-fuselage lamp, first followed by 'Q' (which meant we required assistance to find the nearest aerodrome) then the aircraft identity letter – which was another 'Q'. All of this brought no reply whatsoever from the ground. We had been led to believe at briefing that, if it became necessary to use a beacon, a string of lights would be illuminated near that beacon which would indicate the direction to an aerodrome. Remember on this occasion, though, we were unaware of the red alert in progress.

A faint row of lights (subsequently found to represent a dummy railway siding!) was spotted next. Peering along the direction indicated by these faint lights, I could vaguely make out what appeared to be a flare path a few miles away. Much relieved, I headed towards it. Circling these lights I flashed the underside lamp for permission to land. Once again – no response. I was now pretty low on fuel, with the needles bending against the stops – so I decided to hell with it, I'd land anyway!

My last recollection on approach was that the obstruction lights on buildings seemed very close to the ground and … Crikey!! that's a helluva short flarepath. As the Hudson touched down I applied full brakes. Then we started to bounce over rough ground, finally coming to an abrupt halt in a ditch with the wings at ground level. This actually saved us, as the undercarriage had not collapsed and was relatively intact in the ditch itself. Hudsons were notorious for catching fire in a crash as it had a 'wet' wing [no separate fuel cells, the wing surfaces forming part of the fuel tank walls] and any fracture of the wing usually caused petrol to spray forward onto the hot engine. Combined with a high magnesium content in the alloy skin [for lightness] this made for an immediate conflagration, frequently with fatal consequences for the unfortunate crew.

We had landed – or arrived – upon Potterhanworth Fen 'Q'-site, a decoy airfield!! Having already collected ninety-six enemy bombs and one Whitley crash, the Q-site staff was naturally cagey about letting off signals and in the middle of a raid, made no attempt to warn off our Hudson. The situation was not helped by the fact that codes given us at briefing were incorrect anyway and therefore unrecognisable by the Q-site staff.

Having deposited four more bombs and one more aeroplane on the Q-site, Bill Shankland, second pilot Sergeant W. Goulding and Wireless Operator/Air Gunner Sergeants Sutherland and Conlin all walked away from the bent Hudson with just bumps and bruises. Showing signs of strain from continuous operations, Bill Shankland, by way of a rest, was sent off on a blind flying course. 'It was not good to be away from my buddies at Christmas,' he said, although he rejoined the squadron on 27 December. More operations followed until, on 6 January 1942, he was struck down by an attack of appendicitis in the middle of a sortie over the North Sea. In great agony he managed to get the aircraft back to base and was hospitalised. It was at this point that his time with No.407 Squadron came to an end, and while Bill was on sick leave, the Squadron – having taken a beating for three months – was moved from North Coates to Thorney Island to re-group.

Subsequently, Bill Shankland saw much and varied war service. For example with No.1401 Met Flight flying the venerable Gladiator; with No.3 General Recce School flying Bothas ('not my favourite aeroplane!'); instructing on Hudsons in Durban, Aden and Aboukir; on Baltimores and Ansons in North Africa and back onto operations flying the Baltimore III with No.454 Squadron around the Mediterranean. Later Bill flew Baltimores and Mosquitoes for radar calibration in the eastern Mediterranean; Wellingtons fitted with the odd-looking anti-magnetic mine ring and flying Wellingtons on supply drops to the Chetniks in the

Lockheed Hudson V, AM619, RR-Q of No.407 (RCAF) Squadron, after its crash landing on Potterhanworth Fen 'Q'-site on 11 December 1941. (Peter Green)

Balkans. Varied indeed! Bill Shankland's war ended with him being posted back to Canada in September 1944 as an instructor specialising in converting RAF crews to operate American equipment in B-24 and B-25 aeroplanes. He retired from a senior post in air-traffic control in 1978 and lived in Vancouver until his death in 2002.

The Whitley crash to which Bill referred was that of Z6495 in which Sergeant Moorcroft from No.78 Squadron also 'landed' on the Potterhanworth decoy site on 17 August 1941. When his bomber suffered engine failure he mistook the lights for nearby RAF Waddington and the undercarriage collapsed on the rough ground of the decoy site. On that occasion the 'Q' site staff got a rocket for not taking the correct action to warn off the Whitley pilot.

Entering operational service with No.7 Squadron at RAF Oakington in February 1941, first among the new four-engine 'heavies' was the Short Stirling. Also based in Cambridgeshire, at RAF Bourn, was No.15 Squadron, which received its Stirlings in April of the same year. Being based to the south of The Wash region it is to be expected that most operational unit sortie routes would take them east across Norfolk and Suffolk or even further south. This probably accounts for why the Stirling was a relatively 'rare bird' over the area covered by this book and therefore why only a small number of incidents involving this type are recorded. One incident, however, that shook No.15 Squadron to the core, happened on the morning of 29 October 1942.

'Q-Queenie', Stirling Mk I, BF386, lifted off from RAF Bourn at 11.10a.m. for an air-test with some night-flying training thrown in for good measure. Unusually, in addition to a full crew of seven commanded by Squadron Leader Charles Fisher, it carried four passengers: Flight Lieutenant Harry Salter (padre); Sergeants Charles Barrie, an air gunner and Roland Ponting, and Corporal Donald Cleaver. It seems likely the latter two were ground crew and that all four were taken along for the ride. Sadly it was to be their last. Forty minutes later, eyewitnesses on the ground at Salter's Lode, a village three miles west of Downham Market, said that when the Stirling emerged from cloud it appeared to be flying quite normally. It was then seen to make a steep turn, which tightened until it dived into the ground and was destroyed. All eleven men on board perished.

The light soil structure in the area meant much of the wreckage became buried quite deeply. As was often the case in such circumstances and in rural locations, little time was spent in recovery other than for the bodies of the unfortunate crew. In 1980 FAWNAPS undertook a successful excavation of the site, unearthing many large components including two Hercules XI engines, propeller blades, the distinctive twin-tailwheels, two parachutes in their packs, four Browning machine guns from the rear turret (suitably dealt with), a compass and a fully equipped survival dinghy. The items are all now displayed in their museum near Wisbech as a poignant reminder of that awful day.

Giving joy rides might be nothing unusual, but perhaps youthful exuberance could get the better of common sense when there was an audience. In addition to the eleven men above, nine more 'went west' in a similar mishap not so very far away in November 1941. Sergeant George Bruce took off from No.115 Squadron base at RAF Marham just before midday for an air test on Wellington 1C, Z8863. With him that fateful day was his usual crew: Sergeants Percy Taylor, Henry O'Shea, Percy Crosbie, Bill Evans and Ernest Lawrence, plus three ground crew: Sergeant Jack Dix, Corporal James Fox and AC2 Gordon Wakefield. An official summary of the incident indicates the passengers were not authorised to fly, nor was low flying authorised. Precisely what happened prior to the crash will forever remain unknown, but suffice it to say that in this case 'low' means low! The Wellington flew horizontally into a railway embankment at an estimated speed of between 160 and 200mph, smashing into goods trucks on the railway line that ran between March and Spalding, killing everyone on board.

By 1943 the Stirling Mk I bomber was being relegated to training units or for less arduous operations. They were somewhat underpowered and had difficulty operating above 15,000ft altitude, which made them very vulnerable to flak. However, having beaten a worthy path for the RAF's four-engine bomber force, it was time for the Stirling to step aside for the Lancaster and Halifax. There was still much useful life left in these Stirlings, though. Sixteen, for example, were allocated to No.1657 Heavy Conversion Unit at RAF Stradishall where they provided the means of bringing new heavy-bomber crews – fresh out of OTU, perhaps having flown Wellingtons – up to proficiency on a four-engine bomber prior to being posted to an operational squadron.

It was in the Heavy Conversion Units that raw crews had the chance to improve their skills and on 14 February 1943, Sergeant R. Watson and his crew certainly got a feel for a 'dicey situation'. Their aircraft that day, W7451, had begun its service life on 26 October 1941 on the strength of No.149 Squadron at Mildenhall, but was transferred to No.7 Squadron, Oakington after just two weeks. The bad luck that was to dog this aeroplane began on 9 December that year, when the twin tailwheels failed to lower due to flak damage sustained during a daylight anti-shipping sortie off the Dutch coast. The pilot on that occasion, Flight Lieutenant Crebbin, was able to land his aircraft despite extensive damage to the rear fuselage. This aircraft was badly damaged again on 15 May 1942 when its pilot overshot the runway while landing at Oakington. Lengthy repairs at the Sebro works in nearby Cambridge were followed by a spell with 218 Conversion Unit at RAF Marham, before being transferred to 1657 HCU at RAF Stradishall, where it finally had one too many mishaps.

Short Stirling I, W7451, in markings of No.7 Squadron before it was transferred first to No.218 CU then to No.1657 HCU with which it had its final mishap near King's Lynn on 14 February 1943.

On a clear sunny Sunday morning, briefed to carry out a full-load climb test to get the feel of coaxing a heavily laden aeroplane to altitude, Watson had just lifted Stirling W7451 off Stradishall's runway when things started to go haywire. First the undercarriage would not retract and, realising he was in trouble, Watson headed for The Wash to jettison the bomb load. Now the port outer engine burst into flames! Having laboured to only 1,400ft, W7451 wavered and began to lose height. Desperate to get rid of the bombs, as soon as they were over water, Watson ordered the bomb doors open. But the doors would not budge! Too low to bale out, rapidly losing height, unable to drop the bombs and with the wheels locked down, Sergeant Watson took the only course left to him – to turn inland and force land the ungainly bomber. To his credit, he pulled off a fine landing in a ploughed field at Saddlebow, three miles from King's Lynn. Although the Stirling ended up nosing into a pond, Watson and his crew all emerged unhurt. It transpired that the undercarriage failed to retract due to a faulty accumulator and the port engine had a hole punched in a crankcase that caused the fire to start. The overall damage proved so extensive that W7451 was declared a write off.

In due course even the bigger-engined Stirling IIIs were found wanting in terms of performance in the cauldron that was the enemy's night sky. Once again, therefore, Mark IIIs found their way to the HCUs and other second line units. What follows now are two Stirling Mark III accidents, both non-operational, which serve to re-emphasise that, despite the dangers inherent in venturing over enemy territory in out-moded aircraft, accepted then as 'an occupational hazard', things could go terribly wrong – even without the enemy trying to shoot down our crews!

The MOD Accident Record for the loss on 17 October 1943 of Stirling EH960 was very succinct: 'This aeroplane took off [from RAF Witchford] at 10.50 hours on an air test. The pilot reported excessive vibration then the aeroplane was not heard from again.' Even the location was vague: 'In the UK, unknown location.' Flying Officer James Deans DFC and his crew were originally posted missing without trace, but perhaps not *entirely* without trace, since – on occasion – The Wash gives up its grim secrets. While scanning the pages of the Operational Record Book for Central Gunnery School during its period at RAF Sutton Bridge, the following entry appeared dated 12 November 1943:

> The body of 1851312 Sgt [James] Lane of 196 Squadron was recovered from The Wash. He is believed to have been in the accident on 15 [*sic*] Oct 1943. Sgt Lane was an air gunner and his body was recovered from a Stirling [found] on Gat Sand.

Indeed, Sergeant James Lane, aged nineteen, was the mid-upper gunner in EH960 when it went missing, and he is now buried in Abney Park cemetery in north London. After his body was discovered, two other members of the crew were found at later dates. Flying Officer Frederick Chapman, navigator, was interred in Cambridge City cemetery while Sergeant Ken Wallace, the flight engineer, was buried in the military section of Great Bircham parish churchyard. The bodies of Flying Officer Deans, wireless operator Sergeant Terence McDonnell, Canadian rear gunner Warrant Officer II Nolan Butts DFM and Flight Lieutenant John Griffith, the squadron engineering officer, were never found, and they are remembered on the Runnymeade memorial.

Flying Officer Deans and Warrant Officer Butts were each the holder of a gallantry award and the story of their final sortie now allows that earlier bravery to reach the light of day. Both airmen were gazetted on 5 October for acts of gallantry during an operation that took place on 23/24 September 1943, and the joint citation in the *London Gazette* reads as follows:

One night in September 1943, Fg Off Deans and Sgt Butts were pilot and rear gunner of an aircraft which attacked Mannheim. Shortly after the bombs had been released the aircraft was attacked by enemy fighters. In the first attack the bomber was hit and Sgt Butts' guns suddenly failed to operate. Nevertheless this airman coolly gave his pilot directions in offensive action and at the same time cleared his guns of stoppages. Further attacks were made by the enemy fighters but, owing to Sgt Butts' skilful commentary, Fg Off Deans so manoeuvred his aircraft that one of the attackers was shot down. This officer and airman displayed great skill and courage.

Another sort of heroism provides the theme for another stirring Stirling tale. At two minutes past midnight on 28 July 1944, the sleeping town of March in Cambridgeshire was saved from disaster by the bravery of a young Australian pilot. Pilot Officer Jim Hocking and his NCO crew were on their final cross-country exercise before being posted to an operational squadron from No.1651 HCU at RAF Wratting Common. After several weeks of training on the Stirling, the time had come for the final long navigation exercise across country, out over the North Sea, followed by a run over a Lincolnshire bombing range. Take-off was 11.30p.m. on 27 July in Stirling III, LJ451, coded QQ-C. Thirty minutes into the climb out from base, the course took this aircraft towards the Fenland town of March. On the ground, in Royal Observer Corps post 'Juliet One' near March, Observers Titus Lewis and Fred Fovargue reported the Stirling's progress across their patch of night sky.

It was at this point that Jim Hocking's problems began in the form of an engine fire. First the starboard inner caught fire, followed by a complete failure of the starboard outer. Even feathered, the props continued to windmill and with such an asymmetric loss of power, Jim was unable to maintain height and gave the order to bale out, which the crew did successfully. The fire quickly spread to engulf the whole wing. As the last crew member, wireless operator and fellow Aussie Flight Sergeant Stan Tebbutt, left the aircraft, Jim Hocking shouted to him that he would avoid the town below then follow him out. But the Stirling was now a fireball and losing height rapidly. By staying with his aircraft for those extra minutes to clear the town, Jim lost the chance to parachute to safety, thus sacrificing his own life. Stirling LJ451 plunged to earth in a field at Knights End on the outskirts of March. This field also contained the ROC post and the exploding aircraft showered burning fuel and wreckage onto the post, severely injuring the two observers on duty. By his heroic action, Pilot Officer Jim Hocking saved the town of March from disaster that night, but paid the ultimate price. He is buried in the Commonwealth War Graves Commission plot in Newmarket Road cemetery, Cambridge.

Few of the towns and villages around The Wash are very far from the site of an aeroplane crash site, but the west Norfolk villages of Clenchwarton and Hilgay can claim to have no less than five and seven Second World War sites respectively within their parish boundaries. In the case of Clenchwarton, first of these was a Hurricane from nearby No.56 OTU at RAF Sutton Bridge on 21 January 1942. Next came Stirling I, W7473, from RAF Marham on 23/24 April 1942, followed by Halifax II, HR832, of No.405 Squadron at RAF Gransden Lodge on 16 June 1943, then Mosquito DD717 of No.141 Squadron at RAF West Raynham on 29 May 1944, and finally Oxford PH414 of No.7SFTS, also from RAF Sutton Bridge. A plaque on the village hall wall was unveiled in April 2000 to commemorate the nineteen airmen who died in the five crashes, and we can take a look at the two bomber incidents in more detail now.

On the night of 23/24 April 1942, the moon shone brightly as Stirling W7473, one of a mixed force of bombers, was setting out on a sortie to the Baltic port of Rostock. Shortly after take-off the port inner engine failed, and when the pilot Sergeant Vincent Davidge could not maintain height, he jettisoned the bombs. Immediately, he made a turn towards the u/s engine, but the turn became tighter and the aircraft dived into the ground. All seven airmen on board died when the Stirling crashed into Ingram's field about a hundred yards from Clenchwarton school.

During 1942 the Halifax, second of the four-engine bombers to enter service, was the principal equipment of Bomber Command's No.4 Group. It began to be seen across the Fens, a hundred miles to the south of its Yorkshire bases, usually as a result of cross-country training flights. While No.4 Group expanded its use of the Halifax, greater production capacity helped to widen its use geographically, notably by the new Pathfinder Force based in Cambridgeshire. Opening as a satellite of RAF Tempsford, RAF Gransden Lodge to the west of Cambridge became home to No.405 (Vancouver) Squadron when it moved in with twenty Halifax bombers in April 1943. One of this number, HR832, fell victim to a weather-related accident on 16 June 1943 during a cross-country navigation exercise. Once again, little explanation was forthcoming, since all seven crew died when the aeroplane crashed at Clifton Farm, Clenchwarton, between Sutton Bridge and King's Lynn – one of the five incidents commemorated by the aforementioned plaque. Being seen on fire and apparently diving out of control, it was surmised the Halifax may have been struck by lightning, as witnesses told of a storm going on in the area at that time.

Captained by Flight Lieutenant Christopher Lawson, the others of his crew were: Pilot Officer Lawrence Frewin (B); Sergeants Arthur Faulkner (WOp/AG) and Malcolm Holliday (FE); Canadian Flying Officers Roland Agassiz (N) and Walter C. Davies (RG) and American 'Canadian' from New York Flight Sergeant Clinton L. Pudney GM, the mid-upper gunner (MUG). The last three are buried side by side in Sutton Bridge churchyard, and this gives rise to some anomalies that are ever the bane of researchers because there is also here a grave for Flying Officer Max Howard Davies, a WOp/AG victim of yet another local Halifax crash, No.78 Squadron on 31 August 1943, and the grave of pilot Pilot Officer William Lee Davis (18 March 1941), another American 'Canadian' from St Louis buried nearby.

The award of the George Medal to Clinton Pudney was gazetted on 13 July, just about a month after his death, and curiosity as to the reason for this high honour uncovered yet another anomaly. On St George's Day in April 2000, due largely to the efforts of the King's Lynn branch of RAFA, a memorial was unveiled to the memory of Lawson's crew and indeed to the nineteen airmen who had died in five air accidents occurring within the parish boundary of Clenchwarton, the village closest to the Halifax crash site. CWGC records show Clinton Pudney's rank as Flight Sergeant at the time of his death. The *London Gazette* citation recording the award of a George Medal for his actions in an incident on 28 January 1943 while holding the rank of Sergeant, reads:

> While engaged on a local practice flight, the Halifax in which Sgt Pudney was flying as mid-upper gunner struck high ground, crashed and burst into flames. Three members of the crew were killed and the others, with the exception of Sgt Pudney, were too severely injured to extricate themselves from the burning wreckage. Though suffering from severe lacerations on his face and in spite of loss of blood and shock, Sgt Pudney entered the blazing aircraft several times and finally succeeded in bringing all of his companions out. He then struggled over rough moorland for two miles to obtain help.

On that fateful night, Pudney's crew was in the final stages of its training and took off from RAF Leeming, North Yorkshire, in a Halifax II, W1146, of No.1659 HCU, for a cross-country navigation exercise. On the return leg to Leeming, the Halifax struck the ground of Great Shunner Fell that rose above the village of Thwaite, in Swaledale. Three of the seven men on board – Flight Sergeant Joseph Beliveau, navigator; Sergeant Richard Drago, bomb aimer and Sergeant John Stone, wireless operator – died in the initial impact, while the pilot, Pilot Officer Edmond LeFebre, flight engineer, Sergeant Hugh McGeach, and gunners Flight Sergeant John Askew and Sergeant Pudney suffered injuries. Sergeant Pudney managed to escape from the burning aircraft but re-entered the blazing machine several times to rescue the other, more injured, airmen. LeFebre, McGeach and Pudney all survived, but Sergeant Askew died of his injuries.

Liberator V, FL950 managed to clock up thirteen hours in the air before it finally ran out of fuel over Whittlesey, near Peterborough. What was an RAF Liberator doing in this part of the East Midlands anyway? Once again, the answer has its roots in our old friend – or should that be old enemy – the weather. Acquired by the RAF in 1941, the B-24 Liberator operated both as a long-range heavy bomber, in this role generally in the middle- and far-east theatres, and as a very-long-range maritime patrol aircraft. By 1945 ten Coastal Command squadrons were equipped with later marks (IV, V, VI) of this aeroplane. With a potential range of over 2,000 miles, Liberator crews of No.224 Squadron, for example, were no strangers to long-duration sorties roaming far out into the Atlantic, hunting for U-boats.

Hidden away in that picturesque corner of England between the New Forest and the sea, Beaulieu Airfield was home to No.224 (Coastal) Squadron. It was there at 10.30a.m. on 29 March 1943 that Flying Officer C. Moore hauled the heavily laden FL950 into the air, heading down-Channel for yet another routine patrol over the grey waters of the Atlantic. While most of the time such patrols were uneventful, to maximise time and area coverage, fuel state always had to be watched most carefully. If the weather turned nasty or a target had to be chased, things could get critical for the return leg. Approaching England that evening, FL950 ran into thick cloud right down to sea level. With the radio going u/s intermittently, Flying Officer Moore was unable to locate the welcoming lights of Beaulieu runway. Fortunately the radio perked up long enough for a signal to be received, diverting them to RAF Mildenhall of all places! Fog must have blanketed the whole of the south of England for hundreds of miles in all directions, since Mildenhall is all of 150 miles north of Beaulieu. When they reached Mildenhall it too was absolutely fogged-in. Now desperately short of fuel, Moore flew round the area searching for a break in this dense blanket – but to no avail.

When the petrol gauges read 'empty', he gave the order to bale out. Everyone cleared the aircraft safely, but five of the crew were slightly hurt when they hit the ground. Moore's crew that day included: Flying Officers J.E. Jenkinson (co-pilot) and K.B. Seal (nav); Pilot Officer R.C. Randall (WOp/AG); Sergeants J.P.R. Paquin RCAF (WOp/AG), J.R.L. Thompson (WOp/AG), G.H. Shaw (flight engineer) and T.D. Wade (WOp/AG). Liberator FL950 crashed in Elderneth Wash, Whittlesey, near Peterborough, fortunately without causing any damage to life or property. Following the usual pattern the aeroplane had punched quite a hole for itself and only debris on or near the surface was cleared away, the hole then being filled in. Evidence of the whereabouts of the crash first came to light post-war when, in 1977, drainage contractors unearthed an engine and propeller, but it was another ten years before FAWNAPS undertook a more detailed examination of the site. During the following year, 1988, they began digging, and by August 1989 had recovered another engine and propeller, oxygen bottles and a survival dinghy, together with numerous quantities of smaller artefacts. Of the crew on board that day, it is known that new Zealander Flying Officer James Jenkinson was posted missing in action on 12 June 1944, and in 1991 Pilot Officer Randall was living in Wigan.

Specialising in low-level attacks over water, high-level precision bombing and precision target marking were the main bolts of lightning in No.617 Squadron's arsenal. Retained as a special duties unit after the epic Dams raid, The Wash became the regular training ground for No.617 while it was based at Scampton and later on, Woodhall Spa. Wainfleet bombing range was used intensively day and night as 617's crews practised hard to master the new Stabilising Automatic Bomb Sight at altitudes up to 20,000ft so that they could not only drop bombs like the special aerodynamic 12,000lb 'Tallboy' with precision from high altitude, but also put target markers down with an accuracy of forty yards from altitudes of between 3,000–6,000ft. In between all this, No.617 was still tasked for attacks on potential targets requiring a similar 'on the deck' technique as that used in the Dams raid. It was one such training sortie in this latter role that caused the demise of ED918 AJ-F, the Lancaster bomber previously flown by Flight Sergeant Ken Brown in the attack on the Sorpe Dam.

Operational losses during 1943 had sadly depleted the squadron, yet recruiting new crews was not always easy, since the squadron's fame – or notoriety – often worked against it in Bomber Command. However, pilot Flight Lieutenant Tom O'Shaughnessy and his crew were among those accepted by Wing Commander Mickey Martin, the CO, and agreed – no one was ever forced to accept the posting – to join 617 in the autumn of 1943. In November 1943 command of 617 passed to Wing Commander Leonard Cheshire just in time to organise the squadron's second attack on the Antheor viaduct that carried the coastal railway link between France and Italy. On 11 November, Tom O'Shaughnessy and his crew, flying Joe McCarthy's old ED825, were one of nine aircraft, each carrying a 12,000lb Tallboy, despatched to that target.

In an effort to break the stalemate on the Italian front, Allied landings were made at Anzio in January 1944. However, when the army became stuck on the beaches someone in Bomber Command had the bright idea that if a large dam just north of Rome could be breached, the ensuing flood might disrupt German communications sufficiently to help the imminent breakout from the Anzio beachhead. Thus the order went out for No.617 Squadron to step up training on its low-level, bouncing-bomb routine in preparation for the target.

This target required a different approach technique, though. Surrounded by high hills, the Italian dam required a bomb run to be made at night by an aircraft first slipping over a hill, losing 1,800ft of height in only 3,000yds then steadying at 60ft over water in time to drop its spinning bomb. Where better to practice this than over The Wash? Coming in over a mark then dropping like a stone to cross another mark at sixty feet, often under the eagle eye of the CO, this was what 617 was all about, and the pilots practiced keenly. But disaster struck on the wintry evening of 20 January when Flight Lieutenant O'Shaugnessy was briefed to carry out one of these simulated low-level sorties over The Wash, off Snettisham.

A No.617 Squadron crew in January 1944. Flight Lieutenant Tom O'Shaughnessy (extreme left) with (from left) George Kendrick, Arthur Ward, Jock Hutton, Chunky Stewart, Bert Holt and (crouching) Arthur Holding.

The trip did not get off to a good start because three of his crew, the flight engineer and two air gunners, failed to turn up at dispersal. When the missing three had not shown up by ready-to-roll time, Tom decided he would do the sortie without them and duly took off at 7.30p.m. Bomb aimer, Pilot Officer George Kendrick handled the flight engineer duties and since it was a training sortie, they could manage without the gunners. This particular exercise only required the pilot to dive at a shallow angle from 600ft down to 60ft, then with guidance from navigator, Flying Officer Arthur Holding, peering out of the cockpit at the image cast by the downward spotlights in each wing, Tom had to maintain that height during a simulated bomb run above the water. George Kendrick took up his usual place at the bombsight down in the nose of the aircraft, and at 8.05p.m. wireless operator Pilot Officer Arthur Ward sent a message to base that they were starting their first run.

The next thing Arthur Ward heard and felt was a tremendous crash and being engulfed by clouds of smoke. Thinking they were about to ditch, he clambered to his crash position against the main spar and braced himself. Strangely, no water came in; only the horrifying sound of metal being ripped apart and the aircraft shuddering like a mad thing. Flung violently against the spar, he was knocked out and when he returned to consciousness and regained his faculties next day, he discovered himself in hospital with arm and leg injuries, but had no idea how he got there.

It transpired that the Lancaster had 'mushed' at the bottom of the shallow dive, hit the water like a skimming stone, first rising up and then plunging down onto Snettisham beach, sliding along on its belly until it hit the sea wall at speed. Fortunately some American airmen were close by – there was a US air gunnery school firing range located on that beach. They were able to remove all four British airmen before fire took hold on the wreckage. For Tom O'Shaughnessy and Arthur Holding it was too late; they had died in the crash. George Kendrick, extremely vulnerable in the nose of the aircraft, miraculously survived the crash, but suffered massive head and other injuries from which he was not expected to recover. Pilot Officer Ward had got off comparatively lightly.

By May 1944 Arthur Ward had recovered sufficiently to be declared fit for flying and went back to 617 at Woodhall Spa. However, as a 'spare bod', while he flew occasional training flights and some operational sorties as a gunner, it took a while for him to get back into the air as a radio operator and regular member of a crew. It was during this period he also discovered what had happened to the three airmen who missed the disastrous flight. They turned up late at the crew room, just missing the bus that took crews out to the aircraft. Unaware that anyone was missing, the WAAF driver completed her round and drove straight back to the MT section leaving the three airmen stranded. While Ward and Kendrick were in hospital all three re-crewed with Flight Lieutenant Bill Reid VC. Eventually, Arthur Ward's patience paid off when in August 1944, the new 617 CO, Wing Commander Willie Tait, asked him to join his crew as wireless operator.

Lady Luck plays cruel tricks, though. Against all the odds, Flying Officer George Kendrick recovered from his serious injuries by the end of 1944 and was declared fit for operations once more, only to lose his life flying as bomb aimer in a Lancaster shot down over Bergen on 12 January 1945. Having crewed up with Bill Reid, the three wayward members of Tom O'Shaughnessy's crew – flight engineer Flight Sergeant Donald Stewart, mid-upper gunner, Flight Sergeant Albert Holt and rear gunner Warrant Officer John Hutton DFC – also fell victim to another tragic accident. Tasked with dropping a 12,000lb Tallboy from 12,000ft onto a railway tunnel at Rilly la Montage on 31 July 1944, Reid's Lancaster was hit by bombs dropped from an aircraft flying above him. All three airmen died in the stricken aircraft, and only Bill Reid and one other survived to become a Prisoner of War. Thus it was that, after this amazing series of incidents, from O'Shaughnessy's original crew only Arthur Ward, now with fifty-three operations to his name, managed to cheat death by the end of the war.

'Cookie' was a euphemism for the RAF's 4,000lb high capacity (HC) bomb. In its thin-case version it was a highly effective demolition tool designed to explode on impact, razing whole groups of buildings to the ground with its tremendous blast shock wave so that incendiaries could set the resulting debris ablaze. The 4,000lb HC bomb was basically a non-aerodynamic metal cylinder with an explosive charge to overall weight ratio of about 75 per cent. As an operational weapon it had been around since late 1941, entirely filling the bomb bay of a Wellington and making it hard work to haul it to more distant targets. Even in the larger Lancaster and Halifax, crews were still keen to see the back of this lethal monster. Being sensitive to impact, or even a strong airflow blowing over the fuses, it was one big headache if it hung up or had to be jettisoned if aircraft problems forced an early return to base.

Canadian Warrant Officer II Francis McGrath of No.50 Squadron encountered just such a problem on the night of 10/11 April 1943 when Main Force sent 500 bombers to attack Frankfurt. On this occasion, the target was hidden safely beneath an impenetrable layer of cloud, but twenty-one aircraft (4.2 per cent), including five Lancasters, were lost – but with practically no effect on the city of Frankfurt itself. Taking off from RAF Skellingthorpe just after midnight in Lancaster ED478, Warrant Officer McGrath set course for the target. At 1.30a.m. a radio message was picked up at Waddington saying ED478 was returning to its base. No reason was given. An hour and a half later – presumably nearing the English coast – the pilot requested permission to jettison his 4,000lb cookie in the designated dumping area in The Wash, between Skegness and Hunstanton, before attempting to land. This was granted. There seemed to be some confusion on the ground as to which of the returning bombers was trying to communicate with base. Twenty minutes passed and the Skegness Observer Corps post reported an aircraft crossing the coast heading inland. Then faint radio transmissions were picked up suggesting ED478 was around sixty miles out to sea off Skegness. That was the last that was heard of ED478, its pilot or its crew (Flight Sergeant Peter Mansfield and Sergeants Robert Wilson, Ronald Coulson, Cyril Birtles, and Alfred Jeffery). A subsequent air and sea search in the area of the last transmission found some small pieces of aircraft wreckage, but it was never established if they belonged to ED748.

Pilots were advised to jettison cookies at not less than 5,000ft altitude over the sea, in order to avoid being caught in the tremendous blast effect when the bomb exploded – even if thought to be 'safe', these weapons still had a nasty habit of exploding! If McGrath's aeroplane was already in difficulty, perhaps unable to gain height to a safe altitude before the cookie was released, he and his crew may have become such victims. Alternatively, ED478 may simply have flown into the sea. The Air Ministry decided that, as there were no reports of a massive explosion at sea, the latter option was more likely to have been the reason for this particular loss.

The estate lands of Houghton Hall, home of Lord John Cholmondeley, collected a couple of Lancasters during the Second World War – one in 1944, and the other in 1945. The first of these was on the night of Monday 23 October 1944, when a huge force of 1,055 bombers launched not only the heaviest attack so far directed against Essen, but also the greatest number of aircraft sent to any German target to date. Amazingly, from this immense force only eight aircraft were lost (0.7 per cent). Among the massive 4,538 tons of bombs dropped that night were 509 of the 4,000lb 'cookie' type. In this 'maximum effort' raid, RAF Binbrook despatched twenty-six Lancasters from No.460 (RAAF) Squadron. One of this force was Lancaster BIII, PB351, AR-H[2], fully laden with an awesome destructive force: 1 x 4,000lb cookie; 5 x 1,000lb and 6 x 500lb HE bombs; and 1,000 x 4lb incendiaries. The crew of PB351 was briefed to bomb a specific wing of the Krupps factory from 18,000ft altitude.

As they crossed the French coast this Lancaster flew through a cold front with much cloud up to and beyond the bombing height, but as they approached the target at 7.35p.m., the pilot, Pilot Officer Denis Richins, saw the first markers go down. Encountering neither fighters nor

A typical Lancaster bomb load of 1 x 4,000lb 'cookie', 8 x 1,000lb and other bombs. (Bob Reid)

searchlights and only moderate flak during the bombing run, the crew blessed their luck, but it did not hold. Shortly after the bomb load was released, PB351 took a flak hit in the fuselage, the explosion knocking mid-upper gunner Flight Sergeant Jack Cannon unconscious.

Setting course for home via Holland, the pilot found he could not climb above the cloud brought in by the cold front and the aircraft became severely iced up. An SOS radio call was sent out and an instruction received to divert to RAF Bircham Newton. Just before 10.00p.m., while attempting to land at Bircham, 'Harry Two' hit the top of a tall beech tree in a wood near Houghton Hall and crashed, disintegrating into a flaming wreck. With .303 ammunition crackling off all around, Lord John Cholmondeley – home on leave from the Navy – ran to the scene with his gardener Fred Dye but, driven back by the intense conflagration, they could do nothing for the crew. However, one of those airmen, Flight Sergeant Jack Cannon, was incredibly lucky that night.

Unconscious in his turret and oblivious to everything throughout the whole of the return flight, it is thought Jack Cannon was flung out through the top of his turret when the Lancaster exploded. The surrounding trees cushioned his fall and he finally dropped to earth on a patch of damp bracken. When he came to, he had sustained leg and head injuries, acquired as he fell through the branches. Bizarrely – but in the circumstances, not unreasonably – Jack thought himself to have crashed somewhere in Germany and started to hobble towards the wreck to see if any more of his crew had survived. It was only after he had stumbled upon poor old Fred Dye and threatened him with his escape knife that he discovered he was just outside King's Lynn in dear old England! Next morning Sergeant Cannon's parachute harness and unopened parachute pack were discovered hanging in the trees some distance from the wreck, but all six of his compatriots were dead.

Gelsenkirchen was another Rühr target that came in for Bomber Command attention on 25/26 June 1943. It had not been bombed directly since the dark old days of 1941, but even with sophisticated marking now available, this raid was not a great success due to half the marker Mosquitoes suffering *Oboe* equipment malfunctions. The bomber loss rate from 473 aircraft despatched was 6.3 per cent, with thirteen Lancasters among those lost. Among them was W4830, QR-E from No.61 Squadron, based at RAF Syerston and captained by Sergeant

D.H. Pearce. Over the target, his aircraft was badly damaged by flak bursts that started a fire in the wing and eventually put the port outer engine out of action. He managed to nurse the bomber all the way back to England before losing so much height that it was impossible to coax it the final few miles to base. Soon he realised it would be too low to bale out and discounting a forced landing without proper control over the aircraft, he ordered his crew to bale out. One after the other they dropped out of the Lancaster and landed safely – all, that is, except the navigator Sergeant Kenneth Lloyd and mid-upper gunner, Herbert Beasley. Lloyd died when his parachute failed to open and Beasley, who was last out, was too low for his 'chute to deploy and break his fall.

The abandoned bomber crashed at 4.00a.m. on 26 June on land belonging to Deeping Fen Farm at Baston Common, nine miles south-west of Spalding. Having landed strung out in a line from Spalding Common to near the crash site, it was some time before the crew were rounded up, but despite a wide search by police, air force, fire brigade and civilian personnel, Sergeant Beasley simply could not be found. Then, in May 1945, the local newspaper carried this short report:

> The body of Sgt Herbert William Beasley, navigator, RAuxAF with No.61 Squadron, aged 31 of Lincoln, was discovered in a field. He had been missing since 26 June 1943 when his aircraft crashed.

The loss rate for the raid on Cologne on 9/10 July 1943 was much lower – 2.5 per cent – than the raid mentioned above, and is a good illustration of the beneficial effect that the new electronic navigation device *Oboe*, when used in conjunction with PFF, could have. It would be a decisive weapon in this campaign, and it did its job well on this occasion. But all of this relative sophistication was academic to the crew of Lancaster ED360 of No.106 Squadron from RAF Syerston. Their aeroplane had crashed after take-off with the loss of five of the seven airmen on board. An engine caught fire on the outward leg and the pilot, Flight Sergeant Arthur Bristow, was unable to prevent his aeroplane diving into the ground at Church End, Parson Drove near Wisbech. As might be expected, the 4,000lb 'cookie' on board 'went up', although fortunately, in that sparsely populated area, its blast dissipated in the rural night with infinitely less devastation than intended for Cologne. Local man Gordon Fennelow recalled that night and said some cottages were demolished by the blast, while a building some distance away housing Land Army personnel was severely damaged, with most of the occupants luckily escaping with just cuts from flying glass. One wall of his bungalow still has a 'pot-belly' appearance from the effect of the explosion.

Survivors of the accident were the bomb aimer Sergeant L.J. Hazell and flight engineer Sergeant F. Scattergood, who managed to bale out. In the aftermath of such a tremendous explosion, their comrades were initially posted as 'missing', until the body of the navigator Sergeant James Johns was recovered on 14 July, and air gunners Sergeant Clifford Simm and Flight Sergeant Kenneth Murphy on 21 July. The latter, a Canadian, is buried in Sutton Bridge parish churchyard. Sadly the bodies of pilot Flight Sergeant Bristow and wireless operator Sergeant Wilfred Worthington were never found. It is this aspect of wartime accidents, where the wreckage can be seen and examined, which prolongs the sadness in a very different way to the comparative finality of losses over enemy territory. Confirmation of the location of this incident was found by FAWNAPS, during an excavation in 1978, when they were able to extract two engines, tail wheel assembly, a pair of Browning machine guns and a propeller blade and boss, from the main point of impact.

By contrast, an earlier raid by 600 aircraft on Dortmund on 4/5 May was still considered highly successful, although more costly (5.2 per cent) in terms of losses. Bad weather marred the return to England, with thick fog contributing to seven crashes. Among the latter was

Lancaster ED715, GT-J, of No.156 (PFF) Squadron, whose story begins a run of Pathfinder-related accidents in the Fens, where the number of parachute escapes almost matched the number of aircrew deaths. One of the trade-offs for Bomber Command pressing for an ever greater individual aircraft bomb load, was that because fuel loads were so carefully calculated, margins for emergencies became small in consequence.

Acting Squadron Leader B.L. Duigan DFC found RAF Warboys fogbound on his return from the first PFF-led raid on Dortmund. 'Stooging around', he could find no break in the dense blanket of low cloud and decided to try to land at RAF Wyton. It, too, was shrouded in fog so, before his fuel ran dry, Duigan gained some altitude and ordered his crew to bale out. This was achieved successfully with only Flight Lieutenant Rogers suffering slight injury while ED715 flew on to crash near Chatteris. Those energetic diggers in FAWNAPS also excavated this site in 1977, recovering many large components that are now preserved in their museum near Wisbech. In addition, a propeller blade from ED715 was presented to the military cemetery in Bergen-op-Zoom in Holland in 1980 where, mounted atop a small plinth, it became a fitting memorial to aircrew that never made it home.

Historians sometimes differ over dates when one 'phase' of the bomber offensive passed into another, but there was, for example, a period beginning in August 1942 that Gordon Musgrove called the 'Pathfinder era'. Targets were selected from a wide range of major German and Italian cities as the new Pathfinder Force (PFF) learned its trade, and Main Force also grew in numbers. Then the phase that became known as the Battle of Berlin opened with a raid on that city in August 1943. It required the longer autumn and winter nights, preferably with no moon, to cloak Harris's bombers with sufficient darkness to make these deep penetrations into Germany. They needed all the cover they could get in order to avoid the attentions of night fighters and flak. Consequently, aircrews fought this campaign under the most adverse weather and severe conditions in their aeroplanes. As Musgrove wrote:

> Long hours at sub-zero temperatures dulled the brain, slowed reflexes and increased mistakes
> … frostbite was common and … conditions in the aircraft were often severe beyond belief.

As if that was not enough, just at the time when mental and physical exhaustion would be reaching its peak, weather conditions over England might be less than helpful on the return.

With ten-tenths cloud over the target, 'Black Thursday', 16/17 December 1943 became the worst night of the war for bomber accident losses over England. Pathfinder Force was hit particularly badly, both over enemy territory and England that night, losing a total of almost fourteen crews – a severe loss of experienced airmen. Research shows that from 483 Lancaster bombers despatched to Berlin, twenty-five were lost to enemy action but no less than thirty were wrecked in collisions or crashes or abandoned by their crews in bad weather over England and thick fog from Yorkshire to Suffolk. Apart from those aeroplanes managing to crash-land on their home airfields, four of these aeroplanes, all from PFF squadrons, crashed on Fenland soil around midnight. Take-off had been early – at 4.00p.m. – to avoid moonlight over the target on the 16 December.

Arriving back at RAF Bourn in fog and low cloud, Pilot Officer Robert Mooney in command of Lancaster JB482 from No.97 Squadron, judged a landing attempt as far too risky and ordered his crew to abandon the aeroplane. All seven airmen did this successfully and came down near Wyton Airfield while JB482 flew on to crash in the North Sea. Mooney may have survived this one but he was killed in action on 2 January 1944. A second No.97 Squadron Lancaster, JB531, was also abandoned near Ely without injury to any of its crew: Pilot Officer F. Smith and his six comrades. In an interview with author Martin Middlebrook, Smith's navigator, Pilot Officer John Arthurson, recalled that terrible night:

We were stacked high, circling as other planes attempting to land using Standard Beam Approach were [all] making more than one try. The flight engineer said at this rate we'd run out of petrol before we landed so the pilot called on 'Darkie' for assistance. We were given a course and time to fly to another aerodrome and when over this one, a flare was fired but none of the crew saw it. We flew around at zero feet with wheels and flaps down and the bomb aimer in the nose giving instructions: 'up a bit – down a bit', amid exclamations of relief at something just missed.

We came upon FIDO and glimpsed a runway – cheers! The pilot did a turn that should have lined him up for a landing, but we came upon it [the runway] sideways. Other 'split-arse' turns failed to find it and when the flight engineer said we had only enough petrol for fifteen minutes flying, I said let's get up and bale out. The rear gunner agreed. Our pilot was loath to do so but after a few more minutes trying to find a runway, he agreed too. Setting the aeroplane on an easterly heading at 8,000ft the pilot waited until the crew baled out safely, then jumped himself.

The Lancaster then crashed near Orford Ness.

While one crew might escape disaster, Fate might not be so kind to another. So it was for the Canadian crew of JB369 LQ-D, one of thirteen aircraft despatched to Berlin by No.405 (PFF) Squadron. Unable to land at RAF Gransden Lodge in that same atrocious fog on the 16/17 December, this aeroplane ran out of fuel, crashing near Ely with the loss of six out of the seven-man crew. Sole survivor was rear gunner Warrant Officer S.H. Nutting DFM, who managed to bale out just in time. What kind of game was Fate playing that night? It was Warrant Officer Nutting's forty-fifth and last operation as a member of PFF (he was screened from operations when he came out of hospital) and his Canadian pilot, Flying Officer Burus McLennan's seventeenth operation. The rest of the crew who died were: Sergeant Herbert Cornwell (FE), Flying Officer Walter Sheppard (N), Warrant Officer II Gordon Schneider (B), Sergeant Eric Halliwell (W), and Sergeant Maurice Roobroeck (AG).

Six more airmen died that night when JB282 of No.156 Squadron crashed on the Earith to Sutton road while trying to get into RAF Warboys, killing Flight Sergeant William Watkins and five of his crew. Only the rear gunner, named in some records as Sergeant L.F. Darlison but as Dalton by the Squadron association, escaped by parachute. A lucky night for rear gunners, for a change! All in all it was indeed a black night for PFF, losing six aircraft over Germany (forty-two airmen) while a further twelve crashed in England with casualties of fifty-three killed and nine injured.

Berlin was taking its toll in more ways than one. It was not just the Main Force and Pathfinders that had problems that night. Mention of RAF Tempsford earlier, particularly in the context of Halifax operations, brings to light a stirring tale in which that enduring and typically British soft spot for animals comes to the fore. The story begins at Tempsford, known mainly for its role as a departure point for clandestine operational flights, including agent dropping and pick-up or supply drops to various resistance groups; it ends when the icy waters of The Wash swallowed up Halifax LL120. Scheduled for the night of 16/17 December 1943, 'Operation Wheelwright' involved three Halifax aircraft of No.161 (Special Duties) Squadron in a mission to drop supplies to the French resistance in the vicinity of Angouleme. One of the three was Halifax LL120, MA-W, which left Tempsford at 9.15p.m. with Warrant Officer W.A. Caldwell at the controls, his crew of six and their mascot, a fox-terrier puppy.

Visibility deteriorated soon after take-off but was good enough for them to map-read to within forty miles of the target area. Flying conditions then deteriorated even further but Caldwell pressed on, relying now entirely on instruments. Estimating his position to be over the target area, he circled in the hope of picking up a pin-point, but cloud cover was so thick it was impossible to determine if they were anywhere near the right place. For this reason Warrant Officer Caldwell decided not to risk dropping the supplies. Part of the load comprised bundles of propaganda leaflets so, turning the aeroplane towards where he believed Angouleme lay, the crew kept themselves busy by casting leaflets to the four winds. While appearing productive it was often felt by aircrew that dropping leaflets was 'just a way of providing the enemy with free toilet paper!' Setting course for home, conditions were so appalling there was little cause to fear attention from either searchlights or fighters. Tempsford was now shrouded by the same impenetrable cloud and a radio message diverted Caldwell to RAF Woodbridge. Even there the weather did not relent, making a descent through cloud and a blind landing in darkness completely out of the question. A hurried consultation between Caldwell and his crew brought him to the conclusion that the flatlands of Lincolnshire around The Wash offered the best chance of survival in a forced landing.

After nine hours in the air, many of which were without the benefit of a decent 'fix', the actual position of the Halifax still remained in doubt. Believing them to be somewhere in the area between Boston and Spilsby, Warrant Officer Caldwell finally gave the order to bale out, shouting to the crew: 'and don't forget the pup!' First man out stuffed the little dog unceremoniously into his flying suit, secured him with his left arm – leaving the right for his rip-cord – and jumped into the blackness. Warrant Officer Caldwell undid his straps, eased clear of his seat and waited anxiously for the last man to disappear. Then, trimming LL120 on a course that should take it out to sea, he let go of the controls and baled out himself, leaving the Halifax to its fate. The only mishap to the entire crew and their precious fox-terrier was a broken ankle suffered by Flight Sergeant Morris. Halifax LL120 itself was seen by members of the Observer Corps to crash into the icy waters of The Wash.

It was a bad night all round for the special duties squadrons. Many airmen, highly experienced in this difficult and dangerous work, were lost on this night of atrocious weather. Both the other two Halifax Vs on 'Wheelwright' crashed, LK899 near Bawdsey and DK206 near Woodbridge, each with fatalities. Two 161 Squadron Lysanders were also lost and three more Halifaxes, LL115, LL119 and LW280 from No.138 Squadron crashed. Though by no means unusual, this scale of casualties is a measure of the vital importance placed on this work and the lengths to which these airmen went to carry it out. Any bomber returning from operations that night was likely to be caught out by the impenetrable fog. Stirling III, EF163 from No.75 Squadron, despatched on a 'Gardening' sortie to the Freisian Islands area, returned with one mine hung up so the crew, already facing a difficult landing, now had their troubles magnified by the fog that enveloped their Mepal base. Flight Sergeant C.J. Kinross made it back into the circuit, but the 'hung up' mine was always likely to make the aircraft tricky to control at the best of times, and during one circuit, EF163 simply flew into the ground and exploded. Only one airman, Sergeant S. Newman, an air gunner, survived the crash at Beddington Farm, Sutton near Ely. It had been a grim night indeed.

Much mention has been made of main force and pathfinder operations by four-engine heavy bombers, but we should not overlook the efforts and price paid by the crews of DH Mosquito aircraft belonging to the Pathfinder, Light Night Striking Force and Bomber Support squadrons. Not least because of their performance capabilities, as well as the skill of their crews, in many well-known summaries of these Mosquito raids there is often the remark 'no aircraft lost'. That may be true with reference to losses over enemy territory, but until 'engines off' there were still losses even in the closing stages of a sortie.

No.139 Squadron converted to the bomber version of the Mosquito in 1942 and joined No.8 Group for Pathfinder duties in April 1943. Operating from RAF Upwood it was used variously to drop target markers, *Window* or HE bombs and quickly gained a reputation as a good 'all-purpose' night bomber unit. This came at a price, though, since it suffered the highest percentage loss of aircraft and crews among No.8 Group's Mosquito squadrons.

Australian pilot Flight Lieutenant Graeme Keys earned his DFC – gazetted in July 1943 – while flying main force operations with 460 (RAAF) Squadron from RAF Binbrook. Having completed that tour he was posted in early 1944 to No.139 Squadron to fly the Mosquito IV bomber as a Pathfinder. On the night of 4/5 May 1944, a small force of twenty-eight Mosquitoes was despatched to raid Ludwigshafen and Flight Lieutenant Keys and his navigator, Flying Officer Arthur Hamlin, were one of five *Oboe*-equipped Mosquito crews briefed to mark the aiming point from 25,000ft with red Target Indicators (TI). Only moderate flak came up over the target and no aircraft were lost on the raid itself but, after a sortie lasting three and a half hours, at 200ft on finals Flight Lieutenant Keys lost control when DZ646, XD-Y stalled during the approach to land. It was believed the ASI inlet may have iced up and contributed to the crash near Ramsey that tragically claimed the lives of both airmen.

No.5 Group also wanted to operate its own Mosquito Pathfinder squadron and in April 1944, No.627 Squadron was transferred – Don Bennett felt it was 'stolen' – from No.8 Group to No.5 at Woodhall Spa. On 26/27 September 1944, Main Force was due to raid Karlsruhe with 627 Squadron acting as target marker. Flying Officer Andrew Mathieson was briefed and with his Australian navigator, Flying Officer Allan Fitzpatrick DFM, they prepared to take off from Woodhall Spa in Mosquito IV DZ521, AZ-M. Although Main Force bombers had taken off some time earlier, the Mossie's superior speed meant that Mathieson could lift DZ521 off the runway at 2.10a.m. on 27 September, overtake the Lancasters and still be on time putting down the markers.

Disaster struck just twenty-four minutes into the flight when DZ521 crashed, inverted and burned out at Tilney St Lawrence, near King's Lynn. Wreckage was found strewn across a two-and-a-half mile swathe, indicating that the Mosquito had broken up in flight. It was suspected that an undercarriage door broke away and destroyed the tail unit, causing severe loss of control and the disintegration that killed Flying Officers Mathieson and Fitzpatrick. Fitzpatrick's DFM was awarded while he was also a member of 460 (RAAF) Squadron.

No.608 Squadron, based at RAF Downham Market, was part of Don Bennett's 8 Group Light Night Striking Force, frequently employed, for example, on diversionary and 'spoof' raids during which fake night fighter flares, route markers and *Windows* were dropped on the way to targets upon which they might drop TIs and 4,000lb 'cookies', driving the population into shelters and simulating a Main Force attack that did not materialise. While Main Force actually went to Bochum on 9/10 October 1944, the Mosquitoes of No.608 and others raided Wilhelmshaven. Among their number was Mosquito XX, KB261, 6T-D, flown by Flight Lieutenant Reginald Gardner with his navigator, Flying Officer Oswald Sweetman DFM who bombed the target with no difficulty. At 9.30p.m., with their sortie almost over and beginning their circuit to land, KB261 inexplicably dived into the ground from a height of 1,000ft near Wimbotsham, exploded and killed both airmen.

No.608 lost another Mosquito XX, KB360, on 10/11 November 1944 as it was setting out from Downham Market for an operational sortie to Hannover. The port engine failed ten minutes into the flight and despite jettisoning bombs and drop tanks, Canadian Flight Lieutenant Stuart Webb could not maintain height and the bomber crashed into a field on Maltmas Farm, Friday Bridge near Wisbech. Webb died but his navigator, Flying Officer Campbell, although injured was pulled from the wreckage to survive the crash and the war.

No.128 Squadron was also part of 8 Group's LNSF equipped, in January 1945, with Mosquito B Mk XVI and operating from RAF Wyton. On the night of 14/15 January, along with another eighty-two Mosquitoes, Australian pilot Flight Lieutenant Alan Heitmann took MM194 on the long trip to Berlin and back – a round trip of five-and-a-half hours.

The weather that night had been stormy to and from the target and visibility back at base was bad. Feeling his way carefully down the approach funnel, he must have heaved a sigh of relief as the main wheels touched the tarmac, but in that final minute tragedy struck. The throttles jammed and Heitmann decided to go round again. Not knowing if the throttles would respond again and getting low on fuel, he climbed and ordered his navigator to bale out, which he did safely, but Heitmann himself was unable to abandon the Mosquito and died when it crashed near Chatteris. That night, from the total of 1,214 sorties undertaken by all Groups, seventeen aircraft were lost to enemy action but, including Alan Heitmann's Mosquito, a further fourteen aircraft crashed in England.

In mid-1943, British night fighters went on the offensive against their German counterparts who were wreaking havoc among RAF bomber streams over Europe. The radio frequency of current German airborne (AI) radar had been discovered and a receiver, code-named *Serrate*, was developed that could home into radio signal emissions from German airborne radar sets. Used in conjunction with RAF AI Mk IV, British long-range night fighters were able to detect and attack German night fighters. Initially a single squadron, No.141, operated within Fighter Command and built up experience with *Serrate*. These operations were known as Bomber Support and squadrons equipped first with the Beaufighter then the Mosquito with later versions of AI, patrolled RAF bomber streams or roamed over known enemy airfields and assembly points, seeking out German night fighters. It proved to be a very effective weapon against Luftwaffe night fighters as Hauptmann Wilhelm Johnen, a Luftwaffe night fighter ace, confirmed:

Fast Mosquitoes … lived up to their name … and wreaked havoc among the German crews. The radar equipment of this wooden aircraft surpassed anything previously seen. It was so technically perfect that at a distance of five miles they could pick German night fighters out of the bomber stream like currants out of a cake. They pursued us in the bomber stream [and] waited for us at our airfields as we took off or landed.

At the beginning of 1944, No.141, plus two new Mosquito squadrons (169 and 239) and all *Serrate* operations were transferred to Bomber Command under the control of a new radio countermeasures unit designated No.100 (Bomber Support) Group. So successful were these intruder-type activities that Bomber Command created its own experimental unit: Bomber Support Development Unit (BSDU) based initially at RAF Foulsham in Norfolk, and a training school: No.1692 Bomber Support Training School (BSTU). This latter unit was based at RAF Great Massingham, west Norfolk, where its main purpose was to give new crews joining the *Serrate* squadrons a few weeks' training in the use of the equipment and techniques for its employment on operations. It was staffed by tour-expired crew from the *Serrate* squadrons who could pass on their hard earned experience to the newcomers.

Thirty years after these events, the summer of 1975 was a very dry one, and pushing our way in single file through tall reeds was easy, as the usually soggy ground had completely dried out. The current writer was following Flight Lieutenant John Tagg, a Victor tanker navigator from RAF Marham, and we were making our way through shoulder-high reeds to the site of Mosquito II, DD736, from No.1692 BSTU that crashed on 22 November 1944 about a mile north of the hamlet of Fair Green, near King's Lynn. Normally inaccessible, the recent dry spell, together with new drainage work in the area, had caused the water table to fall and John was brought in when workmen spotted a propeller during November 1974. He was a recovery enthusiast who was also 'keeping an eye on the project for the RAF', and he invited me along to see the beginning of a recovery project involving the East Anglian Aviation Society.

June 1975. Cadets from Wisbech ATC Squadron hold one of the prop blades from the starboard engine of Mosquito DD736, later presented to the Squadron. The recovery dig is under way in the background while the tip of a prop blade on the port engine is just visible.

Unable to get heavier equipment to the site, over a period of six months EAAS laboured with hand tools to uncover the wreckage. At the start the only piece visible above ground was the tip of a port propeller blade, while the port elevator and fin were found in a bush about a hundred yards away. Soon after digging began, a large quantity of live 20mm ammunition was turned up and the dig had to stop to allow an RAF bomb disposal team (BD) to clear the ordnance.

The first major items recovered were the port main wheel with tyre intact, the top of the port engine, propellor blades and various metal fairings. Gradually the site was oriented and marked out with tape and with digging down to four feet, larger items came to light. Digging in the peat was initially quite easy, but as the depth increased the soil became thick with oil and aviation fuel and was criss-crossed with cables and wires. Self-sealing rubber foam that covered the fuel tanks also caused spades to bounce back out of the soil when it was hit! All four cannon were recovered in good condition, but one with a round jammed in the breech had to be destroyed by the BD team. The cockpit area was completely destroyed, although the control column was eventually pieced together from several broken parts. Seat armour and other cockpit items, including oxygen bottles, fire extinguisher and Very pistol, were also unearthed. Oil cooling radiators were intact but very compressed by the impact. Close to the surface, the port engine was heavily corroded but showed some signs of fire damage. The starboard engine was extremely difficult to dig out, being buried beneath ten feet of peat, two feet of clay and two feet of gravel. It was finally hauled out by hand winch.

All useful components having been recovered, the by now large and waterlogged hole was filled in and the salvaged remains taken to EAAS museum at Bassingbourn for cleaning, assessment and disposal. Few wooden components remained, but a section of wing skin a couple of yards square and several chunks of main spar survived the ravages of time, and these were sent to Ciba-Giegy's museum, the original manufacturers of the wood glue. The fuel pump went to Hawker Siddeley for possible use on their airworthy Mosquito, while exhaust stubs and other engine components were donated to the BBMF. The barrel of the destroyed cannon found its way to the Belgian Air Force to help in the renovation of its Hurricane, and the Mosquito Museum at London Colney received three cannon and what was left of the engines.

But what of the crew and circumstances that thirty years earlier had led to this crash? Mosquito II, DD736 was built at Hatfield in August 1942 and was used as a trials aircraft until it suffered an accident in September 1943. Repaired, it then went to No.141 Squadron in March 1944, and then to No.1692 BSTU in July 1944. Canadian pilot Flying Officer Charles Preece took off from Great Massingham Airfield at 2.35p.m. in DD736 for an air exercise with Nav/RO Flying Officer Fred Ruffle DFC. Less than an hour later, the aircraft was seen to emerge from cloud in a spin and crashed at 3.20p.m., killing both members of the crew. An official inquiry failed to establish the cause. Fred Ruffle had only recently been posted in to No.1692 BSTU as it has been noted that his DFC was awarded immediately after flying a special operation with No.515 Squadron – another Bomber Support unit – in October 1944.

The fact that there was some sign of scorching on one engine might indicate that one engine could have failed and contributed to the crash. In his autobiography *Pursuit Through Darkened Skies*, former radar operator Michael Allen DFC** wrote of his experiences in No.141 (Bomber Support) Squadron:

> The Mosquitoes which were delivered to us were NF IIs. They were old, worn out and much used aircraft from Home Defence night fighter squadrons. Ultimately they had to be re-engined, but only after several crews had been lost and others had crawled back on one engine.

Relegated to the training unit, DD736 had been worked intensively for two years and maybe it was just worn out.

Bravery in the air was not something that Flight Sergeant Leslie Chapman or his contemporaries would have given much thought to; they just got on with the job. Born in the village of Saracen's Head in south Lincolnshire, by 1944 Leslie was wireless operator of Avro Lancaster, R5856, serving with No.61 Squadron at RAF Skellingthorpe near Lincoln, and took part in the last major raid of the Battle of Berlin. This was the ill-fated attack on Nuremberg on the night of 30/31 March 1944.

Flight Sergeant Leslie Chapman CGM, No.61 Squadron RAF. (Derek & Pam Brown)

Much has been written about the strategy, planning, execution and statistics of this notorious operation because Bomber Command suffered its greatest single loss of manpower and aircraft during the raid. From an attacking force of 795 aircraft despatched, ninety-five were lost and sixty-four of these were Lancasters. Among all the statistics and all the stories of heroism to emerge from that raid – and there were many – Flight Sergeant Chapman's story gives just one glimpse of what bravery meant on that fateful night. It was only the crew's third operation and there is no better place to begin than with the joint citation in the *London Gazette*, of 9 May 1944, for the award of the Conspicuous Gallantry Medal (Flying) to wireless operator Sergeant Leslie Chapman and of the Distinguished Flying Cross to his pilot, Flying Officer Desmond Freeman:

> This officer and airman were pilot and wireless operator of an aircraft detailed to attack Nuremberg one night in March 1944. During that operation the aircraft was attacked by a fighter. It was driven off but shortly afterwards two more enemy aircraft attacked. Before they also were driven off the bomber had sustained much damage. The starboard wing, the flaps and the undercarriage nacelle were all hit by bullets. The windscreen was shattered and other parts of the airframe were shot away. Four members of the crew were wounded. Most of the navigational equipment was useless but course was set for home. Sgt Chapman had been wounded in the back, neck and head but bravely remained at his post obtaining fixes which were of inestimable value in establishing the aircraft's position at various stages on the return flight. Finally the English coast was reached and Fg Off Freeman landed the aircraft safely, although a tyre on one of the landing wheels had been punctured. Fg Off Freeman displayed great skill, courage and determination throughout; Sgt Chapman also proved himself to be a gallant member of the aircraft crew. It was not until the aircraft had been safely landed that he informed his captain of his wounds. He set a splendid example.

Sergeant Derek Patfield was the bomb aimer in the Lancaster with Leslie Chapman and, interviewed in 2001 by Steve Snelling from the *Eastern Daily Press*, Derek gave his version of what it was like that night. He recalled it was near Frankfurt, a brilliant, moonlit night and the sky was full of bomber contrails because it was so cold. German fighters dropped flares, illuminating everything – bombers and fighters alike. His own position was up in the nose of the aircraft, reporting any aircraft shot down so that the navigator could enter it in the flight log.

Suddenly there was an enormous bang followed by a violent lurch that threw him onto his back but left him unhurt. Enemy fighters had attacked the Lancaster from astern and below and caused havoc in the aircraft. The pilot's windscreen was shattered, half the front turret had disappeared; the mid-upper was damaged; the flight engineers panel was on fire and there were holes everywhere. When Sergeant Patfield clambered back into the smoke-filled fuselage, he found the flight engineer with one arm smashed, beating out the flames on his panel with his gloved hands. The navigator was slumped unconscious over the remains of his table, with one hand almost torn off and most of his equipment in ruins. Leslie Chapman was still at his wireless set, although it was damaged and he had blood streaming down his face. The mid-upper gunner was also wounded but he and the rear gunner remained in their turrets. The pilot, Flying Officer Desmond Freeman, had escaped with minor scratches but with a howling, freezing gale blasting through the shattered windscreen; the navigator and engineer incapacitated and the wings and fuselage riddled with large holes, it was going to be touch and go finding England again – let alone reaching it.

Sergeant Chapman's face was covered in blood, his helmet was torn and blood was splashed all over his flying suit. Despite his face, neck and back being peppered with shrapnel, he told Derek Patfield that it looked worse than it was and after Patfield cleaned him up they both carried the navigator back to the rest bunk and made the engineer as comfortable as possible. Sergeant Chapman then went back to his damaged set and managed to get it going again while the bomb aimer, Sergeant Patfield, faced the task of trying to find where they were, using a few scraps of the navigator's maps that had not been blown away.

Now Leslie Chapman set about trying to obtain the all-important radio 'fixes' and after half an hour, got the first of these, which Patfield plotted on a map. However, at this crucial point Sergeant Patfield himself now collapsed unconscious. He was unaware that shrapnel had damaged his oxygen mask and oxygen supply and he passed out. Leslie Chapman was left to operate the wireless and attempt to 'navigate' entirely alone, which he did successfully, passing bearings to the pilot that helped bring them across the North Sea to within R/T range of RAF Horsham St Faith. But it was not all over yet. Having contacted Horsham, Leslie was told that a crashed aircraft would prevent other aircraft from landing and Desmond Freeman had to divert to RAF Foulsham where, with Chapman and Patfield – the latter having regained consciousness shortly after crossing the coast – shielding their two seriously wounded colleagues with their own bodies, he brought the aircraft down for a dicey crash landing on one good wheel – but from which they all emerged safely. A later inspection of Lancaster R5856 found her fuselage and wings riddled with no less than 280 holes of assorted shapes and sizes. As was usual in the circumstances, the crew split up after the Nuremberg raid and Leslie Chapman, now recovered from his own wounds, went back on to operations with another crew during that summer but sadly never lived to receive his gallantry award personally.

In the late afternoon of 1 February 1945, No.61 Squadron began to take off as part of a No.5 Group force briefed to attack railway and other transportation targets in Siegen. Sergeant Chapman was now getting near the end of his tour and his experience made him a valued member of his flight commander's crew. Shortly before 4.00p.m., Squadron Leader Hugh Horsley AFC lined up Lancaster I, NF912 and set off down Skellingthorpe runway. Just as the Lancaster became airborne, the port engine cut out. Exercising considerable skill, Horsley nursed the heavily laden bomber round a very tight circuit and put it down, wheels-up, on the airfield grass. As the bomber touched down there was an explosion, quickly followed by a conflagration from which only the rear gunner, Sergeant R.T. Hoskisson, though badly injured, escaped with his life.

Giving an order to bale out was always going to be a gut-wrenching effort for any aircraft captain, but that's the decision Australian captain Flying Officer Bill McNamee took on the night of 7/8 January 1945. He and his crew were never seen again – not so, though, for their No.467 Squadron Lancaster, JB286, coded PO-L. McNamee took off from RAF Waddington around 18:00 hours on 7 January, part of a force of 645 Lancasters setting out for the last major air raid on Munich. Ten hours later, at 4.15a.m., the village of Eye on the outskirts of Peterborough was rocked by a large explosion. RAF Wittering was alerted and a crash tender was quickly despatched from the station but it never reached the incident because it crashed at Market Deeping en route. The local fire service was called out, too, and fireman Fred Dighton recalled: 'it made quite a crater but there was very little of the aircraft to be seen, just a big smouldering hole.' Strangely though, the crash investigation team could find no evidence of any bodies of the crew in the wreckage.

Extending the range of their enquiries, a picture began to emerge. Having completed the bombing attack, the crew turned for home but from radio messages exchanged with RAF North Coates for bearings, it seems they had became lost in thick cloud and snow showers. During the investigation some misgivings emerged about the accuracy of bearings given by North Coates, but it was assumed that the pilot judged there to be insufficient fuel to reach England and, in the atrocious weather conditions, it was presumed the crew then abandoned the aircraft.

Bearing in mind the probable routing of the return flight and that the ground war was pushing towards the Rhine at that time, Bill McNamee may have thought that even though they were lost, there was a pretty good chance of his crew parachuting behind Allied lines and perhaps this hope is what convinced him to give the order to bale out. As no aircrew – alive or dead – traceable to JB286 were reported as found on land, they were listed as missing. As it seems fairly unlikely that none of the seven would be found if they had baled out over land perhaps, because they had so badly miscalculated their position, they came down in the inhospitable sea. Flying Officer McNamee's largely Australian crew included: Sergeant Henry Kirsh, the flight engineer and only Englishman in the crew; Flight Sergeant Herbert Williams, navigator; Flight Sergeant Stephanos Servos, wireless operator; Flight Sergeant John Gloury, bomb aimer; Flight Sergeant Laurence Saulwick, mid-upper gunner; and Flight Sergeant Max Bruckner, rear gunner. Meanwhile JB286 flew on until, after ten hours in the air, its fuel finally exhausted, the bomber crashed to earth at Eastwood House Farm, near Peterborough.

The author first became aware of the incident in 1977, when a Mr Moore from Holbeach St Johns sent a letter with a sketch map of the location. A visit to Eastwood Farm later that year yielded little as the occupants were newcomers to the area and knew nothing of the crash. The land was then owned by London Brick Company and used as arable land and there was a brick pit close by. As years passed by, the farmhouse was demolished, the brick pit became a landfill site and both the site and a new local road scheme gradually ate into the arable part. Then, in June 1995, workmen excavating the clay with mechanical diggers accidentally came across the last resting place of JB286. Four engines, three propellers and other debris were unearthed, but not much of the fuselage area was in evidence. Members of the Fenland Aircraft Preservation Society (now FAWNAPS) were brought in to help sort out the wreckage and try to identify what it was from. It was suggested at the time of the crash that the size of the explosion on impact may have been due to some bombs being left on board, and this may account for little of the fuselage being found. What was unearthed is now on display in the FAWNAPS museum near Wisbech.

The scene now moves north to RAF Balderton near Newark, home of No.227 Squadron. It is 1.00p.m. on 8 February 1945. The crew of Flying Officer George Edge's Lancaster, B-Baker, are all in their 'pits', sleeping the sound sleep of the exhausted after the previous night's operation to the Dortmund-Ems canal at Ladbergen. Sweet dreams were soon shattered, though, by the raucous blare of the 'tannoy', summoning all crews to report to the crew room at 2.00p.m. Ops again tonight!

Shaking the sleep from his mind, Pilot Officer Bob Reid dressed and went off to the navigator's briefing where he found the target for that night was the synthetic oil plant at Politz, north of Stettin. Twice they had been briefed for this target in the past few days and twice it had been scrubbed, each time due to a suspected intelligence leak. German oil production targets had never really left the priority target list since those dark days back in 1940/41, but the difficulty of hitting such selective targets had made good weather a requirement to mounting these raids. However, by this stage of the war, improved bombing techniques and availability of precision navigation aids now rendered 'bad weather' no excuse for 'Bomber' Harris not to divert his bombers from area bombing to more selective targets.

At the main briefing it was announced that that night's operation would be another 'maximum effort' for Bomber Command. As many as 475 Lancasters and seven Mosquitoes, of Nos 1, 5 and 8 Groups, were to attack in two waves, led by No.5 Group aircraft. Eighteen Lancasters from No.227 Squadron, including Flying Officer George Edge's B-Baker, were part of this force. With take-off scheduled for 17.00 there was no time to check their aircraft with the usual thoroughness. Ground crews had been beavering away in order to ready the

No.227 Squadron Lancaster B for Baker's crew in 1944. Back row from left: George Mitchell, bomb aimer; Harry Piper, flight engineer; Len Davy, mid-upper gunner; Bob Reid, navigator. Front row from left: Charlie Davis, wireless operator; George Edge, pilot; Dizzy Desborough, rear gunner. Sergeant Twitch Ling took Sergeant Harry Piper's place as FE on 8 February 1945. (Bob Reid)

squadron's aircraft – 2,000 gallons of fuel and 11,000lb of bombs were on board and final checks were hastily made before the aircraft taxied from dispersal at the start of a nine-and-a-half-hour round trip.

It was a fine evening with a strong west wind as George lined up PD348, 9J-B at the end of Balderton's runway 26. As usual the A1 Great North Road, which ran close to that end, was closed until all bombers were airborne. By Bob Reid's watch it was 5.03p.m. when George Edge pushed the throttles firmly forward and the heavily laden bomber began to roll. Flight engineer 'Twitch' Ling followed these movements and as the skipper concentrated on take-off, Twitch held the throttle levers wide open as the speed built up. At 105mph, Edge eased B-Baker off the tarmac, but even as the bomber cleared the perimeter hedge, black smoke suddenly began streaming from the port inner engine. Calmly, Edge told Ling to shut the engine down and feather its propeller. Still climbing, now mid-upper gunner, Sergeant Len Davey, reported black smoke coming from the starboard inner. It was overheating and so it was throttled back, while both outer engines were opened up to compensate. As power to the starboard inner was reduced, so was the temperature, but still it did not run smoothly.

At 700ft, seven minutes after take-off, all attempts to re-start the port inner failed and the bomber could not be coaxed higher. With a 4,000lb cookie, fourteen 500lb bombs, 2,000 gallons of fuel on board and two sick engines threatening to catch fire, B-Baker was in no fit state to make a long flight into enemy territory, so the skipper aborted the trip and set about the task of pure survival. While pilot and flight engineer applied all their skill to keep the aircraft under control, the remainder of the crew quietly got on with their own jobs. Behind his curtain, navigator Bob Reid plotted the aircraft's position. All his navigational aids were

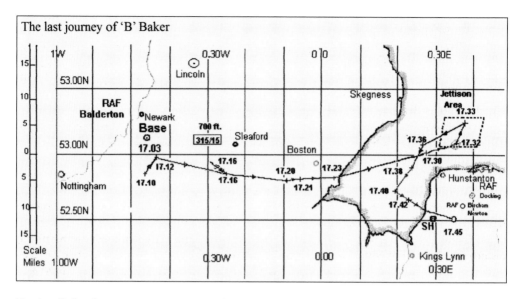

The last journey of 'B' Baker

The last flight of Lancaster PD348 on 8 February 1945.(Bob Reid)

working fine and *Gee* was available to fix the position throughout the emergency. Bomb aimer, Flight Sergeant Mitch Mitchell, lay in the nose watching for landmarks while mid-upper gunner, Len Davey, and rear gunner, Sergeant Dizzy Desborough, were keeping a sharp lookout for other aircraft. Behind the navigator, wireless operator Sergeant Charlie Davis was listening out, ready to relay messages to and from the ground. As always, intercom talk was limited to the job in hand and for efficiency and discipline, the crew always addressed each other by their respective trades. Just fourteen hours after landing from their last raid, these men were now fighting for survival against a different enemy.

Skipper George Edge weighed up the options quickly. One: he could land back at Balderton fully laden on two engines; two: set the Lancaster on a course for the sea and abandon the aircraft over land; or three: drop the bombs at 'safe' over the sea and return to base. He discarded the first option since, at best, the all-up weight would damage the runway and at worst, there was a 99 per cent chance of the cookie going off and devastating the airfield. The second option was also a non-starter because they were already below 700ft and the parachutes would not function fully below 600ft. If the aircraft dived in quickly, there was also a possibility that the blast from the cookie could injure the crew. Even the last option was 'dicey'. Safe minimum height formula for dropping 500lb bombs is weight plus 50 per cent in feet, i.e. 500 + 250 = 750ft altitude. On this basis, the cookie's safe release height is 6,000ft, and even then it could be expected to detonate on impact. Anything less than 6,000ft would be very dangerous indeed for the aircraft.

When the skipper told his crew what the options were, they all elected to stay with the aircraft so, his mind made up, he asked Bob Reid for a course to steer for The Wash jettison area. His plan was to get rid of the 500 pounders first, try to gain enough height to drop the cookie without damaging B-Baker, then return to base or land at the most convenient airfield. Simple! 'Steer 100° true, running distance fifty-five miles,' replied the navigator. Altitude was still hovering around 600ft and, reaching 150mph, at their current weight there was not much margin between that and stalling speed. Pilot and flight engineer continued to nurse the two outer engines and the sick starboard inner, but all three were overheating badly now.

Six miles to run to the drop zone, but still only 600ft on the clock. The skipper decided to let the 500lb bombs go in two balanced sticks of seven and told the bomb aimer that, come what may, the bombs had to go at 500ft. That would lighten them by 7,000lb and, together with fuel being used up, they might be able to claw some more altitude and get rid of that damn cookie. B–Baker reached the southern edge of the jettison area and turned onto 020° for the bombing run. Bomb doors open – airspeed dropping – nose down to prevent a stall – 500ft – let 'em go! Bombs gone and bomb doors closed. Back in the rear turret, Dizzy Desborough let everyone know he was not a happy chap: two of the fourteen bombs exploded on impact and they gave him a right shaking. But no damage done, and they were still airborne – just.

Turning into wind, Edge altered course to 246°, back over The Wash, still juggling with controls, trim and throttles, but the Lancaster stubbornly refused to gain altitude. He made one last effort but the engines overheated dangerously and he reduced power to bring the nose down again. B–Baker was now at 400ft, and the skipper, deciding enough was enough, made for land – cookie and all. He was initially aiming for a belly landing, trusting not to disturb the cookie, but Mitchell persuaded him to try it wheels down, with the undercarriage being released on landing to cushion the impact. At 5.43p.m. in fading light, the Lancaster crossed the Norfolk coast. It was now at 200ft and the skipper wanted a flat glide into the first big space that could be found, because if – heaven forbid – the cookie went up, it would devastate a two-mile radius. Meanwhile, the crew calmly prepared to abandon the aircraft, anxiously turning off all their equipment – they didn't want any sparks setting off the 1,600 gallons of fuel still on board, let alone the cookie!

At 5.44p.m. and at 100ft, B–Baker slipped between the unsuspecting villages of Dersingham and Snettisham when Mitch, down in the nose, spotted a big open space to starboard. As the skipper called 'crash stations', Twitch removed the flight deck escape hatch and stayed to help the skipper; Dizzy turned his turret to port; Charlie clambered to the rear of the main spar;

Lancaster PD348, 9J-B, looking forlorn after its pilot had pulled off a brilliant forced landing with a live 4,000lb cookie still on board. (Bob Reid)

Len left his mid-upper turret and joined Charlie. Bob Reid sat facing forward with his back rammed against the forty-inch main spar. Mitch removed the front hatch then hurried back to sit next to Bob. The drill took a mere twenty seconds and with only seconds to spare, they braced themselves in the blast of cold air rushing back through the open hatches. It was all down to the skipper now.

At 5.45p.m., B-Baker crash-landed. In the dusk, farm workers on land south west of Bircham Newton looked up when they heard the drone of engines coming towards them. It was a Lancaster bomber, very low down and heading towards a field called Brush Heath a few hundred yards away. Bob Reid recalled the sequence of events over the next few minutes:

> With the wind on the port side, George made a slow flat descent, desperate not to run out of space, and pancaked the bomber. The rush of cold air turned into choking dust and the sound of rasping metal. Then an eerie silence and darkness pervaded the fuselage except for shafts of light through the open hatches.

George had brought the Lancaster down in the field, intact and with 300yds to spare, slewing through 90° before it came to a full stop. Time to get the hell out! The skipper's first thought was the overhead hatch, then he looked at Twitch and saw he was bleeding from the face. Waving Twitch to get moving, he helped him stand on the pilot's seat and exit through the hatch. Twitch, followed by the skipper, dropped onto the wing near the two hot, smoking engines then they both ran to the nearest road to look for a telephone. Mitch the bomb aimer was next:

> I was sitting in my crash position thinking that if, by chance, the cookie doesn't explode on impact and the fuel doesn't go up, I must move quick up the ladder, out of the hatch and down onto the wing. As I poked my head through the hatch I saw the skipper was already out and sliding down the wing into the field. Smoke was coming from the port inner so I clambered out and we ran as fast as our legs would carry us to the gate about two hundred yards away, throwing off our kit as we ran.

Bob Reid said:

> I thought Mitch was in a helluva hurry, then I suddenly remembered the cookie and shot after him. In my rush through the hatch my parachute harness snagged so I turned the buckle anti-clockwise, hit it hard and climbed through the gap down on to the wing – and came fourth in the race to the road!
>
> Down in the fuselage, the DR compass and navigational equipment had all come adrift and the H2S scanner was smashed to smithereens. Charlie the wireless op stumbled back through the debris and made his exit through the rear door, a jump of normally about six feet but now only one foot down. Len, the mid-upper gunner, affectionately known as the old man of the crew, followed hard on Charlie's heels despite being encumbered by his Mae West, harness and flying suit, all of which kept snagging on things en route. Dizzy, although probably first out, went out the rear door but had then gone round to the front of the aircraft to see if everyone was clear, so he was actually last to reach the comparative safety of the road.
>
> With us all panting for breath by the gate, the skipper said five of us would make for a farmhouse about a quarter of a mile down the road and telephone the nearest RAF station to tell them the situation and get medical aid for Twitch's facial injuries. He told Charlie Davis and me to stay at the gate and make sure no one approached the aircraft.

So Charlie and Bob kept a watchful eye on the bomber, which was about 200yds away. They reckoned they would be safe as long as it did not catch fire and explode the cookie, but the road they were standing in was sunk about three feet below the field level so, at the first sign of fire, they agreed they would lay down in the gutter and hope it all passed over. Night was falling as they watched the five airmen disappear round the bend, and what happened next can only have been the release of the enormous tension of the last hour – the pair of 'guards' began to play cricket with an imaginary bat and ball!

Mitch recalled:

It was almost dark when we reached Heath Farm house and knocked on the door. Mr J. M. Turner, the farmer, had heard the aircraft crashing and he and his wife made us very welcome. George rang RAF Bircham Newton to tell them what had happened and that there was a 4,000lb bomb still on board. We were offered tea or whisky to help us cope with the shock and not wishing to offend, all five of us had a large tot of whisky while we settled down, chatting to the couple and being topped up at intervals.

Meanwhile, the imaginary cricket match was interrupted by an RAF warrant officer who materialised out of the blue and must have thought this pair were definitely 'Harpic' types (i.e. 'clean round the bend'!) However, quickly explaining the situation to him he agreed to stand guard himself and gave instructions as to how Bob and Charlie could navigate their way, in the dark, to the farmhouse. Upon arrival they were led to comfortable chairs by the fireplace in the large kitchen and joined in with a glass of whisky each.

Soon there was another knock on the door. This time it was an RAF Medical Officer (MO) who, gratefully accepting a glass of medicinal whisky, duly inspected each of the crew in turn. According to Bob:

Twitch looked much better now, sitting at the large kitchen table, grinning from ear to ear clutching a glass of whisky in his hand. Dizzy sat next to him; Len and Mitch lounged on the sofa and Charlie and me tucked in near the fire. All very convivial. Then the phone rang. It was the RAF telling Mr Turner that, because of the bomb, he and his family would have to leave. He mentioned we, the crew, were all in his kitchen and was told we would soon be collected and taken to Bircham Newton.

Next to arrive was the local bobby, confirming the evacuation of the farmer to Great Bircham village, which would be the same for everyone within a two-mile radius of the bomber. It was expected that the bomb would be de-fused and removed next morning. Mrs Turner fetched their youngsters downstairs and got ready to leave while Mr Turner set another bottle of Scotch on the Welsh dresser and asked us to lock up when we left.

Now an RAF nursing sister turned up, looking in amazement at the broad smiles on our rosy faces. Then she had a right go at us for drinking alcohol when in a state of shock before turning to vent her wrath on the MO. We were rescued by the arrival of the transport to Bircham Newton. There the MO gave us all another check-over then, after a de-briefing about the crash landing, Twitch Ling and George Edge went into sick quarters while the rest of us went gratefully to bed.

Early next day, the 4,000-pounder having been defused, Mitch, Bob, Charlie, Dizzy and Len were driven to B-Baker to collect personal belongings. Mitch recalled:

In the light of day we could see what had happened. The track of our landing was fairly clear, with the nose ploughing a furrow as it dug in, smashing the perspex. This caused the aircraft to swing through ninety degrees as it came to a halt. I came to the conclusion that this sudden turn as it came to a halt saved us from being blown sky high because the fuses were at the front end of the bomb, which had come off sideways in the bomb bay. I went to collect my parachute from the nose compartment which was partially filled with soil and rye from the field crop. I kept a piece of that perspex and the bomb release trigger as souvenirs.

Bob Reid gathered up his leather case and green canvas bag with his maps, charts and navigational tools and retrieved his parachute harness from the escape hatch. As he did so, Dizzy remarked: 'I wonder if these parachutes work; let's try; Bob will get the blame!' They did work, but Bob did not get the blame.

On 9 February at 4.40p.m., with George and Twitch still in Bircham sick quarters, the other five flew back to Balderton from RAF Docking as passengers in Flight Lieutenant Croker's Lancaster. The consummate skill with which George Edge had crash-landed B-Baker that day is evident from the fact that (a) the crew walked (ran) away from it virtually unscathed, and (b) B-Baker was taken apart, removed from the field in April 1945, repaired and after hostilities had ceased, took to the skies again in the Middle East theatre. Skill had got them down, but surely Luck had stopped them being blown sky high.

Clearly, hauling 'cookies' around was always going to be a problem if anything went wrong with the aircraft and almost without exception, the loads being carried in the latter years of the war included this blockbuster weapon. By the end of the European war, about 90,000 'cookies' had been dropped by the RAF, distributed fairly evenly over the last three years.

No.44 Squadron lost Lancaster III, ND869 when Flight Lieutenant Wilfred Shephard and his crew went missing on 16 March 1945. Loaded with a 4,000lb cookie and 5,400lb of incendiaries, this aircraft set off from RAF Spilsby at 5.45p.m. to raid Wurzburg. At 6.00p.m. it was seen by Observer Corps personnel to come down in The Wash off Skegness where an almighty explosion followed, in which everyone and everything was sent to oblivion.

The final operational 'cookie' incident in the region occurred on 20 March 1945, and that dubious honour goes to Lancaster RA530 of No.57 Squadron. Synthetic oil plants at Bohlen were the target for Australian Flying Officer Charles Cobern and his crew. Heavily laden with one 4,000lb bomb and fourteen 500-pounders, Cobern hauled 'Y-Yankie' off the East Kirkby runway. Suddenly, at just 250ft altitude, the port inner engine seized and caught fire. Unable to feather the propeller and losing height rapidly, the pilot had no chance of recovery. RA530 crashed into a house in Stickney village killing Flying Officer Cobern, Sergeant Ken Ashun (FE), Flying Officer William Calderbank (Nav) and Sergeant Alan Ramsbottom (AG). The bomb aimer, Flight Sergeant William Searby, succumbed to his injuries nine days later, while wireless operator Sergeant R. Bates and another air gunner, Sergeant E. Lawrence, were both fortunate to escape with only slight injuries.

Since replacements were some years off, Avro Lancaster and Lincoln bombers continued to grace post-war skies, but eventually the RAF piston-engine bomber era came to a close. It will be rounded off here with the story of the loss of a Boeing B-29 aircraft, a type brought into the RAF inventory in 1950 to prove to its NATO allies that Britain was serious in its commitment to modernise its air force, but needed to bridge the gap until the new British Canberra bombers and V-Bombers entered service.

Only eighty-eight Boeing B-29 Super Fortresses, designated Washington B1 in RAF service, were acquired and No.15 Squadron at RAF Coningsby was one of eight Bomber Command squadrons equipped with these long-range aircraft. Training in January 1953 consisted principally of continuation training for pilots and co-pilots involving instrument flying, let down and approach procedures and ground-controlled approaches (GCA). For a unit that was a major part of Main Force Bomber Command, the squadron diary makes a

B-29A Washington, WF553, of No.15 Squadron, RAF Coningsby, before its accident on 5 January 1953. (Chris Howlett via Peter Finch)

somewhat worrying disclosure that during January no practice bombs were dropped by day and only three by night. In addition, six simulated bombing runs using on-board radar were made during the month.

Just before 6.00p.m. on the wintry evening of 5 January 1953, Flight Lieutenant Fred Rust hauled Washington WF553 off Coningsby's runway at the start of one of these radar-bombing exercises. Four hours later Mary Ashton, relaxing in front of the fire in her home at Claxby Dairy Farm, heard an aeroplane fly low over the house. It was followed by a distinct thud and the noise of the engines stopped abruptly.

> I ran out and saw a 'plane in a field on the Miningsby side of our house. Part of it was in flames. I heard people shouting and ran across the fields to help them and I saw five airmen coming towards me. I helped two of them into our house and the other three went back to try to rescue those trapped inside. My father joined them at the wreckage while I attended to the two airmen, who had minor injuries. It was not long before fire engines from Horncastle, Spilsby, Skegness and RAF Coningsby and ambulances arrived.

Blacksmith George Hill, his son and a neighbour ran for about half a mile to the scene and found airmen and civilians already trying to get people out and they, too, gave assistance to extricate Flight Lieutenant E. Read, who was alive but trapped by an engine. The centre section of the bomber was well ablaze and next morning, daylight revealed a large blackened hole where the wing roots and fuselage either side of the wings was reduced to ash. Five airmen died but six had escaped – although one was badly injured – when the aeroplane ploughed into the ground at a shallow angle.

By the time WF553 returned to Coningsby's circuit, the weather was foul. The pilot overshot from a controlled descent in the poor visibility, then carried out bad weather circuit procedure. Coningsby's air traffic controller described it as 'a bad evening, there were snow showers, hail and rain and visibility was very bad. It would be very difficult to pick up airfield lights.' He said the pilot was given permission to land and he made three GCA attempts to do so. The first time he was not correctly lined up with the runway and went round again. On the second attempt he was lined up but came in too high. He went round again on a left-hand circuit and it was on the base leg of this third attempt that the bomber flew into the ground. In addition to Flight Lieutenant Rust, those who died were: Flight Sergeants Eric Matthews (2nd Pilot); Robert Howes (Nav); Gordon Tomlin (FE); Leonard Lloyd (Signaller).

With the cessation of hostilities, the sky around The Wash region seemed eerily quiet for a while – but it was by no means the end of aerial incidents or tragedies, and for those living in the region, the sky was never still.

Chapter 3

SECOND WORLD WAR
USAAF Accidents

ON A WING AND A PRAYER

The year was 1943. Second Lieutenant Royal D. Frey, just nineteen years old, was a fighter pilot and an officer in the US Army Air Force who, in his own words, '… had the world by the tail!' Since arriving in England in August 1943, Royal and his buddies in the 55th Fighter Squadron of the 20th Fighter Group (55 FS, 20 FG) took any opportunity to buck the rules during training flights across the Fens from their King's Cliffe base. Reminiscing about those days, Royal said:

> Once I went onto ops and got my ass shot off a couple of times, I soon realised it was a deadly game and we were not playing! I remember well, flying over those flatlands criss-crossed with canals [*sic*] to the south of The Wash. One day, smoking along down on the deck, with 400 indicated on the clock, I spotted a small auto going down one of those long

P-38 J Lightning, 43-2843 KI-N *Jeanne*, of 55th Fighter Squadron, 20th Fighter Group USAAF based at Kings Cliffe in 1944. (Merle Olmsted via Mike Bowyer)

straight roads. Since we had been told we would soon be doing some ground strafing on our missions I decided to get in a little practice on this truck. Well, I guess the poor guy must have looked up and seen me coming right at him and he swerved off in panic, promptly driving right into the canal alongside the road! When I pulled up over him at about twenty feet, that little ol' truck was still sinking with the driver just scrambling clear. I kept right on going down there on the deck because if I had circled to see if he got out OK he would sure as heck have seen the 'KI-W' markings on the booms of my P-38. Boy – would I have been in hot water then!

Always in the thick of the US daylight bombing campaign, there were few days when the 20th's P-38s were not flying escort missions to targets in France or Germany and Lieutenant Royal Frey had much cause to remember a mission to Brunswick on 10 February 1944. It was the day he was shot down! The 55 FS war diary records:

Today's mission is one we will long remember. We were to escort bombers to Brunswick. Made landfall at 10.50 near Alkmaar (Holland) at 23,000 feet. An Fw190 was seen to make an attack on Lt Lundin in the vicinity of Hazelunne, NW Germany. He spun down but some of the squadron think they saw his 'chute open. Made rendezvous with the bombers at 11.17 near Quakenbruck, altitude 24,000 feet. Over the target at 11.30 and withdrew fifteen minutes later. The squadron fell behind the bombers at the target area because of bounces by two Me109s, an Me110 and between fifteen and twenty Me410s just north-west of the target. Here, Capt Maurice McLary and Lieutenant William B. Taylor joined combat and got the better of the engagement. Capt McLary claimed a '110 and a '410 destroyed with a '190 and a '110 damaged. His wingman Lieutenant [W. B.] Taylor claimed a '109 destroyed.

It is thought that Lieutenant Frey also went down to make a bounce during this encounter. He was not heard from again and it is believed he was shot down by an enemy aircraft. The squadron crossed the Dutch coast between Ijmuiden and Alkmaar at heights between 8,000 and 13,000 feet and headed for home.

Weather over Eastern England was bad today, with many snow flurries. The flight to which Lieutenant J. [Jack] Taylor was attached ran into one of these snow showers and he lost contact. Lieutenant Taylor was later found to have crashed near RAF Sutton Bridge and was killed.

Royal Frey was luckier than his two buddies. He was indeed shot down, but not by an enemy aeroplane, nor did he go down to make a 'bounce'. Writing of his experience that day, he recalled:

Buddies to the end. Lieutenant Jack Taylor (left) and Lieutenant John W. Lundin of 55FS, 20FW pictured at RAF Wittering in October 1943. Both pilots died on 10 February 1944. (Royal D. Frey)

John Lundin was the first to go, just east of Munster. I saw an Fw190 sneak up on him and yelled at him to 'break!' but it was no use. My transmitter was acting up – the first time ever – and nobody heard me. Then I lost power in one of my engines (we often had trouble with those Allison's at high altitude) and started to go down. Limping along at low level over enemy territory with one sick engine was no joke. Every ★★★ was taking a shot at me! Finally my luck ran out when I was picked off by light flak near Ludinghausen. I managed to bale out though and spent the rest of the war as a Prisoner of War.

Another 55 FS veteran, Chris Pannell from Knoxville Tennessee, filled in some detail about the loss of Lieutenant Jack Taylor:

Jack Taylor was a very good friend of mine, the pair of us having gone all through flying school together, then both being assigned to 20 FG before coming to England in August 1943. No-one is too sure exactly what happened to Jack, except he got separated in thick cloud and snow shortly after crossing the English coast. He must have become dis-oriented in the cloud because he was seen spinning out of low overcast near Sutton Bridge.

Lieutenant Jack Taylor's P-38J Lightning, 42-67729, crashed close to Strathmore House at Friday Bridge, near Wisbech about thirty miles from King's Cliffe. Chris continues:

It was another very cold, bleak day when I attended Jack's funeral at the American cemetery in Cambridge. The real sad thing was that his wife had given birth to a baby just a week before his death. We were having pretty rough going at that time and next day, 11 February, the Group took another beating losing eight more pilots to flak, fighters and engine trouble.

It was not until mid-1942 that the US Army Air Corps despatched the first aircrews that would in rapid time grow into the 'Mighty Eighth'. It is not proposed to re-write what has already been written, but rather to complement it with some of the many stories of bravery and tragedy in the East Midlands skies still to be told. Most relate to a side of this momentous daylight campaign rarely dwelt upon at length or, at best, perhaps dimmed by the glare of 'hot battle.' What follows, though, are also battles in their own right: stories from training missions; formation assembly prior to raids; struggles to make the final few miles back to base and battling with perverse British weather. Like the story above, these are the unsung battles by unsung heroes, fought out often before or even after tangling with the enemy.

Among the first of the Heavy Bombardment Groups to reach England was the 306th Bombardment Group (Heavy) (306 BG) in September 1942. Arriving with a complement of thirty-five B-17Fs at its base, Thurleigh in Cambridgeshire, it was not long before the Group considered itself ready to begin operations. Training missions were a daily occurrence in order for aircrews to become acclimatised to aircraft, the geography of the local area, British weather, and flying at operational altitudes. The latter included learning to form-up and formate, processes always fraught with danger. It was during one such practice formation flight over south Lincolnshire on 2 October 1942 that 306 BG took its first casualties in Europe.

Heading for The Wash at dusk, the Group climbed steadily to an altitude of 24,000ft. All went well until the oxygen supply tube to one of the waist gunners in B-17F, 41-24492, began to ice up. When the gunner passed out due to lack of oxygen, pilot First Lieutenant William Ely, took impulsive action to reach denser air in an effort to save the man's life. Pushing the control column hard forward he sent the B-17 into a steep dive. Down and down they went, ever steeper and faster. After losing 9,000ft in quick time, Ely hauled back on the yoke. That's when things started to go wrong. The violence of the pull out first caused the elevator control cables to snap. Then, excessive strain caused the airframe to break up. Part of the starboard wing folded back, taking an engine with it and starting a fire in the fuselage. Now, the ferocious airflow of the dive tore off the bomb bay doors, which struck the underside of the rear fuselage with such force they sliced off the entire rear section – including the gunner's compartment with Staff Sergeant William Kellum trapped inside!

With the B-17 plunging to earth in an uncontrollable spin and on fire, there was virtually no chance of the crew overcoming centrifugal force to grab a parachute and bale out. Ball-turret gunner Sergeant Raymond McAskill stood in the waist of the aeroplane, hanging on desperately as it began to break up in the dive. Fate certainly smiled on him that day. With his 'chute already in position, he was sucked out through a hole in the bottom of the fuselage, as he put it 'just like a darned cork out of a bottle.' Falling safely to earth he landed in a farmyard narrowly missing a tractor, with nothing more than a slight cut on his scalp and a grazed ankle to mark his passage. Such was the height of this formation – and it being a relatively new phenomenon over the district – that the accident was watched by a number of people in Spalding, some three miles distant. Dennis Fell recalled seeing the drama unfold while watching the group of aeroplanes up high, making long white contrails. Suddenly a large puff of white smoke appeared, a bit apart from the rest:

> As a small boy I remember standing with my brothers in our back yard in Pennygate watching this formation. It was very high up and an aeroplane started to fall on fire. It came down, twisting and turning and one parachute opened [Sergeant McAskill]. We shouted excitedly to each other, as boys will, saying: 'Gosh! Fancy trying to get out of that!' Then just before the 'plane vanished from our view, another parachute [Staff Sergeant Kellum] opened.

Unable to smash an exit through the turret windows, Kellum frantically tried to kick a hole in the metal fuselage. Having succeeded in this desperate attempt, he wriggled out feet-first only to become stuck by his shoulders. Then, by some miracle, he broke free, opening his parachute with just a few hundred feet to spare. He landed, without a scratch, in the middle of an Army searchlight battery. Together with British soldiers and farmhands, Kellum ran across fields to the wreckage, the main components of which had crashed about a hundred yards away. Beaten back by flames, they searched in vain for survivors. In addition to First Lieutenant William W. Ely, the other airmen who died that day were: First Lieutenant E.F. Patteson; Second Lieutenant W.F. Kuhlman; Second Lieutenant R.P. Cameron; Technical Sergeant D.E. Fuller and Private First Class C.M. Goller.

From later interviews it emerged that Kellum, after a restless, nightmare-filled night, revisited the scene of the crash with his CO. In the light of day it was a macabre sight and one he would never forget. Kellum was no quitter though – far from it. He joined up with another crew, fighting his fear of confined spaces and the anguish he felt on hearing wind noises that reminded him of his ordeal. He flew several more combat missions, each one with some event bringing back those bad memories, until his CO, aware of his worsening condition, sent him to a medical board. This brave airman had never once asked to be relieved from flying duties but finally admitted to the doctors that he wished he never had to get into an aeroplane again. The medical board granted Staff Sergeant Kellum his wish.

This US attitude in 1942 inevitably invites comparison with the RAF 'lack of moral fibre' (LMF) – or, more correctly, 'forfeiting the confidence of his Commanding Officer in the face of danger in the air' – policy at that period. In August 1942 the subject of RAF aircrew morale was investigated, under the title of 'Psychological Disorders In Flying Personnel', by an Air Ministry team led by Air Commodore C.P. Symonds. The subject itself is naturally a highly emotive issue – sometimes misunderstood, misquoted or riddled by myths – and will not be further commented upon here, other than to draw attention to part of a post-war observation made by Wing Commander J. Lawson who, although acknowledging that the issue existed, remarked: 'it is, however, clear that less than 0.3 per cent of the total aircrew have been classified [as LMF]. This is indeed a grand record.'

Tragedy soon fades or by necessity is pushed into the background. On 9 October, 306 BG had more pressing matters on its plate. That was the day the Group sent twenty-three B-17s to bomb Lille for its first operational mission. With this one under its belt, the 306th continued the grind of daily training exercises.

It is customary, though not exclusively so, to associate US B-17s with high altitude flying. However, the war diary of 306 BG for 22 October records experiments with the B-17 'as a hedge-hopper' [*sic*] – with some alarming results!

> Four crews from 423rd Bombardment Squadron (423 BS) were ordered to fly [from Thurleigh] to The Wash and back at under 500 feet. Upon completion much evidence was brought back in the way of tree branches and leaves to show the altitude had not been exceeded.
>
> On 27 October another, two-ship, low altitude mission was ordered. This time Lieutenant Check's aircraft hit a tree and the 'plane was demolished. Four of the crew were slightly injured.

While taking a sizable chunk out of a Fenland tree (and there are not that many about!), Lieutenant Raymond Check, also from 423 BS, made rather a mess of B-17F, 41-24508. The nose glass was smashed in, control surfaces damaged and a variety of holes torn in wings and fuselage. By good fortune, good flying, or both, he was able to remain airborne sufficiently long enough to make an emergency landing at RAF Graveley.

It was not long before these risky flights were abandoned, possibly influenced by the fact they were turning into an excuse for high jinks at low level and 'rides for the boys'. Lieutenant Check, for example, was carrying a full crew plus two privates as 'passengers' on his little jaunt. Raymond Check's luck ran out flying what would have been the twenty-fifth and final mission of his tour on 26 June 1943. He was killed when his aeroplane was hit by flak during a raid on Tricqueville.

Returning to base on 20 May 1943 after practice bombing on The Wash range, B-17F, 42-29786, flown by First Lieutenant Maxwell V. Judas and his crew, was one of a five-ship section flying at low altitude. Judas, it seems, had taken the opportunity to indulge in a little hedge-hopping, and had come to grief in Rippingale Fen. Returning, rather sheepishly, to Thurleigh, the crew received a blast for writing off a perfectly good aeroplane. It came as no surprise, therefore, to find their names on the roster for the next day's mission to Wilhelmshaven – a mission from which they failed to return.

By April 1943, pre-assignment training in the USA was substantially improved compared to that acquired by ETO-bound crews a year earlier. Arriving at Grafton Underwood in mid-April, 96 BG was pitched into battle almost immediately, its first war mission being scheduled for 13 May against St Omer Airfield in France. It was also to suffer its first aircraft MIA in unusual circumstances. Easing B-17F, 42-29752 off the Grafton runway at the start of that first raid, Captain Darryl W. Rogers concentrated on the climb to formation altitude while his crew went through the drill of checking equipment. Back in the fuselage, the two flexible .50 inch-calibre waist guns were in their stowed positions either side of the fuselage. Their barrels were inboard, parallel with the fuselage and pointing rearwards when the two gunners began checking them over.

Suddenly, the starboard machine-gun began firing! Still pointing inboard, a stream of fifty-calibre shells swept through the rear fuselage. Pandemonium broke out before the lethal spray of about fifty rounds stopped. Much of the starboard tailplane was shot to pieces, severing some control cables in the process while the waist gunner himself was injured and the tail gunner seriously wounded. Abandoning the climb, Captain Rogers found his aeroplane difficult to control in anything other than a turn. He struggled back towards Grafton Underwood and ordered his six NCO crewmen to bale out, which they did successfully. With a full bomb load aboard an unstable aeroplane there was little chance of getting the B-17 down intact so, once more, Rogers fought with the controls to head back towards The Wash. Sinking ever lower, The Wash was reached with just enough altitude to jettison the bomb load. Keeping the aircraft steady, Rogers now ordered the bombardier and navigator to bale out near King's Lynn and these, too, did so safely.

Aiming the stricken bomber out to sea, Captain Rogers and co-pilot Second Lieutenant Norville Gorse lashed the control column to keep it on course, then prepared to bale out themselves. The B-17 became uncontrollable again and ordering Gorse to jump, the pilot returned to the cockpit to re-secure cords holding the steering column in position. When Rogers finally baled out, he was too low for his parachute to deploy fully. His lifeless body was recovered from the sea some hours later.

During the latter half of 1943, an increasing number of B-17s seemed to be falling victim to fires originating in the top turret. Constant rotating movement frayed electrical and oxygen lines in the central spigot of the turret, often resulting in short circuits and fire.

Since the accident in May 1943, 96 BG had relocated to Snetterton Heath in Norfolk, where it was to remain for the rest of the war. It was from their new base that the group set out on 19 August to bomb Woensdrecht Airfield and it would lose a B-17 to one of these turret fires at the very start of this mission. Fortress 42-30172, *Black Heart Jr*, was being flown that day by Second Lieutenant J.A. Attaway from 339 BS and carried Lieutenant Colonel James Travis (403 BW Exec) on board as air commander for the mission. While forming up over north Norfolk, a fire broke out in the top turret causing an oxygen bottle to explode. Fearing more explosions, Lieutenant Attaway dropped away from the formation, ordering the crew to bale out while he set course for the sea. Believing all the crew had jumped Attaway set the autopilot and baled out through the forward hatch. Meanwhile a drama was unfolding back in the fuselage: co-pilot Second Lieutenant Matthew Vinson had gone back to find his parachute and discovered it was missing! The bombardier, Second Lieutenant John Miller, who had also not yet left the aircraft, offered to jump with the co-pilot holding on to him. Vinson dismissed this as far too dangerous for both of them and told Miller to jump. Unable to find a parachute and suffering from minor burns, Vinson decided to stick with the bomber and try to make a forced landing. Draughts from all the open hatches had by now cleared the cockpit of smoke and the fire, although well alight, was being blown rearwards.

Crouching over charred seats, Lieutenant Vinson disengaged the autopilot, but now down to 2,000ft altitude, he could hardly see through the smoke-blackened windscreen. Vinson had enough control over the big bomber to bring it quite gently down on to a sand bank in The Wash off the Babingley river near Snettisham where, still on fire, it slewed to a halt amidst a shower of sand. Matthew Vinson made a very rapid exit through the cockpit window, putting as much space between him and the burning aircraft with its full bomb load. Just fifteen minutes later that bomb load exploded. For the bravery he displayed that day, Second Lieutenant Matthew Vinson was awarded a Distinguished Service Cross.

Having acted as a holding unit for combat replacement crews for nine months, first at Bovingdon then Alconbury, 92 BG returned to operations in May 1943. Subsequently

Alconbury was chosen as the base for a new USAAF *H2S*-equipped Pathfinder group and 92 BG relocated to Podington. Port installations at Nantes came in for some attention by the USAAF in September and the 92nd was involved in a couple of these missions. One of these, on 23 September, was plagued by bad weather from start to finish.

Podington B-17s usually headed towards south Lincolnshire to form up and assembly in poor conditions was a process always fraught with danger. For reasons that remain obscure, a 92 BG B-17F, 42-3183 exploded while climbing through the murk, the aircraft crashing at Deeping St Nicholas, close to the River Welland. As the aeroplane, from 327 BS, broke up, seven crew including pilot Second Lieutenant Henry Ogden managed to bale out, but three men died in the crash. One complete wing fluttered to earth in Cloot Drove on the distant side of the river, while the remainder of the wreckage was scattered on farmland owned by the Atkinson family at Four Mile Bar – an area that was to collect rather a lot of aeroplane 'tin' over the war years. Farm labourer Charlie Chapman, who lived in the village, remembers seeing a wing leaning precariously against outbuildings at Bleak House Farm. Six unexploded 500lb bombs, released during that fatal dive, fell onto Atkinson's and Pick's land where, marked by red flags, they remained for a week before being blown up by a bomb disposal unit.

The sheer scale and complexity of US daylight bomber operations is often difficult to comprehend, and the scale of USAAF human and material loss is equally mind-numbing. It is therefore useful to consider the thinking behind these huge geometric US bomber formations, which may be summarised in two notions:

1. To place the largest concentration of bombs onto a target in the shortest time possible, thereby maximising damage while minimising exposure of the bombing force to defensive AA fire.
2. To bring the maximum amount of defensive fire to bear on enemy aeroplanes attacking the bomber formation.

In January 1944 General Jimmy Doolittle made his views on the subject of close-formation flying very plain in a letter to his Air Division Commanders. He said:

Two points must be impressed firmly upon every pilot in our formations. First, the integrity of each group must be maintained. Formations must be kept closed-up and there must be not one avoidable straggler. Second, the group leaders must reduce the length of the Combat Wing columns.

That was the theory, at any rate. But formation flying in these big four-engine monsters was not easy. Holding a tight formation on element leaders, hour after hour, required mental concentration, piloting skill, physical stamina and teamwork between pilot and co-pilot. Pilots leading three-ship elements in a 'low group/squadron' position had a particularly difficult task. They had to look upwards, often into the sun, for the duration of a mission. As a result this unit often took up a looser formation. Furthermore the number three ship, on the left of the 'low' element of these twelve-ship formations always seemed to have a hard time holding position anyway. Because of its vulnerability to being singled out by enemy fighters, that particular position became known as 'Coffin Corner.' Early in 1944, as the overall numbers of bombers available increased, a twelve-ship formation unit was adopted within Groups. It was considered more effective than earlier eighteen-ship formations, proving to be more compact defensively, easily manoeuvrable and delivering a compact bombing pattern. This was also the time when Groups acquired an additional, fourth Squadron.

One example of a strategically decisive mission, when the sky above the East Midlands was crammed with bombers and the Lincolnshire town of Spalding in particular became a pivotal route checkpoint, was the day the Eighth Air Force mounted an unescorted, deep penetration attack on a vital German industrial target. On 14 October 1943 – what would become known as Black Thursday – the 8th Air Force despatched 164 B-17s from its 1st Bombardment Division (BD), together with 160 B-17s from the 3rd Bombardment Division – a total of 324 bombers – against the ball bearing plants at Schweinfurt for the second time.

These were the days before Allied fighters could escort bombers all the way there and back to German targets and US daylight bomber losses had become alarmingly high. In this case, the 1st BD force was quickly depleted by fifteen and the 3rd BD by eighteen bombers turning back due to assorted technical reasons, leaving a total of 291 B-17s (escorted up to the German border by 103 P-47 Thunderbolt fighters) to carry out the Schweinfurt attack. From this number, no less than sixty bombers were lost due to enemy action, five more crashed in England and twelve more were written off in crash landings at the various bases – a total of seventy-seven aeroplanes (26 per cent). An estimated 121 of the remaining aircraft required battle-damage repairs. In human terms this meant that 600 airmen were killed or made Prisoners of War, and it was reported that five dead and forty-three wounded airmen were removed from those aircraft that struggled back to England. One bomber actually crashed in the region under discussion while trying to return to base, and that will be mentioned a little later, but events unfolding over the East Midlands right at the beginning of the mission had a serious knock-on effect on the vulnerability of the aerial armada when it reached enemy territory.

The majority of the 1st Bombardment Division of the 8th Air Force was located in the East Midlands, and as such its formations were a regular sight over the Fens and around The Wash. It is the intention here to show how that Division assembled prior to departing these shores for the notorious second mission to Schweinfurt, and also to demonstrate the part played by one of its Groups, the 305th, in particular. This in turn will serve to illustrate the complexity involved in getting these missions under way in the air – day in, day out – and to highlight some of the hazards that could potentially arise.

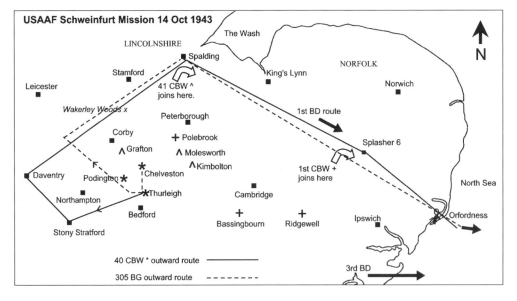

Map of the assembly route for the 1st Bombardment Division for the mission to Schweinfurt on 14 October 1943.

The Schweinfurt mission of 14 October 1943 was originally assigned to three Bombardment Divisions (BD): 1st BD (B-17); 2nd BD (B-24); and 3rd BD (B-17). Within this force, the 1st BD comprised three Wings: 1st Combat Bombardment Wing (1 CBW), 40 CBW and 41 CBW.

1 CBW comprised:	91st Bombardment Group (91 BG)	Bassingbourn
	351 BG	Polebrook
	381 BG	Ridgewell
40 CBW comprised:	92 BG	Podington
	305 BG	Chelveston
	306 BG	Thurleigh
41 CBW comprised:	303 BG	Molesworth
	379 BG	Kimbolton
	384 BG	Grafton Underwood

Commanded by Major Charles Normand, who was flying with First Lieutenant Kane in the lead aircraft, eighteen B-17s of 305 BG took off from Chelveston at 10.15a.m. and circled base in cloud, rain and bad visibility prior to joining up with 92 BG (Podington) and 306 BG (Thurleigh) which together would constitute the 40 CBW formation. Even at this early stage, though, things started to go wrong. In poor visibility, the 305 BG lead-ship navigator, although glimpsing several aircraft flying around the Thurleigh area, could not see any of the usual identity flares to show him who was who or who to tag on to. However, while the 305th was still circling indecisively, some distance away the other two Groups had formed up and departed the Group assembly beacon near Thurleigh at 11.32a.m., on time, at the correct altitude of 13,000ft and steering 247° on the first leg to Stony Stratford. It was during this first leg that the three component Groups of 40 CBW should take up their Wing formation and 'tighten up' as they progressed between each checkpoint en route.

On leg three the armada would grow in size as 40 CBW joined up with 41 CBW. Then, on leg four, the 1st CBW would later join on behind these two to complete the 149-ship, nine-Group, three-Wing 1st Bombardment Division formation. This Division would fly an independent timetable and route to the target, bomb and leave the target area, then – if all the timings and routings worked out correctly – it would be followed over the target about five minutes later by the 3rd Division. In order to achieve the tight formation structure necessary for mutual self-protection and an effective bombing pattern, each aeroplane, Squadron, Group and Wing occupied a predetermined place in 'stepped and staggered boxes' within the Division formation. To achieve that compactness, all this had to be completed with great discipline and efficient flying, in radio silence and to a tight timetable that would bring the 1st BD to 'coast out' at Orfordness at 12.30p.m., i.e. in the space of about two hours from take-off. A similar process was also happening elsewhere over East Anglia to the B-17s of the 3rd BD and the B-24s of the 2nd BD.

For some, though, the timetable began to go awry. At 11.39a.m. the bombers of 92 and 306 BGs (40 CBW) were in formation above cloud and crossing the Stoney Stratford checkpoint at the end of the first leg – but still their missing 305 BG was nowhere to be seen. Now steering 325°, 40 CBW flew the short second leg to Daventry, which was passed at 11.46a.m. – still with no sign of the 305th.

Having failed to rendezvous, Major Normand decided to leave the Thurleigh area at 11.41a.m., so his seventeen-ship 305 BG was now nine minutes behind schedule. It was already an aircraft down due to one crew being unable to locate any formation at all to tag onto! Knowing he had to make up lost time, Normand steered the Group on 280° at 12,000ft directly for Daventry, where he hoped to join up with the other two Groups. However, while still short of Daventry, Major Normand ordered a right turn onto 322° and reduced speed to slightly below that set down in the published orders. He appears to have decided to try to 'cut the corner' and intercept the 40 CBW formation as it flew the seventeen-minute third leg from north-east from Daventry to Spalding. Despite breaking radio silence in an attempt to find each other, the two formations were unsuccessful and in poor visibility, remained about fourteen miles apart, quite oblivious to each other. At 11.48a.m. the 305th crossed the track of the third leg but, unbeknown to them, it was now pulling ahead of Col Budd Peaslee's main formation. Thinking he would 'catch up' with 40 CBW at the major turning point over Spalding, Major Normand turned the 305th onto a heading of 052° that would take them to Spalding – but by using his 'short-cuts', he had now actually overtaken 40 CBW!

At 11.59a.m. Major Normand reached Spalding at 15,000ft, seven minutes in front of schedule. Realising he was early, Major Normand ordered his pilot to lead the Group in a 360° turn over the town to lose some time, but this manoeuvre only took about two minutes. He was still unable to contact Colonel Peaslee by radio and when the turn was complete, he spotted a large formation nearby, but because he could clearly see it comprised three complete Groups, he deduced it could not be his elusive, two-Group 40 CBW. Peaslee's 40 CBW was assigned to lead the whole 1st Division on this mission, and so that is why the whole of 41 CBW was 'hanging around' Spalding. That Wing had formed up successfully over the Molesworth assembly area, then made its way to its next rendezvous point over Spalding to await the arrival of Colonel Peaslee's formation in order to slot in behind it. This situation could have suggested to Major Normand that (a) his own Wing was behind him and not in front, and (b) that if he orbited until at least the Spalding checkpoint scheduled departure time of 12.06, he would almost certainly be able to join his Wing formation. But this was not to be. Having lost just a couple of minutes by the 360° turn, Major Normand appears to have believed 40 CBW was still up ahead and so the 305th departed Spalding, heading 130° across Norfolk on leg four, for the 'coast-out' point at Orfordness in Suffolk where, now down to fifteen aircraft because of two more 'turn-backs', it would be the last real chance to find his Wing. In the event, he never did, and when his Group caught up with 1 CBW it simply tagged on in the 'low Group' position.

The rest of the mission over enemy territory is a matter of history and will not be discussed in detail here, but the way in which this mission assembled over England is representative of what was going on above this region day in, day out. The statistics, mentioned earlier, speak for themselves, but the ferocity of the European daylight air battles and the magnitude of this day's mission losses was exemplified when 305 BG came home to Chelveston with just two bombers out of the fifteen that set out for Schweinfurt. It had lost a staggering eighty-seven per cent!

Among the second formation (41 CBW) seen orbiting Spalding that day, was B-17F, 42-3037, *Windy City Avenger*, coded SU-Z from 384 BG based at Grafton Underwood. Commanded by Lieutenant William M. Price, *Windy City Avenger* bombed Schweinfurt, but not without taking battle damage from repeated enemy fighter attacks. Price knew the elevator control cables were shot up but it was not until the crew made it back to England after the seven-and-a-half-hour mission and he began to slow down for approach to Grafton Underwood, that the full extent of the damage became apparent. At approach speed and needing to make full use of the elevators, the aircraft became uncontrollable and it was soon

B-17F 42-3037, *Windy City Avenger,* from the 384th BG crashed near Corby on return from the Schweinfurt raid on 14 October 1943. (Fred Preller/384thbombgroup.com)

clear that there was no way Lieutenant Price would get *Windy City Avenger* down in one piece. Gently coaxing the bomber back up to 2,000ft he made a wide circuit to the north, well away from the airfield and ordered everyone to bale out. This went without a hitch except for co-pilot, Lieutenant Lee B. Coleman, who broke his leg on landing. The bomber plunged into Wakerley Woods, between Stamford and Corby.

Now resident at Grafton Underwood, 384 BG mounted a twenty-two-ship mission on 31 December to bomb a blockade-running ship, the *Osorno*, in the River Gironde near Bordeaux. It was a long eight-hour haul for these B-17s that made landfall back in England in darkness and thick cloud. Other Groups were busy in that part of France, with Merignac Airfield coming in for some close attention at the same time. No less than eighteen bombers were lost in crashes that day, among them B-17F, 42-31073, from 547BS 384BG, flown by First Lieutenant George Stier. Off course, in overcast and almost out of gas, Stier ordered eight of his crew to bale out while he and co-pilot Second Lieutenant Harold R. Bertram stayed with the aircraft to bring it down for a crash landing at Whittlesey, a few miles from – but well clear of – the city of Peterborough. Sadly, Bertram died as a result of the crash landing.

There is quite a story behind this seemingly innocuous mission that, in fact, made it far from ordinary. Some months earlier, Bletchley Park boffins broke the enemy's *Sunfish* and *Shark* codes – used by German supply surface ships and submarines working to the Far East and Japan – sufficiently to be able to disrupt their movements. Between November 1943 and

January 1944 no German surface supply ship succeeded in getting away from the French Atlantic ports without being sunk in the Bay of Biscay area. During this period, five German freighters tried to run the inward gauntlet from the Far East and in a complex piece of international air and sea co-operation named Operation *Stonewall*, various Allied naval vessels intercepted all en route – except the *Osorno*.

The SS *Osorno*, 6951 tons, escaped from Bordeaux in April 1943 and sailed to Kobe, Japan, where it took on a cargo of raw rubber. With Captain Paul Hellmann in command, *Osorno* made the hazardous voyage back to Europe, evading Allied attempts to intercept her en route. By Christmas 1943 she succeeded in reaching French waters but *Osorno*'s luck ran out when she struck a submerged shipwreck in the mouth of the Gironde Estuary while trying to reach Bordeaux. The ship was beached among the sandbanks in the estuary where the work of offloading the valuable cargo into shallow-draught lighters began with much haste. Six German destroyers and six torpedo boats stood guard during this operation. It made a juicy target for Allied bombers.

Both the USAAF and the RAF mounted bomber operations to try to destroy this ship and its cargo of rubber. RAF Coastal Command had a go on 24 December then, on the night of 30/31 December, No.149 Squadron mounted an unusual mine-laying (Gardening) raid in front of the ship's path. Delayed action mines were to be dropped from high level on this occasion. When daylight came on 31 December, it was the turn of the Americans to try and sink the freighter, and this is how First Lieutenant George Stier and his crew became one of the pawns in this dangerous game. Despite the air attacks, under cover of an intense flak barrage, the Germans managed to unload the freighter's valuable cargo.

The Americans sent the 41st Combat Wing against the ship but, on what was its longest mission thus far, it had little to show for the effort. The 384 BG from Grafton Underwood despatched nineteen aircraft plus three flying spares, but encountered bad weather and thick cloud up to its bombing altitude all around the target area, so they took their bombs home again. The weather over England was particularly bad for the returning aircraft and only four of the 384th made it back to Grafton Underwood directly; two – including Lieutenant George Stier's aircraft – crashed in England and the remaining thirteen were scattered across various airfields. The 303 BG at Molesworth sent twenty aircraft plus two spares and had a similarly unproductive result. That same thick clag was encountered at its bombing altitude of 16,000ft and having flown around three alternative targets without seeing a glimmer of anything, they, too, went home with their bombs. Second Lieutenant Vern L. Moncur, pilot of a 359 BS B-17F, 42-3131 *Flak Wolf*, wrote:

> We were in the air about eight hours. Upon reaching England, we ran into the kind of weather pilots dread. We found very adverse weather all the way in from the English coast. All of our flight back over England, we flew at about 500 feet and were unable to see the other ships in the formation. With several hundred bombers [*sic*] doing the same thing, it became a ticklish business. We gradually dropped out of formation and struck out on our own, figuring it was much safer than flying formation on instruments. We got a radio bearing from base [but] on reaching the field it was next to impossible to see a runway. We buzzed the field at about 100 feet and finally felt our way through the rain and fog until we found where the runway was. Nineteen planes were landed in this fog and rain in little over twelve minutes. Slight battle damage to the plane from flak but no injury to the crew.

In those days, it was not often that an individual aeroplane became a 'star'. *Memphis Belle* springs most readily to mind in this context, but there was another, if perhaps less well known, B-17 that flew across the silver screen.

A tired-looking Captain Clark Gable (on right) chatting to Captain William R. Calhoun after landing back from an operational mission to Antwerp with the 351st BG on 4 May 1943. (Gary Moncur)

Polebrook was originally home to 97 BG, but another heavy bomber group, the 351st, took up residence from April 1943. One of the latter's claim to fame was that, during September and October 1943, Hollywood film star Clark Gable flew five combat missions as an air gunner with the 351st while he was involved in making a training movie about air gunners. Gable had flown another combat mission, his first, on 4 May, with 303 BG at Molesworth. The resulting film, entitled *Combat America* (still available, sixty-five years later, on DVD) featured prominently one of the Group's original B-17Fs, 42-29821 *Argonaut*, an aeroplane that was attached to 508 BS of the 351st.

The interior of the B-17 struck chill in the dim light. Hot breath from the exertion of boarding came out as vapour in the cold air. Settling into position, First Lieutenant Harvey Anderson (on attachment from 511 BS) and his crew would each be handling the pre-start tension in his own private way. It was well before dawn on 7 January 1944 and their mission was to bomb the I.G. Farbenindustrie chemical works in Ludwigshaven. Lieutenant Anderson began the start-up routine, but one engine refused to fire. Anxious not to miss the operation and with time running out on him, Harvey had no option to declare the aircraft unserviceable and called control to ready a spare aircraft. This was 29821, YB-F, named *Argonaut*, assigned to the 508th. Making a rapid transfer to their new mount, all was fine this time. Quickly catching up with the Group, Anderson's mission went well despite the earlier bad start. That is, until he re-crossed The Wash coast, when events took a sudden turn for the worse.

Descending through cloud, on course for base, *Argonaut* flew into the turbulent slipstream of an unseen bomber. It must have been a close call for, in an instant, Anderson's aircraft was thrown into a spin from which it never recovered. So violent was the spin that *Argonaut* disintegrated as it fell and only four of the crew managed to bale out: co-pilot Second Lieutenant Benjamin Finnell; top-turret gunner Technical Sergeant William Reilly; radio operator Technical Sergeant Domenick Garcia; and right-waist gunner Staff Sergeant Buddie Wolfe. First Lieutenant Anderson and five of his comrades perished when the B-17 hit the ground between Moulton and Whaplode Drove, seven miles south of Spalding: Lieutenant Douglas E. Webb; Lieutenant William H. Udick; Staff Sergeant Richard J. Allen; Staff Sergeant Frank H. McNamara; and Staff Sergeant Leonard Edwards.

Confirmation of the location came from Mrs Dorothy Aubin, at that time a volunteer ambulance driver with the Civil Defence in nearby Holbeach. Quoting from her wartime ambulance log-book, she said:

> I received a call at home about 10am on 7 January 1944: 'Plane crash, Whaplode Drove and step on it!' My partner and I raced to the scene and picked up four men who had baled out. It had apparently blown up in mid-air. We took the survivors to Holbeach hospital and I think they were transferred to an RAF hospital in Ely next day.
>
> I remember the rear-gunner [*sic*] was eighteen years old and suffered a broken leg. The co-pilot tore off the chinstrap of his helmet and handed it to me. He said he would never forget what we did for him that day. The strap, bearing the words 'United Carr, M-199', is still a treasured possession to this day.

While on the subject of movie stars, one of the most famous among those serving in ETO was actor James Stewart, who flew many combat missions as a pilot with 453 BG from Old Buckenham before moving to Tibenham. On the day Lieutenant Royal Frey – whose story opened this chapter – was shot down, 453 BG was tasked for a diversionary raid on the Luftwaffe airfield at Gilze-Rijen, Holland. For crew No.46, led by First Lieutenant Robert R. Bickerstaff, it would be an eventful trip, too, but at least they would make it back to England.

Take-off was 10.35a.m. In B-24H, 41-29254, everything looked normal, except that the revs on number-three engine were jumping around between 2500 and 2700rpm. Bickerstaff reduced power on the wayward engine and it seemed to settle down ok. Approaching the enemy coast, the aircraft generators started to play up, too. In order to reduce the electrical load, flight engineer Technical Sergeant Paul Harper asked the crew to turn off their heated suits. Each aircraft carried a small petrol-engined generator for such emergencies, usually known as the 'put-put' after its distinctive sound. Harper unshipped this motor and tried to start it up. Before he could do so, number-three engine finally gave up the ghost and stopped. The electrically operated feathering gear was inoperative so the propeller had to be left to windmill. Hydraulic pressure was also lost when the engine packed up.

Bickerstaff wisely decided it was time to turn around and head for home; the B-24 was not noted for its ability to maintain height once an engine was out. It was just as well that he did so because, due to the loss of electrical power, the engine intercooler shutters would not work and before long the carburettors to numbers two and four engines iced up. Then they both stopped, too! Approaching The Wash but sinking earthward rather rapidly, Lieutenant Bickerstaff realised there was no way he was going to make it back to Old Buckenham. Emerging from low cloud into flurries of snow and rain – too low now for a bale-out – he picked out a field in which to set the B-24 down. Wheels down, Bickerstaff suddenly saw the field was obstructed. Yelling at Harper to get the gear up, the pilot coaxed the nose up, aiming for another field just beyond. 'No hydraulic pressure!' came the reply. No time to dither, either. Down went the nose and the big bomber ploughed another deep furrow in Fenland soil at Hilgay Fen, south of King's Lynn. Damaged beyond repair, 41-29254 was finished, but although five crewmen were injured, they had all lived to fight another day.

A grim truism of the war was that, for tens of thousands of aircrew casualties and Prisoners of War, the air war was over. For those who got back to base, mission after mission, sometimes unscathed, sometimes 'on a wing and a prayer', combat flying imposed an immense cumulative mental and physical strain. Second Lieutenant Harry White was but one man among thousands of Americans who flew bombers in the Second World War, and his story offers an insight into the mental strain that a typical American bomber crew had to cope with in those days. Major Myron Keilman, CO of 579 BS, 392 BG was Harry's squadron commander at Wendling and this is his version of events in that summer of 1944:

Our new crews arriving in England in 1943 and 1944 had very little training in formation flying. The number of hours allocated to it were limited and for the most part, their instructors themselves had little or no four-engine formation training. Not until tour-expired 8th AF and 15th AF pilots returned to USA in sufficient numbers was this aspect of training improved. Harry White was assigned to my squadron as a 2/Lieutenant early in May 1944. I flew with him and his crew for the first time on his formation and assembly procedure indoctrination flight, which showed me they were all working well together as a team. It was not long after that check flight that they went onto operations.

Within the space of just sixty days Harry flew seventeen missions, lost seven of his original ten crew, baled out of one stricken B-24 and crash-landed another! To put this into context, the 392nd Bomb Group mounted 285 operational missions in its twenty months in England. This represents an average of one mission every other day – not the highest rate in 8th AF but pretty close to it. There were times, for example on the run up to D-Day, when the 392nd flew missions five days in a row. It was tough on all the crews, but 392 BG was by no means an exception. As far as the airplanes are concerned, it has also been suggested that by mid-1944 the average life-span of a bomber aeroplane in 8th AF combat groups was 145 days – and that included time on the ground.

On Sunday 4 June 1944, the target for thirty-six B-24s of 392 BG was St Avord Airfield, just south of Paris. Flying B-24H, 42-100261 named *Sweet Chariot*, it was Second Lieutenant Harry White's eighth mission, and he takes up the story now.

It was only a short trip but it counted towards our mission total just as much as the long ones. We did not take off until 16.00 but everything went well. Procedure en route to the target was to warm-up and trim the Sperry auto-pilot [C-1]. Well, with all of seven missions under my belt, I was a 'seasoned pro' by this time wasn't I, so I didn't bother with all that stuff!

392nd Bomb Group, Lieutenant Harry White's crew in 1944. Back row from left: William Forde, navigator; John Martin, co-pilot; Harry Green, bombardier; Harry White, pilot. Front row from left: Glenn Barnes, flight engineer; James Reynolds, radio operator; John Braccoforte, waist gunner; Robert Weitkemper, ball-turret gunner; Robert Dunbar, waist gunner; John Wehunt, tail gunner. (Harry White)

During our bomb run the flak came up pretty heavy and we took hits from several near misses. Shrapnel from one or more of these tore through our rudder cables putting the rudders out of action. Throwing on the C-1, which took effect immediately, it was still a struggle to keep the wings level. I was alternately twisting the turn control from full left to full right, with the 'plane levelling for a few seconds before it started to turn the rudders full opposite.

Still in formation, when the time came to open the bomb bay doors we discovered our hydraulic system had been shot out too. However, there was the manual bomb release to fall back on, so no sweat. When the order came for 'bombs away' I pulled the handle and out they went. Unfortunately the bomb bay doors went with them – I'd quite forgotten about them! Now there was quite a draught as well as extra drag, all the way home.

On the flight back I had so much trouble keeping the 'plane stable that I felt more of a danger to the squadron than the enemy. Gradually, though, the rest of the boys pulled away from me and then I began to worry about being picked off by enemy fighters. It was about 20.00 when, trailing the rest of the squadron, we crossed the south coast of England; dusk but not yet dark.

My first idea was to try a landing on that big, long runway at Manston. Down at 1,000 feet altitude, to keep under the thick cloud, I spotted the airfield; had a quick think as to how to approach, then turned the Sperry control. No response! She just kept going straight on. Several attempts later it dawned on me I had virtually no control over this ★★★ airplane.

By now we were heading roughly in the direction of our base at Wendling, which was reached still just under the cloud base. Well, I was not about to try a landing on autopilot so I decided to abandon ship. At that altitude we were too low for the crew to bale out safely so, circling base, I coaxed *Sweet Chariot* up to 3,000 feet, sent everyone, except my co-pilot John Martin, to the rear fuselage and told them to prepare for bale-out.

Bale-out! Hell, we had all practiced it many times in training, but it's still not for the faint-hearted. Three short rings on the alarm bell, then I gave them one long one to GO! Putting ole '261 on course for the sea, I waited my turn to go, too.

Dead silence! Then, after what seemed an age, over the intercom came: 'Skipper! Dunbar won't go!!' Cpl Bob Dunbar, one of my waist gunners should have been the first to jump. Jeez; this was not going according to practice!

This scene was repeated several times, during which I had to persuade the darned 'plane to circle towards Wendling again while the crew argued in back. I ordered the second man to get the hell out, then everyone, including the reluctant Dunbar followed. We found out later that, in spite of all we had been through, Dunbar was convinced we were playing a practical joke on him and that if he had jumped we would just turn right around and fly back to Wendling! How about that guy! What with that fiasco, the fast fading light and having to coax *Chariot's* head once more towards the sea, I turned to John Martin and in all innocence said: 'Which one of us goes first?' Eyes opened wide in amazement he replied: 'Me, you dumb ★★★★' (that was insubordination, right?) and baled immediately. Humour can surface at the most odd times. It's also surprising how quiet and lonely it is to be left all alone in a big airplane. Doing my best to trim the airplane, I checked my harness, unbuckled from the seat and headed for the bomb bay.

All of this was taking only minutes but confusion seemed to beset me. For the life of me I just couldn't remember the correct way to go and did several pretty stupid things. First I grabbed hold of the bomb racks and stuck my foot into the slipstream like I was testing the water. Nope, that's not the way! Next, seeing an extension oxygen tube flapping in the breeze, I thought I could shimmy down it until I was clear of the airplane. No dice! Gee, the 'plane's getting erratic again! Grabbing my 'D-ring' I bent over to tumble out. Hang on, what if I jerk the darned thing too soon? Oh, the hell with that; I jumped, into the darkness, somewhere over west Norfolk.

My 'chute opened with a tremendous jolt, knocking the wind out of me. Once again my mind refused to focus clearly and landing procedure escaped me. Rather foolishly I reckoned that if my legs were moving as fast as possible I could simply land and just run to a halt! Well, the obvious happened. I collapsed into a heap, flat on my face and was dragged along until the 'chute snagged a barbed wire fence.

It was by now about 23.00 so, gathering up my parachute, I began walking. About thirty minutes later, coming across a farmhouse, I heaved a sigh of relief and thumped on the door. When it opened there what seemed like the biggest double-barrelled shotgun was pointed at my head. The occupant was a Home Guard who was taking no chances! Eventually, convinced now that I was an American, his wife fed me hot milk and crackers (it was twelve hours since I had last eaten). Later, insisting on driving me back to base, he stopped en route at a pub, knocked up the landlord and they toasted my good fortune with rounds of good Olde English nut-brown ale. Morning was breaking when I arrived back at Wendling, where to my amazement, I discovered that due to all that circling, I had landed only five miles from base.

Reunited with the rest of the crew it transpired that my tail gunner, John Wehunt, had dropped into an AA encampment and was given the 'third degree' all night. Bombardier, Harry Green and navigator, William Forde landed together in the backyard of a house whose owner had been saving a bottle of Scotch for some special occasion and decided this was it. Everyone else got down safely and quite uneventfully.

Sweet Chariot 42-100261 when Harry White was her pilot in June 1944. By this time the 392nd was displaying the last three digits of the serial number on the nose of its aircraft. (Robert Harned)

But this is not the end of the tale of *Sweet Chariot*. Contrary to the official version, she did not come down: 'in the water north of The Wash.' In fact she crashed quite some distance inland, having covered another sixty miles after Harry baled out. It seems likely that *Sweet Chariot* took up a course of her own which, had it continued, might well have taken her dangerously close to the built-up areas of Newark, Mansfield or Sheffield. In the event, however, '261 finally 'landed' in open countryside in Willoughby Walks outside the village of Silk Willoughby, near Sleaford. Her descent was not without incident, though, as Mrs Audrey Woodford (nee Brown) recalls:

> I was eighteen, living in a pair of semi-detached cottages, one of which was unoccupied; the only buildings for quite a distance around. My parents, my sisters, Frances, Mary, Joyce and I were upstairs asleep on the night an aeroplane hit our house. One wing crushed the outhouses while the other completely destroyed the ground floor of both cottages. The upstairs floor collapsed, suddenly depositing us at ground level, covering both my sister Mary and me in rubble. She was unconscious but I was able to cry out for help. Father came and uncovered us and said we were saved from serious injury by our blankets which were blown over our faces.

All the family escaped serious injury, but they lost most of their possessions. Audrey remembered the most frightening thing for her was the sound of ammunition exploding in the fire that consumed the remains of the aeroplane. In 1991 LARG carried out a 'dig' at this site from which a number of components from *Sweet Chariot* were recovered, including a section of an engine with parts of the cottage brickwork still embedded in its cylinder gills.

Returning now to 1944. After de-briefing and medical checks on 5 June, Harry's crew was granted seven days' rest and recuperation leave (R&R). But it was not to be. At midnight on 5 June 1944, Harry White and his crew were roused from dreams of seven beautiful days in London by shouts of 'WAKE UP! WAKE UP! Briefing in one hour!' Surely there was a mistake?

'Get the hell outta here, we're on R&R!'

'It's no mistake, sir,' said Orderly Sergeant Vivian with a grin. 'It's 6 June. D-Day. Maximum effort. Everybody flies!' Five more missions had to be flown before Harry finally got his R&R.

On 13 July 1944, just two months after his first combat trip, Harry White was back in the cockpit again, this time for a mission to the railway marshalling yards at Saarbrucken. This would be his eighteenth combat mission, with only Second Lieutenants Harry Green (bombardier) and William Forde (navigator), Sergeants Robert Weitkemper (ball-gunner) and James Reynolds (radio) from his original crew. The rest were new boys. Briefing for twenty-eight crews rostered for the mission was at 1.30a.m., with take-off commencing at 5.30a.m. Weather over England was predicted as 'lousy', with drizzle, low ceiling and freezing moisture-laden clouds up to 12,000ft.

The trail of wreckage left by B-24 Liberator 42-100261, *Sweet Chariot*, at Silk Willoughby, Sleaford on 4 June 1944. Audrey Brown's damaged house is in the background. The tailplane and fins show the aircraft call letter 'A' with a bar above, confirming the squadron as the 579th.

In aircraft '558, flying blind towards The Wash rendezvous, Harry ran into those icing conditions. A build-up of ice on the wing leading edges became so rapid that the aeroplane stalled. Instinctively Harry pushed the nose down, both to pick up speed and seek warmer air. Fearing he might lose control entirely, he rang the alarm bell to warn the crew to standby for a possible bale-out. Still in control, though, Harry was able to level out as the ice cleared at a lower altitude. It was then, on checking round the crew, he discovered to his horror that Forde and Green had gone ahead and baled out without his say so! Aborting his mission, Harry returned to Wendling where a search for the missing airmen was set up. Their bodies were found floating in their Mae Wests in The Wash, but sadly both airmen had perished from exposure.

In July 1944, left with only a fragment of his original crew – rear gunner John Wehunt had also been killed during another mission – and having taken all that the elements and the enemy could throw at him, Harry White was taken off combat duty and returned to America. Serving with the USAF after the war, Harry flew for eight years as an RB-47 aircraft commander with Strategic Air Command and after other postings, finally returned to combat flying as pilot of a C-119 gun-ship in the Vietnam War before retiring with the rank of Lieutenant Colonel in 1970. In 1992 Harry, his wife Nancy and many of his former 392 BG buddies came to England to commemorate the fiftieth anniversary of the arrival of 8th AF in England. In addition to revisiting his old base at Wendling, LARG members arranged a visit to the cottage once almost destroyed by *Sweet Chariot* to meet and talk over old times with local men who, as young boys, remembered the incident vividly.

While the 392nd was ploughing upwards through the murk and ice on 13 July, another aircraft from 579 BS was in deep trouble. At the controls of 42-95103, *Berlin Bitch*, First Lieutenant Norman J. Hunt and his co-pilot First Lieutenant Peter Roetzel were battling against those same icing conditions – and losing. Hunt, too, decided to abort and try to find the nearest airfield. Re-crossing the Lincolnshire coast, Hunt lost the struggle and '103 crashed near the village of Wrangle, between Boston and Skegness. Only one airman, right waist-gunner Staff Sergeant Mark Osment, managed to escape from the stricken aircraft, and he wrote of his terrifying experience:

> We had icing conditions for a while but it soon cleared and the airplane resumed normal flight. A few minutes later, however, the ice reappeared. This time our aircraft, including the propellers, was covered with very heavy ice. The propellers began to 'run away' and when the pilot lost control I attempted to bale out through the waist window. I became stuck, half-in and half-out and was semi-conscious from striking the side of the fuselage. Somehow, a few seconds later I was thrown clear, pulled my ripcord then lost consciousness again.
>
> When I came to I was on the ground. I remember talking to a couple of children and some Home Guard soldiers then I was carried on an ironing board to an ambulance which took me to an RAF hospital. I later learned that no one else survived the crash.

On a warm Sunday in the summer of 1989, LARG members examined the site of the crash with metal detection equipment. Having obtained MOD and landowner permissions, a JCB digger began the task of re-opening that old crater. At a depth of three feet the first signs of corroded alloy was uncovered. Two feet deeper, more tangled wreckage came up and the familiar telltale odour of fuel and oil pervaded the air. It was just below this level that the tip of a propeller blade was uncovered. Careful hand digging revealed a mass of tangled wreckage with markings indicating it was an engine nacelle. Beneath this lay the remains of a badly smashed Pratt & Whitney fourteen-cylinder radial engine, at a depth of fifteen feet.

During the course of the dig, two parachutes, a flak jacket, one Mae West, oxygen masks and an A-1 flight cap were recovered. A further rare find was a pilot silver 'wings' badge. All exhibits and the story of the incident are now carefully displayed in the Lincolnshire Aviation Heritage Centre at East Kirkby Airfield. On 9 July 1994, LARG marked the fiftieth anniversary of the loss of this crew, by arranging for a brass plaque to be unveiled in Wrangle parish church by Professor Bill Wuest, a governor of the USAAF Second Air Division Memorial Trust and dedicated by Major Gary Carlson, chaplain of the US base at Mildenhall.

What's in a name? Aircraft markings and 'nose art' have long been the subject of many books and mention has been made, in this text, of 'personalised' aeroplanes – a practice more generally associated with American aircraft than their RAF counterparts.

Black Heart Jr, Argonaut and *Sweet Chariot* were simple scripts painted prominently beneath a cockpit. Who thought up such names? What significance did they have for the crew? Who knows? Most seem to have been named after pilot's wives, girlfriends or sisters, while others had deeper meanings for perhaps the crew as a whole. In the archives of 458 BG, for example, can be found an official list dated April 1944 submitted to 8th AF Command, no doubt for assessment of the potential PR value of such names as Bad Girl, Dog's Life, Kiss Me Baby, Table Stuff, Bachelors' Bedlam, Lassie Come Home, Royal Flush, Miss Used, Spitten Kitten and Shack Time.

Sometimes a new crew changed the name, as in the case of 44-40277, a 458 BG B-24 originally named *Miss Used* but later re-christened *Heavenly Hideaway*. On the other hand, Harry White's 42-100261 began squadron life in January 1944 as just another un-named B-24. Christened *Sweet Chariot* by Second Lieutenant William Nugent and its first crew, '261 passed to Harry White in June 1944 when Nugent's crew went home upon completion of its combat tour, and Harry chose not to alter the name. Some units, for example the 511th Bomb Squadron of 351BG based at Polebrook, went to great lengths to adhere to a theme when christening their aeroplanes, achieving some notoriety in the process.

Known as 'The Ball Boys', the 511th took its lead from CO, Major Clinton Ball who named his B-17 *Linda Ball* after his daughter. It was a measure of his leadership and squadron morale that many of his pilots chose to have names ending in '– Ball' painted on their own aircraft. Although much favoured, not all were painted as flamboyant, scantily-clad female forms. Again, photographic evidence of an alternative design has been found from the sad demise on 8 September 1944 of 511 BS B-17G, 42-31238, coded DS-A and christened *Devil's Ball*.

In typical English weather, with visibility down to a mile, cloud base less than 1,000ft, light drizzle and the prospect of icing at higher levels, 351 BG took off from its Polebrook base and clawed upwards in the vicinity of Market Deeping to assemble for a mission against Ludwigshaven. It was necessary to climb 8,000ft on instruments and later, many pilots reported controls icing-up, making their aircraft 'soggy' until they broke clear of the overcast. In *Devil's Ball*, Second Lieutenant John C. Haba, a pilot assigned to 509 BS but attached to 511 BS for this mission, is believed to have got into difficulty after encountering icing conditions. At 9.00a.m. his aeroplane crashed three miles east of Langtoft, Lincolnshire, in the area known as Langtoft Common, being completely destroyed when its bomb load of six 1,000-pounders exploded. Of the nine airmen on board, only tail-gunner Sergeant Donald Holihan escaped by baling out of the stricken bomber. In addition to Lieutenant Haba, the other airmen who died that day were: Second Lieutenant Clinton Cavett; Second Lieutenant Eugene Hooks; Second Lieutenant Robert McGlohon; Staff Sergeant Ernest Clinton; Staff Sergeant James Singleton; Sergeant Roy Morrison; and Sergeant Raymond McCloskey.

'Lily Marlene' was a popular song in those wartime days, bringing a measure of joy to anyone who listened or sang along with the words. B-24 Liberator, 42-50907 was named *Lily Marlene,* but on 9 September she only managed to bring grief to her crew. At 11.30p.m., people living in scattered farmhouses on Deeping High Bank were roused from their sleep to the sound of loud crashing noises. An American B-24 of 755 BS 458 BG based at Horsham St Faith, on a night low-level training sortie to RAF Shrewsbury, had smashed through trees bordering Crowland Common before crashing onto a crew-yard and outbuildings at Fleet Hall Bottom Farm, near the River Welland. Just two of the nine-man crew survived, and afterwards they recalled what happened.

While flying on auto pilot (C-1) at 3,800ft over south Lincolnshire, the aircraft became uncontrollable to such an extent that the pilot, Second Lieutenant William Frederick, gave the signal to bale out. The bomber banked into a right-hand turn and began to dive earthwards. Only the bombardier, Second Lieutenant Jack Hibbs, and the navigator, Second Lieutenant Glen Allen, had time to escape by parachute before the aircraft crashed. Glen Allen said:

> We started to lose altitude, slowly at first but the descent became more violent. At 23.10 hours the 'bale out' bell sounded. The last time I looked at the altimeter it showed 3,100 feet. Bombardier Lieutenant Hibbs got his parachute on first and opened the nose wheel door and baled out. I had trouble getting my parachute on and I could tell we were starting to spin as I was being thrown from side to side. I opened the nose turret door next and when I had got my parachute on I tried to go out the door but was thrown back into the nose compartment. Next thing I knew was that I was hanging in my 'chute. I was trying to stop myself from swinging side to side when I hit the ground. I took off my 'chute and harness and started walking towards the fire, which was about a mile away from where I landed. On reaching the fire I met a man and told him we had no bombs on board.

The impact tore the Liberator apart and, engulfed by flames when the fuel tanks ruptured, there was no hope for the seven men left on board.

B-24 Liberator 42-50907, *Lily Marlene* of 755 BS, 458 BG crashed on 9 September 1944.
(Ian Blackamore)

In the farmhouse, Mr and Mrs Maddison and their ten-year-old adopted son George, had a lucky escape as wreckage rained down around their house. The huge main undercarriage wheels catapulted past to land in the next field. The fire set several haystacks and outbuildings ablaze and the family struggled to get their Shire horses from the stables to safety. They placed wet sacks over the frightened horses' heads to prevent them from being panicked by the fire, but one horse suffered slight burns to its face when he broke loose and ran back into the flames.

By now the whole area was alert to the catastrophe. As Jack Wheat, the local Air Raid Warden and a few other men walked across the fields towards the crash site, they came across one of the survivors, navigator Glen Allen. He was taken to a nearby house to await an ambulance and shortly afterwards Lieutenant Jack Hibbs, the bombardier, was put in with him. When the civilian rescue party reached the scene of the crash, one look was enough to tell them nothing could be done for the rest of the crew.

On the fifty-sixth anniversary of the crash, LARG excavated this site and discovered the Americans had done a good clear-up job all those years ago. However, they did manage to find one propeller blade, still attached to the boss and reduction gear and several cylinders from one or more of the Pratt & Whitney radials. The seven airmen who perished were buried in the American cemetery at Madingley, Cambridge, but after the war three families requested that their sons be brought back to the USA. Staff Sergeant Ulysses G. Seymour, flight engineer, was re-buried in New York, while Sergeants William D. Nobles and William F. Casey, both air gunners, are buried in Georgia and Virginia respectively. Still at Madingley are Second Lieutenant William R. Frederick (pilot), Second Lieutenant Lawrence L. Doelling (co-pilot), Staff Sergeant Jack B. Zonker (radio operator), and Sergeant Robert L. Leake (air gunner).

One of the most bizarre American flying incidents in the region during the Second World War began over King's Lynn at around 10a.m. on Saturday 30 September 1944. It involved B-17G *Melancholy Baby* flown by First Lieutenant Clifton W. Eccles and his crew from 728 BS, 452 BG based at Deopham Green (Station 142). Group aircraft loading lists show 42-37878 was assigned to Lieutenant Eccles that day, but because the accident report for this incident is itself missing, there has been much debate over the years as to the identity of this particular B-17 that set out on a normal bombing mission to Bielefeld.

First Lieutenant Clifton Eccles arrived with his new crew at Deopham Green on 24 August 1944, where they were assigned to 728 BS and flew their first mission on 3 September. Eccles's regular crew comprised: co-pilot Second Lieutenant Victor M. Damus; navigator Second Lieutenant Joe Moderick; bombardier Second Lieutenant Ed Palmer; radio operator Technical Sergeant Paul Babb; top turret and flight engineer Technical Sergeant Doug Edwards; and gunners Sergeant Ken Wilson and Sergeant Hoette (waist), Staff Sergeant Ed Lacy (ball) and Staff Sergeant Jack Triplett (tail). By the end of that month, with five missions under its belt, the crew was briefed for the mission to Bielefeld. For reasons that remain unclear, Ed Palmer did not fly on that fateful day and his place was taken by Second Lieutenant William D. Blades.

Fully loaded with bombs, Eccles was taking 'Baby through the process of forming up over the King's Lynn area when a fire broke out in number three engine. Extinguishers could not subdue the flames and with the fire taking a serious hold on the wing and threatening the fuel tanks, Clifton Eccles ordered his crew to bale out. Aware of the potential effect of his bomber crashing to earth with its load of high explosive, he set the autopilot to take the aircraft out over the North Sea, then, while the aircraft was still on an even keel, took to his own parachute. The *Lynn News & Advertiser* in its 6 October 1944 issue continues the story:

Through some mechanical freak the 'plane circled round and began its cross-country journey. An order was flashed to fighters of Air Defence Of Great Britain: 'Intercept and destroy Flying Fortress, last seen heading from The Wash towards Liverpool'. [Some sources give the course as overflying Spalding, Melton Mowbray, Derby, Congleton, Middlewich, Northwich, Runcorn and Bangor.]

It was not intercepted but flew on and on, across the Irish Sea and all the way over Eire, piloted by 'George' the automatic control. Somewhere over the Atlantic its petrol gave out and it crashed to a watery grave.

Air raid sirens were sounded in many towns in the Midlands, North-west and North Wales, sirens that had not been heard 'operationally' for many months, in some cases years. At Liverpool the alert lasted about twenty minutes and strange as it may seem, the 'plane was said to have circled the city before continuing out to sea.

1/Lieutenant Eccles baled out over West Lynn, another of the crew [2/Lieutenant Damus] landed in a field off Gayton Road, Lynn, breaking his leg [he received help from nearby residents; Paul Babb broke his back on landing and Ed Lacy injured his knee quite badly] and the rest of the men came down at Wooton. The seven uninjured gathered at Lynn police station before returning to their base. They were surprised when they learned what had happened to their *Melancholy Baby*.

In view of some modern-day controversy surrounding the identity and mission of this B-17, it should be noted that the *Advertiser's* prompt article specifically mentions the name *Melancholy Baby*, strongly suggesting its reporter actually obtained the name from the crew itself. Ed Palmer recalled that, due to their injuries, Damus, Babb and Lacy were shipped home. Wilson, Hoette, Triplett and Edwards were posted out to the 15th AF in Italy while he, Cliff Eccles and Joe Moderick finished their tour of duty with the 452nd.

In the final stages of the wayward flight, two Fleet Air Arm Seafires from Ballyhalbert in Northern Ireland were sent up to make one last effort to bring it down. Seafire pilot Lieutenant George Boyd RN wrote of the event:

> One day when we were at Ballyhalbert there was an urgent call from RAFNI [RAF Northern Ireland] Command for some of our aircraft to bring down an unmanned American Flying Fortress which was heading for the Irish Free State [Eire]. As we had no live ammunition at Ballyhalbert, my aircraft and another were loaded with 12lb practice bombs and we were sent off to bring down the Fortress. I was not very keen about this, because if I had had to land in the Free State I would have been interned. The two of us found the Fortress and dropped our bombs from above without hitting it and returned to base. We heard that the Fortress over-flew Ireland and crashed in the Atlantic.

Sidney Solomon said it was the sound of footsteps in the dark, on the wooden walkway outside his hut that always filled him with dread. That was when someone came in the early morning to wake him and tell him that Lieutenant William Miller's crew – of which he was the navigator – was rostered for a mission at dawn. 'You always hoped the footsteps would pass by your hut – but they never did,' he said.

At a reunion of the 452nd Bomb Group in Oklahoma City in October 2003, former navigator Second Lieutenant Sidney Solomon (86) and waist gunner Technical Sergeant Paschal (Pat) Powell recalled painful memories of the loss of their crew buddies fifty-nine years earlier. Bill Miller's crew had been together since training in Lincoln, Nebraska, and as Sidney put it, 'We did everything together, we stayed within our crew and didn't socialize with anybody else.' They spent a quiet evening on 11 October 1944 relaxing in their own huts, the officers separate from the enlisted men. Early on the morning of 12 October, however, the footsteps stopped again, but this time it came as quite a shock to be woken up for duty because Miller's regular bomber, *Little Miss America* – in which they had already completed seven missions – was unserviceable with an undercarriage problem. Rousing the sleeping officers from their dreams, the barrack block GI shouted, 'Wake up sir, everything that can fly, gotta fly!' The same thing was happening, equally noisily, over in the enlisted men's quarters where Miller's crew were told, 'The target has changed; the bomb load has changed and you guys are flying!' Lieutenant Miller's crew found they were assigned a spare 728th Squadron aircraft, 42-39973 *Inside Curve*, a veteran of no less than 112 missions. The crew chief told Miller: 'I've just put four new engines in her, sir, and she's the fastest airplane on the field now. This will be her 113th mission and nothing can stay with her.'

Thick fog enveloped the airfield – a real 'pea-souper'. In the near darkness it was impossible to see more than a few of the parked aeroplanes and every metal surface dripped water and felt clammy. In a maximum effort, the 452nd launched thirty-eight aircraft for this mission against tank, lorry and aero component factories in Bremen, but *Inside Curve* was the Group's only loss that day. Take-off went normally and with the aircraft quickly swallowed up by the thick cloud, the crew settled down as Lieutenant Miller took the bomber upwards through the murk, on instruments and a strict heading, to the assembly area at 15,000ft north of The Wash.

Down in the nose compartment, Lieutenant Sidney Solomon was keeping a lookout through the plexiglass nose when, climbing through 14,000ft, he spotted another ghostly shape loom nearby. As Lieutenant Solomon reported the other aircraft to his pilot, almost instantaneously *Inside Curve* began to shake and dance about violently. It was caught in the propellor-wash of another bomber that came so close in front that the two almost collided. Solomon grabbed his 'chest' parachute pack, clipped it to his harness and tried to stop himself from being flung about.

Meanwhile, Technical Sergeant Pat Powell recalled that during the climb, he had pulled the pins to arm each of the bombs and was now back at his station in the waist munching a candy bar when he felt a sort of 'inner voice' urge him to put on the parachute harness he had thrown carelessly onto the floor. Stung by the power of that feeling, he did as the 'voice' bid him and, buckling himself into the harness, also took note that his 'chute was still wedged behind the gun mounting where he usually put it. He described what happened next:

> The ball turret gunner, Earl Bowen – who we nicknamed 'Short Round' – was having trouble with one of his guns and asked me by intercom to check the ammunition feed chute. I told him to roll the turret all the way down and stay like that until I told him to come round again, as I would have to unplug my mike in order to reach the turret. After taking off the top of the turret I saw that the ammo to this gun had not engaged with its feed pawl. As I was working the slack in the ammunition line through the turret chute, the airplane suddenly began to pitch and tilt wildly. Instinctively I knew we were in trouble and I needed to call Short Round and tell him to roll back up and get out of the turret quick.
>
> I had no chance to do anything, though. I was reaching to plug in my mike when I was thrown down on my belly. The 'plane shook violently, spun and seemed to flip over onto its back. Then it started to spin downwards. I felt so sick and so scared; flattened on the floor, hardly able to move under the force of gravity. Then she quit spinning and started on a long steep dive, making the most horrific noises I ever heard in my whole life.

This violent motion followed by the dive put so much stress on the bomber that as the speed built up, she began to break up with explosive force. The tail unit, up to the entry door, parted company from the waist gun section, while the front of the aircraft broke off at the ball turret. This left a short tube of fuselage, open at both ends, in which Pat Powell was left alone, fighting for dear life. Pinned to the floor, being slowly sucked by a howling gale towards the gaping rear fuselage, Pat admitted he thought he was going to die and remembered crying and screaming all manner of things out loud in his despair. Miraculously, he saw his parachute pack slide past him and grabbing it, he forced himself to snap it to the clips on his harness. Scrabbling hard with his hands and feet towards the ragged edge he reckoned he heard that same voice inside yelling at him: 'Hurry! Pull it!' So he did.

> I pulled that red handle on my pack and saw the little pilot 'chute pop out like a kite in the wind, dragging the rest of the parachute out and me with it, clear out of the fuselage. When my 'chute opened I really thought I saw the glory of God.

At that same moment in time, Lieutenant Sidney Solomon was also tumbling through the air. Afterwards, he had little recollection of how he had got out of the aircraft, but thought he must have been blown through the plexiglass nose and injured in the process. He came to and pulled his 'chute at about 1,500ft, landing heavily in the back yard of a cottage near the village of Ingham, about ten miles north of Lincoln. Pat Powell came down in a ploughed field close by, catching a blast of hot air and a shower of earth as a bomb that had broken loose fell nearby and exploded. He was not hurt by the blast, but had suffered a broken nose, cuts and bruises during his ordeal. He landed well clear of the main part of the bomber as it emerged from low cloud, shedding its wings to explode in a great ball of fire on impact as the rest of the bombs and its fuel ignited.

Staff Sergeant Matt W. Ransom, the tail gunner, was found dead far away from the main wreckage impact point. The ball turret, with Staff Sergeant Bowen still inside, fell away when the fuselage broke up and on impact with the ground, rolled into a thicket where it and his body lay hidden until a search party discovered him at nightfall. The other five airmen in the crew went down with the stricken bomber: pilot, Second Lieutenant William J. Miller: co-pilot, Flight Officer Joseph A. Kayatta; bombardier, Second Lieutenant Robert H. Brucks; engineer, Technical Sergeant Charles A. Bacharach and radioman, Technical Sergeant John J. Wilson. The final location can be estimated from the official reference to 'Coates/Ingham two miles west of', and from the fact that three bodies were taken to RAF Hemswell and four more to RAF Sturgate. After several days in RAF Sturgate sick quarters the two survivors went back to Deopham Green and attended the funeral of their friends in Cambridge.

Staff Sergeant Pat Powell soon recovered and returned to duty. Now crew-less, he found himself posted to the 15th AF in Italy, as an air gunner with 483 BG. Pat took to his parachute – the very same 'chute that had saved him from *Inside Curve* – for a second time when his aircraft was shot down on 22 March 1945, on his fourth mission with the Group. He survived that event, too, and spent the final months of the war as a Prisoner of War. Not without difficulty, Pat came to terms with the fact that he had been spared – not just once, but twice – while others had not, and he found solace in religion, becoming a Baptist minister at the age of twenty-five until his retirement. He died in 2005. Lieutenant Solomon returned to the USA for treatment and rehabilitation and spent the remainder of the war at an air base in Texas. He left the Army in October 1945 and became a successful businessman until his retirement took him to Florida.

Yet another example of the dangerous effect of propellor-wash occurred when 44-6816, a B-17 from 728 BS, 452 BG based at Deopham Green, crashed at Hilgay on 30 March 1945 during formation assembly for a mission to Hamburg. The pilot, Lieutenant Willis DuMond and five of his crew died in the accident and their names, together with those of airmen who died in six other aeroplane crashes in the parish, are commemorated on a plaque erected in 2002 adjacent to the village War Memorial.

Compared with bomber incidents, relatively few US fighter mishaps occurred in the region under discussion, mainly due to the fighters working, operationally speaking, more to the south and east, out of East Anglia. In-theatre Combat Crew Replacement Centres (CCRCs) represented a brief but important stop for replacement aircrews training to replace losses in the ETO. From January 1944 to April 1945, the 8th AF 496 Fighter Training group (496 FTG) operated fighter CCRC No.8 at Goxhill in Lincolnshire, where 2,481 pilots received air and/or ground training on the P-38 or P-51 prior to assignment to combat groups in the 8th and 9th Air Forces – a similar concept to an RAF OTU. The only other fighter CCRC in the ETO was the 495th that dealt with the P-47. Examples among Goxhill's commendably small twenty-three fatal casualties (less than 1 per cent) include Second Lieutenant Chester F. Gerrick, who died when P-38J, 42-967211 crashed at Walcott near Sleaford on 29 April 1944, and Second Lieutenant William D. Jolley, who was killed when his P-38 dived in at Old Leake on 2 June 1944. Both sites have been examined by LARG and recovered artefacts can be seen at East Kirkby.

Many fighter accidents in the East Midlands were related to 'squadron training' flights like, for example, the loss of Lieutenant Esburn D. Otis from 79 FS, 20 FG at King's Cliffe, who died on 26 January 1944 when his P-38J Lightning, 42-67492 crashed in The Wash. It was probably a display of high spirits that contributed to the demise of the pilot of a P-47 Thunderbolt when he had to force-land at Salter's Lode on 28 January 1944. Second Lieutenant Edward MacLean was No.3 in a flight of four P-47s from 362 FG being led by First Lieutenant Thomas H. Beeson and based at Wormingford, near Colchester as part of the 9th AF. Since the 9th AF was going to provide tactical support for invasion forces, it would need to give its pilots some ground attack practice. During this cross-country exercise over the Fens, Beeson called his flight into line astern and took them down in a practice strafing run along the Old Bedford river. Third man down was Second Lieutenant Edward Maclean in 42-75407. He put the nose down and as the speed built up he pulled back on the stick to make his dummy firing run, but failed to distinguish a slight rise in the ground in time and 'mushed' into it in the pull out. The belly tank was ripped off and the propeller damaged. The engine ran rough then stopped dead, so he cut all the switches and landed straight ahead on Mr West's Whitehouse farmland, about 200yds from Denver Sluice. Lieutenant MacLean was unharmed.

Encountering overcast conditions during a cross-country training flight on 1 October, First Lieutenant Thomas Dekle from 375 FS, 361 FG based at Little Walden got into difficulty in P-51, 44-14561 and probably stalled. Unable to regain control of the aeroplane he took to his parachute, leaving the Mustang to crash a mile north-east of Manea near March.

Named after Second Lieutenant Robert Volkman's younger sister, *Mary Jane*, 44-14197, from the same Group, came to grief on 29 October while leading eight 376 FS Mustangs on a training flight across the Fens. Engine failure caused Lieutenant Volkman to force-land in a cornfield on Bungalow Farm in the quaintly named Milking Nook district, two miles north of Peterborough.

No.20 FG based at King's Cliffe lost several pilots in accidents around this time, many of them in adverse weather conditions. On 2 August, Second Lieutenant Stephen J. Nelson from 55 FS ran into bad weather returning from a bomber escort mission to the Paris area. It is believed he became disoriented in cloud, spun and died when his P-51, 44-13832, crashed near Werrington, Peterborough. On 27 September, Lieutenant Harry L. Knapp from 77 FS died when his P-51, 43-13992 *Olivia De*, crashed for unknown reasons a mile south-east of Yaxley, while Lieutenant Walter H. (Moon) Mullins, also from 55 FS, died when his P-51D Mustang crashed a mile from Skegness on 18 October.

North American P-51D Mustang, 44-14197 *Mary Jane*, named after Robert Volkman's little sister crash-landed at Milking Nook near Peterborough. (Robert Volkman via N. Harris)

Detached to France for operations from December 1944 to the beginning of April 1945, 361 FG was absent from Fenland skies for a while. However, training exercises for new pilots continued from Little Walden and accounted for the loss of P-51B, 43-24808 on 2 January 1945. Second Lieutenant Marion C. Kelly from 376 FS lost control of his Mustang while practicing combat manoeuvres near The Wash. Attempting an *Immelman* turn at 30,000ft, '808 fell into a spin from which Lieutenant Kelly could not recover, and at 8,000ft the cockpit canopy flew off, hitting him across the eyes. He undid his seat strap buckle just as the port wing broke off, throwing him from the cockpit, but his 'chute opened and he came down without further injury. The Mustang crashed one mile south of RAF Sutton Bridge. On the same day 384 FS of 364 FG, based at Honington, lost Second Lieutenant Edgar A. Knapp (not to be confused with Harry L.) in P-51 Mustang 44-11233. His fighter was completely wrecked when it crashed onto Brest Sand in the marshes off Admiralty Point near Terrington St Clement.

Two days later, Second Lieutenant John R. Wilson from the 374 FS crashed flying P-51D, 44-15036, on a routine training flight in company with Second Lieutenant Felix Kelinske and Second Lieutenant Jack Joss. A few minutes before the crash, the flight ran into some haze and as visibility decreased, Lieutenant Kelinske called on R/T and suggested a 180° turn to avoid the haze. Wilson was last seen by Kalinske doing a steep turn underneath Joss. After losing visual contact, Lieutenant Kalinske orbited the area and spotted burning wreckage that turned out to be Wilson's Mustang. It had crashed into Bowser's orchard in Cranmore Lane, Holbeach, killing the pilot.

Shortly after 361 FG returned to Little Walden, Second Lieutenant R.W. Hobbs of the 361st had to make a hasty exit from 44-13646 *Li'l Larry* on 24 April 1945, when one wing parted company from the rest of his machine. This P-51 crashed at Eau Brink near Wiggenhall St Germans, with Hobbs landing safely by parachute nearby.

The end of the war in Europe saw an exodus of men and machines to America, but 361 FG was one of the last fighter Groups to return Stateside, not leaving England until November 1945. On 22 June 1945 the engine of 42-106638, an elderly P-51B assigned to 376 FS, seized up due to loss of coolant during a local area training flight. Deciding not to risk a dead stick landing, Flight Officer Wade C. Ross baled out of the doomed P-51, which went on to crash and burn out at Ten Mile Bank, Hilgay Fen. This was another case of an aircraft name being changed, since 106638 was originally E9-R *Impatient Virgin*, whose name later changed to E9-B *Eva*, in which guise sadly she crashed and burned. The location of the wreckage was excavated in 2002 by the East Anglian Aircraft Research Group, who recovered many artefacts for preservation.

An entry in the West Pinchbeck fire section logbook reads:

Friday 5 Jan 1945	17:20hrs	Received fire call to plane crash. Bourne Road, Guthrum.
	17:30hrs	Tender X14 left station for plane crash at Guthrum. Sec Ldr Cole, Ldg Fm Sharman, Fm Sneath, Summerfield, Marriot and Hunt. Dakota aircraft; used foam; one body found in debris. All fire extinguished.
	20:00hrs	Returned to station.

P-51B Mustang, 42-106638 served with the 376th Fighter Group at Little Walden as E9-R *Impatient Virgin* before its demise at Hilgay Fen on 22 June 1945. (Steve Gotts via Jeff Carless)

The site of this accident is about five miles west of Spalding. A Douglas C–47B Skytrain, 43–48727, believed with one wing on fire in the air, had plunged nose first into the bank of the River Glen about 400yds from Guthrum Bridge, on what is now the A151 road to Bourne (Lincolnshire). This transport aeroplane was from 48th Tactical Carrier Squadron, 313th Tactical Carrier Group, based at RAF Folkingham and was making the return leg to base after ferrying personnel to Snetterton Heath Airfield in Norfolk. It was completely destroyed and all four airmen on board died: First Lieutenant Harry R. Klaus, pilot; Sergeant Roscoe L. Toms, engineer; Staff Sergeant Leo R. Messier, radio; and First Lieutenant Joseph Pinkoson, who was listed as a passenger but probably occupied the co-pilot seat. At the time of the accident, there were light clouds at 3,000ft and visibility was one to three miles. In view of the degree of disintegration and the fact that the wreckage was at the edge of a major drainage watercourse, despite the presence of US personnel for a couple of weeks trying to remove the debris without further damaging the raised bank, no explanation for the accident was found.

1945 saw no let-up in the 8th AF bombing campaign either. Following hard on the heels of heavy snow falls over Christmas 1944 and New Year 1945 came 'pea-souper' fogs in January, and on 16 January, B–24J, 42–51471 from 855 BS, 491 BG became a victim of the latter. Low on fuel after a bombing mission and unable to locate his North Pickenham base in visibility that was down to less than 200yds at ground level, Second Lieutenant Frank Rose gingerly force-landed his B–24 on farmland at Stowgate Farm, Deeping St James, south of Spalding. He and his crew were fortunate to come down on flat land with nothing more than a few farm buildings for miles around. All nine aircrew (they carried no bombardier on this mission) emerged unhurt as the big bomber slithered to a stop, its progress halted by a dyke about half a mile from the River Welland. Not so lucky, though, were two RAF airmen detailed to guard the bomber until it could be recovered by its American owners, an operation which was not carried out at a hurried pace at this stage of the war. An unhappy event was reported thus in the Peterborough local newspaper:

> The funeral took place on 16 February 1945 of two RAF airmen who were killed by a train near Stowgate railway crossing on 9 February. Cpl Derek Dalton and LAC Gordon Rea were guarding a crashed aeroplane. They were killed while walking along the railway line in fog and darkness as they returned to the site from the Railway Tavern. They were buried in Peterborough's Eastfield Cemetery.

A third member of the group, LAC Healy, said it was around 7.00p.m. when the three of them walked through the fog along the railway track to the Railway Hotel. They left at closing time, 10.00p.m., and returned to the crash site by the same route. They heard a train coming up behind and moved out of its path by stepping towards the 'up' line. He saw the other two airmen standing watching the passing train. He was unaware of a second train, coming on the 'up' line until something touched him. When the trains had gone, he shouted repeatedly but got no reply. The two airmen had been hit by the Grimsby to King's Cross express, the drivers of which were unaware of the accident.

It was mentioned earlier in this chapter that B–17s often suffered damage or loss as the result of electrical fires starting in the top turret pivots. The problem was never entirely eradicated and 306 BG, also featured at the beginning of this narrative, lost B–17G *Hellcat Hattie* in The Wash due to this same cause. When fire broke out under the top turret, Second Lieutenant Wilfred E. Miessler, pilot of *Hellcat Hattie,* dropped out of a thirty-six-'plane formation outbound on a mission. An explosion in the starboard wing sent the B–17 into a dive. While Second

Lieutenant Miessler struggled to steady the bomber, his co-pilot Second Lieutenant Stanley Burns went to the forward escape hatch, kicked off the door and baled out. Navigator Second Lieutenant John Pappas followed, then bombardier Second Lieutenant William Johnson. It is not known if any of the other crew managed to get clear before the bomber hit the water, but only the co-pilot and bombardier were rescued from a life raft dropped by another aircraft from the same formation. The other casualties were Sergeant M.D. Baughaman, engineer; Sergeant W.D. Searles, radio; Sergeant C. Caserta, ball turret; and Sergeant R.L. Harrison, tail gunner. The waist gunner names are not known.

It took just two weeks from VE Day for the 8th AF great trek homewards to begin, with the first aeroplanes departing on 19 May, carrying their normal crew plus a number of passengers – usually ground crew – and all their worldly goods. Roger Freeman records that, 'during the next seven weeks, 2,118 heavy bombers and 41,500 air and ground crewmen arrived in America from Britain.' Bombers were given priority of repatriation in order for some units to prepare for deployment to the Pacific war zone.

Last staging post before embarking on the long over-water leg of the journey back to the States, was RAF Valley in North Wales. Among the first to set out for home was 389 BG from Hethel in Norfolk. In this incident is a poignant reminder that when it comes to battle, it matters not whether it is war- or peace-time as far as the elements are concerned. It does not matter that a crew may have endured and survived the worst flak or fighters the enemy could throw at it or struggled out or home 'on a wing and a prayer'. The weather could still affect the roll of the dice, as it did for the crew and passengers of B-24M, 44-50688, RR-Q, on 20 May 1945.

Climbing through a thick, grey overcast, First Lieutenant James O'Brien concentrated on his instruments as he set course for RAF Valley. Less than half an hour into the flight, he was flying into storm clouds, lit eerily by occasional flashes of lightning. What happened next remains unclear, but there is a possibility the B-24 was either struck by lightning or tossed by ferocious air currents into a stall condition. In its plunge to earth, only two of the thirteen men on board were able to bale out: navigator, First Lieutenant Howard Tomlinson, and radio operator, Technical Sergeant Robert Dymocek. Their compatriots were trapped in the bomber and died when it crashed at Manea Common near March: Flight Officer A.

The sad remains of B-24M Liberator 44-50688, RR-Q+ from 566 BS, 389 BG at Hethel that crashed at Manea Common on 20 May 1945. (Ian MacLachlan)

McNeil, co-pilot; First Lieutenant W.H. Liming, bombardier; Technical Sergeant C.M. Dunn, engineer; waist gunners Staff Sergeant M.E. Conley and J.W. Moss; Private First Class M.B. Scarberry, tail gunner; and passengers Staff Sergeant J.V. Champion, Technical Sergeant T.L. Karman, Corporal R.C. Hopke, and Corporal C.H. Espie.

Although by early 1946 the wartime American Eighth Air Force had officially left English shores, with the arrival of the Iron Curtain, the Cold War and the creation of NATO, it was of course not many years before the post-war USAF took up residence again. For the people of eastern England, though, it never entirely went home, for there were physical reminders in the form of the 122 airfields once occupied by Americans and now in various states of run-down. Despite the growing mutual distrust between East and West by the end of the war, it was chiefly a consequence of the communist blockade of Berlin in 1948 that brought the USAF back to English skies in numbers.

At the end of the Second World War, after closure for a major reconstruction programme, the runways of RAF Sculthorpe, just inland from The Wash, were greatly enlarged. This was in anticipation of a reactivation towards the end of 1948 for units of the US Strategic Air Command to come on a ninety-day rotation programme, and it was the B-29 and later the B-50 that brought back the sight of US heavy bombers to the skies in this part of England.

'Quick, come and look at this!' shouted my sister, pulling me towards the bedroom window in our Spalding house. The author was, at this time, six years old; it was dark, and we both stood, noses pressed to the window, staring out at a trail of flames away in the distance in the night sky. The image of those flames in the sky stayed with me, but not until many decades later, while researching for this book, was I able to relate my dormant childhood memory to the actual incident.

'BLAZING AIRCRAFT DRAMA' ran the headline in the *Lincolnshire Free Press* of 25 July 1949. It continued:

> Hundreds of people saw a blazing American Super Fortress flying for twenty-five miles across the Lincolnshire Fens before it disintegrated and scattered its wreckage over an area of a square mile at West Walton near Wisbech during the twilight between 9.30 and 10pm on Thursday night. The American crew baled out [and] the doomed aircraft continued for eight miles unoccupied, with blazing pieces falling from it, before it blew up.

The aircraft was Boeing B-29A, 44-62141, from 344 BS, 98 BG, based at Spokane AFB in the USA but on a rotational detachment to Sculthorpe Airfield in west Norfolk. On this practice mission the aircraft commander was Captain Thomas Eastman with eleven other men on board, and he was heading back to Sculthorpe when one of the port engines caught fire over Bourne, Lincolnshire. With the blaze becoming uncontrollable and spreading to the wing, the aircraft droned eastwards over the south Lincolnshire villages of Crowland, Whaplode Drove, Gedney Hill and Sutton St Edmund, its fiery trail watched in awe by those on the ground. Unable to prevent the bomber from losing height, Eastman gave the order to bale out and the first man hit the silk at about 1,000ft over Whaplode Drove, followed in quick succession by the rest of the crew. Captain Eastman was last out, landing heavily near the vicarage in Sutton St Edmunds. Given first aid by local residents and a doctor he was then sent by ambulance to Wisbech Hospital, suffering from injuries to his head and a knee, shock and concussion. Of the remaining crew, which included two supernumeraries, Corporals Clyde Painter and Delbert Gallmeyer on board for the ride, only the bombardier First Lieutenant George Willmer, sustained injury. He broke his leg when he dropped awkwardly on the road at Gedney Hill and was taken to Holbeach hospital for treatment. Both injured men were transferred to the military hospital at Ely. All the uninjured men

Boeing B-50A Superfortress of the type that crashed near Isleham on 13 October 1949.

were rounded up by local people and were 'entertained' by the manager of the Spalding Bulb Company premises at Fleet Fen, until transport arrived from their aerodrome early next morning. The aircraft itself finally disintegrated in the air over West Walton, the main part falling in J.B. Horrell's orchard at Walton Salts, although other wreckage was spread over a square mile area, fortunately causing no damage to life and only superficial damage to fruit and root crops.

Lakenheath Airfield was also reactivated after a post-war expansion project, and between 1948 and 1958, over thirty USAF Bomb Groups or Wings took up temporary residence on ninety-day rotations each. Up to August 1949, it was the B-29 in evidence, then came the B-50 until April 1953, when B-47 exchanges began.

The final act in this part of the story was played out as a tragedy on 13 October 1949 when Boeing B-50A Superfortress 46-060 of 65 BS, 43 BG crashed one mile from Isleham with the loss of all twelve airmen on board. The bomber was one of those on a rotational duty in England from its home at Davis-Monthan Air Base in Arizona, USA. It was 9.30a.m. when buildings and the countryside around Isleham were shaken by an enormous explosion as the B-50 crashed onto Mr Thornelly's farmland adjacent to Beck road and its load of twelve 500lb bombs detonated. The huge bomber had just taken off from its Lakenheath base for a practice bombing mission to the RAF range off Heligoland. The force of the explosion caused much structural and internal damage to many houses and set fire to farm buildings and straw stacks, but fortunately no one on the ground was injured, although there were some narrow escapes.

The pilot on this mission was Major George H. Ingham, the Group Operations Officer. His crew comprised: First Lieutenant John A. Dryer, the usual pilot; First Lieutenant Roger M. Stannard, co-pilot; First Lieutenant Robert H. Sport, navigator; First Lieutenant Robert W. Stratfield, weapons operator; Technical Sergeant Paul R. Suller, bombardier; Technical Sergeant Harold S. Morin, engineer; Staff Sergeant Arthur L. Gilbreath, radio; Technical Sergeant Delmas M. Size, CFC (central fire control) gunner; Staff Sergeant Julius Odegard, left gunner; Staff Sergeant Robert C. Williams, right gunner and S2 Davis J. Garrett, a supernumery RAF signaller on attachment from No.3 Group RAF.

Chapter 4

POST-SECOND WORLD WAR
RAF, RCAF & USAF Accidents

FLAMEOUT!

Growling Rolls-Royce Merlin and Griffon engines – and Wright Cyclones – gradually gave way to the *whoooosh* of RR Derwent or DH Goblin and Ghost jet engines as the propeller age made way for the jet age. Still encircled by many active airfields, for a while propellors would remain much in evidence over the region, mainly at the Flying Training Schools.

Meteor F4s and T7s were filtering through to Advanced Flying Schools such as 206 AFS at RAF Oakington, several of whose aircraft were lost in accidents in the early 1950s. Later in that decade, the arrival of the De Havilland Vampire FB5 and T11, at Swinderby, Cranwell and Oakington extended jet training right across the region. Meteor F8 day fighters were in front line service, for example, with 56 Squadron at Waterbeach and 92 Squadron Coningsby, while night fighter Vampire NF10s of 253 Squadron at Waterbeach and Venom NF2 and NF3 aircraft from 23 Squadron at Coltishall were regular sights across the region, even during daylight hours. It is not surprising, therefore, that – with the size of the RAF moving towards its post-Second World War peak – air activity around The Wash was as intense as ever. It was swelled by aerial visitors to the area's live firing ranges, coming not only from airfields all over the UK but also from mainland Europe. Other reminders of past eras, too, came with Canadian and American fighter pilots returning to use airspace around The Wash. Cross-country flights, low flying – authorised and unauthorised – aerobatics and weapons training continued unabated and the region continued to be littered with evidence of the fallibility of both men and machines.

One of the more unusual incidents to befall a flying station in this region was the mystery surrounding the disappearance of Gloster Meteor III, EE316, from RAF Molesworth during the early hours of 20 November 1945. It was what the *Peterborough Advertiser* dubbed 'AIR MYSTERY – Jet Plane Missing From Drome', and the brief newspaper story ran as follows:

> Molesworth RAF airfield is the scene of a mystery which is occupying earnest attention in official circles. Early on Tuesday morning [20 Nov 1945] a Gloster Meteor III jet plane took off from the unlit runway and headed in a south-westerly direction. No trace of the plane or pilot has yet been found. The plane carried fuel for a flight of one hour or about 500 miles. An official enquiry is being held into the mystery.
>
> It is stated that the pilot of the plane is twenty-four-year-old Plt Off John Adam [*sic*] DFM formerly a Typhoon pilot in WW2 and one of the first RAF men to fly Meteor planes. He trained in South Africa and fought over North Africa and over Europe.

It emerged that a corporal in the station guardroom heard an unexpected roar at about 01.00 hours on the morning in question and ran outside just in time to see a Meteor jet trundling down the runway. Not a matter for undue concern at an RAF aerodrome one might think, but there was no flying scheduled that night and everywhere was in darkness. It was rapidly established therefore that the aircraft was making an unauthorised flight. All hell broke loose and a roll call of pilots found that Pilot Officer Adams was missing along with aircraft EE316. Adams was a member of No.245 Squadron, but had been posted to 1335 Conversion Unit at Molesworth for training on the Meteor. During the subsequent investigation it was alleged that his temperament had been brought into question and had resulted in his suspension from training prior to the incident. In the event, since no trace was ever found of the aircraft and it could have continued to fly south-west for an hour, it might be speculated that the most likely location of its end was in the waters of the English Channel or the Bay of Biscay. Pilot Officer Adams is listed on the Runnymede memorial to the missing and it transpires that, curiously (although not uniquely), the RAF Museum library claims to have no accident record card for the EE316 incident.

At this period in the transition to jets, a curious statistic emerges relating to the frequency with which senior officers, several with distinguished war records, appeared in these early jet incidents. In the ten years up to 1956, at least three Wing Commanders and no less than ten Squadron Leaders feature in accidents in the region under discussion here alone. The advent of the jet engine had brought a remarkable leap in aircraft performance. Maybe it was also something to do with the fact that many of these men, with considerable operational flying experience in piston engine aircraft under their belt, had lived through a period only a few years earlier when danger was taken for granted. Some, having reached senior rank, perhaps in an albeit praiseworthy desire to continue to 'lead from the front', may have lost sight of the need – or simply had less opportunities – for continual flying practice and as a result, failed to have all the emergency drills at their fingertips. In the book *From Blue To Grey*, pilots of that era expressed a similar view of this phenomenon:

> The press made a big sensation out of all these jet crashes … We can look back and see two obvious causes. One was simply that the management, only [a few] years after the war just took danger for granted and everyone just 'pressed on regardless.' Accidents were expected. The other was that the new jet engines had given such a huge leap in performance that everyone was on a steep learning curve, from aircraft designers and senior officers down to junior pilots. Aircraft systems, flight instruments, safety equipment and navigation aids had barely advanced since the days of the Spitfire.

For example, as far back as 12 February 1946, a prominent Second World War pilot, Squadron Leader Edward Thorn DFC★, DFM★, attached to the Empire Central Flying School died when the Meteor F3 he was flying crashed at Landbeach, Cambridgeshire. Tasked to carry out handling trials during a cross-country exercise from Hullavington, Meteor EE456 was seen to break cloud at about 400ft and then bank to port at high speed before crashing into some farm buildings on Rectory Farm where it was totally destroyed. The highly experienced Thorn was a pre-war pilot who, with his air gunner Fred Barker, made a name with No.264 Squadron as the most successful Boulton Paul Defiant team of the war.

The 1950s got off to a bad start with the loss of two more senior officers. The first, from RAF Flying College Manby (later College of Air Warfare), was a former Second World War pilot, Wing Commander Roderick McConnell DSO DFC. He was posted missing while on a familiarisation flight in Vampire FB5, VV680, on 16 March 1950. This aircraft was seen going into a vertical spin at 4,000ft from which it seemed to recover momentarily before diving

Boulton-Paul Defiant pilot Sergeant Edward Thorn (left) in the Second World War, with his air gunner Sergeant Fred Barker.

steeply for another 1,000ft. Then it spun in the opposite direction and although it appeared to stop spinning at 500ft, the Vampire failed to pull out of its dive and plunged into the sea some two miles offshore, south of Mablethorpe.

The second example involved ex-Battle of Britain ace Squadron Leader Constantine Pegge DFC★, an experienced instructor at Central Fighter Establishment, RAF West Raynham. Airborne in Meteor F4 on 9 May 1950, Squadron Leader Pegge was acting as number two in a pair formation with CFE student Flight Lieutenant E. W. Smerdon in the lead. They began a descent from 35,000ft as a pair but entered sea fog at 600ft, with a base that turned out to be at less than 200ft. As soon as Flight Lieutenant Smerdon saw the sea he hauled back on the stick and managed to climb away, but Squadron Leader Pegge is believed to have had no time to pull out and died when his Meteor, VT234, hit the waters of The Wash off Hunstanton. After a lengthy but fruitless search three miles out from Hunstanton pier in the Sunk Sand area, Skegness lifeboat contacted Lynn Well lightship and was told a large patch of oil had been reported further south. The lifeboat discovered the oil about one mile NNE of Roaring Middle Light Float, but found no wreckage or survivor. The body of this distinguished pilot was eventually recovered from the sea in Freeman Channel on 13 June.

On 10 April 1951, Meteor F8 WA965 was being flown by Squadron Leader B. Champreys, a Central Flying Establishment instructor from RAF West Raynham, when it ran out of fuel during an air to ground firing practice on Holbeach range. Fortunately he was able to force-land on the marshes without injury. Less fortunate, though, was Squadron Leader Jack Jagger of 92 Squadron Linton-on-Ouse, who died on 14 August 1952. Briefed to carry out a demonstration of aerobatics at RAF Coningsby in Meteor F8, WK657, Jagger intended

Gloster Meteor F4s of No.263 Squadron. VT336, VT273, VT328, VT249.

Fresh from the factory. This Gloster Meteor F8, WE912, went to 616 RAuxAF Squadron at RAF Wymeswold and crashed at Mill Green, Spalding on 27 September 1953 killing its pilot Pilot Officer George Furness. (F.G. Swanborough)

to finish his programme with a flourish by 'bunting' – an outside loop – to inverted straight and level flight. However, he rolled out of the bunt before it was complete, losing so much altitude in the process that the aircraft hit the ground, tore a path through a herd of cattle and disintegrated on impact with a riverbank at Dogdyke.

Squadron Leader Victor Daw DFC AFC saw action as a junior officer in both the Battles of France and Britain, and in 1953 his career had progressed to that of instructor at the Day Fighter Leader School at CFE West Raynham. His combat experience was being put to good use on 24 March when, in Meteor F8, WH358, he acted as target aircraft in a 'rat and terrier' low-level interception exercise over The Wash. During this sortie the Meteor crashed into the sea killing its pilot. The cause of the accident could not be established with any certainty, but with visibility of about 1,000yds at the time, a calm sea and no horizon, this could be a potentially hazardous situation for any fast aircraft manoeuvring at low level.

More fortunate than these was Squadron Leader R.T.P. Davidson DFC. Unpredicted bad weather over south Lincolnshire gave the CO of 421 (Red Indian) Squadron RCAF some problems during a cross-country flight from RAF Odiham in a Vampire FB5, on 26 April 1951. When his radio failed in worsening visibility he decided it was time to make a forced landing. Fortunately he was close to RAF Sutton Bridge and opted to bring WA207 down for a wheels-up landing on the grassy acres of the former wartime airfield. Davidson survived this mishap and as a wing commander went on to become operations officer for No.1 Wing RCAF when it brought its Sabres to North Luffenham over the next twelve months (of which more later).

RAF Sutton Bridge, although not operating as a flying station since 1947, continued to support the weapons range at RAF Holbeach and it was in the context of the range that

DH Vampire FB5. WA124 'U' (foreground) and WA177.

Squadron Leader Davidson's name came to light in an earlier incident. He was on the staff of CFE at West Raynham when, on 25 July 1949, he nearly shot himself down over Holbeach marsh while flying Spitfire XIV, RM737. This came about when the aircraft was hit by debris as he was carrying out air-to-ground rocket firing practice, but Davidson was able to return safely to base.

While on the subject of ricochets and Holbeach range, there were two similar incidents recorded in 1949. Three days prior to Davidson's incident, it appears that Flight Lieutenant G.F. Thornton from CFE had also tempted providence down on the range, when he returned to base with his Vampire FB5, VV670, showing signs of damage by a ricochet or flying debris after a live air to ground firing session. On 11 February, Meteor IV RA485, flown by P1 W.W. Peet of 74 Squadron, was struck by flying mud and sand, kicked up during an air-to-ground firing pass that resulted in the aircraft nose cowling being dented and part of the nose wheel fairing being ripped. Peet kept the machine in the air and landed safely back at his RAF Horsham St Faith base. Ricochet incidents on the Holbeach range were not that uncommon and some are recorded as far back as 1926 when the range first opened. In the early days, ground-target supports made of metal were employed, but were rapidly replaced by wooden poles when pilots found they were flying through their own gunfire! In more recent times, a Harrier jet crashed on the range in circumstances suggesting the hazard could still catch an unwary pilot off guard.

Rather than continue the Vampire airframe/Goblin engine lineage, by the end of the 1940s, De Havilland had designed the more aerodynamically efficient Venom FB1 around its much-improved Ghost engine. This new combination gave the Venom an excellent performance as a high altitude interceptor, but it was also recognised that one of its Cold War tasks would be as a ground attack aircraft and in service it was also found to be very good in this role. Before it was cleared to carry various under-wing ordnance, such as 60lb rockets, or bombs of 500lb and 1,000lb calibre, trials were undertaken by CFE at RAF West Raynham to determine handling procedures for this low level configuration.

This was the background to an incident that occurred on 28 July 1953 in which twenty-eight-year-old Flight Lieutenant Michael Whitworth-Jones lost his life. Michael was an experienced pilot who had seen active service in Korea while seconded to the Royal Australian Air Force. Having flown the Meteor F8 on 160 operational ground-attack sorties with No.77 Squadron, he was posted back to England to put that operational experience to good use as a test pilot with CFE West Raynham. On the day in question he was briefed to fly to Holbeach range in The Wash and carry out an air-to-ground rocket-firing sortie in Venom FB1, WE261, as part of the handling trials. Whitworth-Jones made two dummy runs then advised range control that his next would be a 'hot' (live) pass and he intended to fire a single rocket on each live pass. Entering a dive at about 2,500ft, his first approach looked fine but watchers saw him continue past the usual release height of about 1,200ft without firing a rocket. Just as the Venom reached the normal pull out height around 500ft, it suddenly disintegrated.

The Venom's maximum diving speed was higher than that of its Vampire predecessor and with pull out speeds that could reach over 450 knots it was quite possible to reach +6g, so some care was needed at that point. Ominously, WE261 had not received a modification that would have strengthened its wing root joints, and to signify that it should not be flown above the +6g limit, the aeroplane was marked with red bands on the wings and an accelerometer was installed in the cockpit. Crash investigators, therefore, homed in on the possibility of wing failure. Sure enough, they found that stress cracks had made the port wing progressively unstable, eventually causing the main spar to fail in up-load and the wing to break off, in this case hitting the tailplane as it did so. Despite all the evidence from this accident, the Venom was still cleared for squadron service – albeit with the same +6g limitation.

Mainstays of the RAF jet night fighter force in the early 1950s were the A-W Meteor NF11 to NF14 series, the DH Vampire NF10, but by the end of 1953, the latter was superseded by the Venom NF2. Based at RAF Coltishall, No.23 Squadron eagerly awaited the arrival of its new mount and in order to hurry things along, the commanding officer Squadron Leader Anthony Jacomb-Hood DFC decided to collect their first NF2 from the factory in Hawarden, Chester himself. Early serviceability proved to be quite poor and together with a spell of bad weather, little flying was being done during January 1954. One criticism levied at both the Vampire and Venom was the poor means of escape from the cockpit for the crew, who had no ejector seats to assist them in an emergency. This was in addition to the cockpit itself being a source of crew discomfort due to its decidedly cramped nature.

Perhaps anxious to crack on with the conversion of his crews to the new aeroplane, Squadron Leader Jacomb-Hood took off in WL828 shortly after 09.00 on 21 January for a weather check to see if any flying was possible. Conditions at the time were stratus cloud with a 600ft base, intermittent rain and a light east wind. With him that morning was navigator Pilot Officer Arthur Osbourne. Just fifteen minutes later some builders working in South Wooton near King's Lynn were horrified to see the Venom came screaming out of low clouds and disappear in an explosion that shook the whole area. The jet had crashed into Reffley Wood a few hundred yards from where new houses were being built in Sandy Lane. A scene of desolation greeted would-be rescuers when they reached the muddy wood. All around a deep crater, pieces of metal wreckage, parachutes, a dinghy and other items hung grotesquely from the trees while small fires flickered in the undergrowth. There was nothing that could be done for the two airmen.

Since the Venom was almost completely destroyed, the subsequent enquiry board had little to go on in its investigation of the crash. Some problems had already been found in Venoms relating to an inverter through which electrical current was fed to the artificial horizon (AH).

DH Venom NF2s, WL830, WL823, WL858 of No.23 Squadron. (No.23 Sqn Archive)

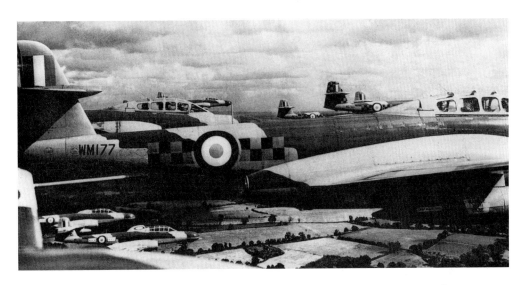

Meteor NF11, WM177, from No.85 Squadron in tight formation for the Coronation Fly-past in June 1953. WM177 was lost in an accident in August 1953. (Key Publishing Ltd)

Furthermore there were instances where a circuit breaker associated with the AH inverter had been tripped when caught inadvertently by the sleeve of a navigator's flying overall. In this case there was speculation that failure of the artificial horizon may have contributed to a loss of control that in turn led to the crash.

Many years later, memories of this crash surfaced again in an odd way. In 1982 the *Lynn News & Advertiser* reported a strange tale related by a fourteen-year-old schoolgirl who lived in Sandy Lane. This young lady claimed to have had recurring dreams involving an RAF aeroplane crash and when she asked elderly neighbours if such an event had occurred in the area, she was told about the Venom that crashed in Reffley Wood, near her house twenty-eight years previously. The girl visited the wood and it was not long before she came across the large crater left by the crashing aeroplane and a little digging turned up some metal and canvas fragments. Helped now by school friends, she returned to the site several times to collect more fragments, the most prominent of which was part of a gold signet ring with part of a crest and the minute but legible engraving, 'Manners Maketh Man', that may have belonged to one of the airmen. Teachers and the local library helped the schoolgirl to piece together the story of that tragic event, but it is not known if the matter was taken any further.

This squadron was not having much luck with its commanders either. Second World War ace, Squadron Leader Michael Constable-Maxwell DSO DFC, replaced Anthony Jacomb-Hood, but after just a few months in post he too was succeeded by Squadron Leader Patrick Engelbach, who also had the misfortune to die in a Venom accident in Norfolk in February the following year.

The second phase of an air exercise codenamed *Momentum* took place overnight on 19/20 August 1953. Vampire NF10 and Meteor NF11-equipped night fighter squadrons were fully operational with crews at ten-minute readiness to scramble to intercept 'attacking' B-29 and Canberra raiders up to altitudes of 40,000ft and with – in the latter case – high Mach numbers.

The Met forecast predicted severe weather and icing conditions by the early hours and widespread thunderstorms rolled in across eastern England. Indeed the weather deteriorated so much that only the most experienced A- and B-rated night fighter crews were allowed to fly these interceptions. It was under these conditions that Flying Officer R.F. Cooper and his navigator Flying Officer M.J. Hart, from No.85 Squadron at RAF West Malling, took off in Meteor NF11, WM177 and did not return. The wreckage of their Meteor was found four miles north-west of RAF Oakington. A court of inquiry considered that the fighter would have been flying at high speed and near its critical Mach number in order to intercept its Canberra target. There was evidence of severe icing conditions that may have affected control surfaces, pitot head or other vital instruments. It crashed into the ground vertically and at high speed and both airmen died.

The following month, thoughts of exercises were put aside and the RAF turned its attention to entertaining the general public with the annual Battle Of Britain 'At Home' displays. Among the participating stations in September 1953 were Binbrook, Hemswell, Manby, Scampton, North Luffenham, Wyton and Coningsby, the latter hosting a crowd of 5,000. The weather was fine and sunny and all was going well at Coningsby until the display was marred by a tragic accident. Flying Officer Patrick Ward of No.74 Squadron from RAF Horsham St Faith thrilled the crowd with a display of aerobatics. Then, glistening silver in the sunlight, Meteor F8, WA836, came in at 300ft from the Boston direction, over the boundary

Panic reigns at RAF Coningsby air display on 19 September 1953 when Meteor F8 WA836 crashes on the airfield.

at an estimated speed of 400mph. An eyewitness said that without warning the jet tremored and the starboard engine tore away as the aircraft disintegrated a few hundred yards from the crowd. Wreckage was scattered across the airfield as men, women and children threw themselves to the ground with the thump of falling debris echoing around them. The VIP party escaped without a scratch when a large section of the engine and fuselage zipped past them and embedded itself two feet into the ground in the space between the control tower and the fire section garage. Miraculously, despite other substantial pieces just missing people, cars and buildings, there were only three people with minor cuts to be treated, slight damage to one car and a hole in the roof of one hut. Flying Officer Ward died instantly and the remainder of the flying programme was cancelled. On the same day, over at RAF Wyton's show, another Meteor F8, WA927, was lost when it broke up as it made a fast low-level run across the airfield. The pilot, Sergeant Warwick from No.56 Squadron, also died.

Sad to relate, since the end of the Second World War, a lengthy list of aircraft have been lost at or while practising for air shows in the UK. This region, for example, saw the loss of two Mosquitos and crew: one at Rempstone (Nottinghamshire) during RAF Wymeswold Battle of Britain display on 20 September 1947, and VA887 of No.139 Squadron, which dived into the ground during a low-level slow roll at Coningsby on 18 September 1948. In more recent times, a Fiat G-91 PAN, MM6254 from the Italian Air Force *Frecce Tricolori* team, with its pilot, was written off when it hit a tree near Eriswell while taking part in the Mildenhall air show on 27 May 1979. A US Navy T-34C Turbo Mentor also crashed at Mildenhall's show in 1983 and the tragic loss of the 'Vintage Pair' at Mildenhall is dealt with later in this book.

In the early 1950s, the Korean War occupied the attention and resources of Britain and the Commonwealth. In order to strengthen NATO air forces guarding western Europe at this volatile time with aircraft that were likely to be more effective against Soviet aircraft than those in the current RAF inventory, the RCAF was called upon to deploy a number of interceptor squadrons to England. Between late 1951 and June 1952, 410 (Cougar), 439 (Tiger) and 441 (Silver Fox) Squadrons of No.1 Fighter Wing RCAF took up residence at RAF North Luffenham in Rutland. Thus, in addition to the usual RAF inventory, an exciting new shape in the form of the swept-wing Canadair CL-13 Sabre – these were US North American F86E Sabres built under licence – could be seen frequently traversing the East Midlands, often at 40,000-plus feet altitude. The Canadians remained at North Luffenham for almost three years, during which time there was an inevitable crop of accidents before the Wing re-deployed to France and Germany at the end of 1954.

As a member of the Canadian aerobatic team *The Acromaids*, Flying Officer Hamilton had to be cool and calm, but this was put very much to the test when he was faced with the sweat-inducing 'will it/won't it?' question high over Skegness on 2 May 1952. The engine of his Sabre flamed out at 36,000ft and with the altimeter rapidly unwinding, he stayed resolutely with the aircraft, managing, after two attempts, to re-light at 12,000ft. The whole squadron thought this was a 'good show' and it gave everyone confidence that all was not lost if the burner went out in the air. However, despite pilot confidence, The Wash collected yet more hardware on 8 July when engine failure forced Flying Officer E.A. 'Al' Seitz of No.439 (Tiger) Squadron to abandon 19112. Flying as No.3 in a formation of four, the engine of his Sabre flamed out and he could not re-light it. He glided from 30,000ft down to 20,000ft before ejecting, and the fighter plunged into the sea off Hunstanton. Seitz ejected safely but he spent a miserable couple of hours being tossed around like a cork in the water because his dinghy would not inflate, since its rusty stopper allowed air to leak out. Skegness lifeboat was launched but could not find him, and it was not until a US Navy Grumman S-16A Albatross from Bentwaters circled the area, that he was seen and picked up by the amphibian

Canadair Sabre 19198 of No.439 Squadron RCAF. (Paul Martin/SPAADS)

and returned safely to North Luffenham. Al Seitz was lucky that time and pushed his luck still further when he ejected from a CF104 Starfighter over the Mediterranean on 13 August 1965. He commented afterwards: 'Well, at least the Med was warmer than the North Sea!' When the Squadron checked its other Sabres, more rusty stoppers were found.

Veteran Second World War pilot, Canadian Squadron Ldr Andrew Mackenzie DFC of 441 Squadron, escaped unhurt from a forced landing in Thurlby Fen, near Bourne (Lincolnshire) on 12 June when his Sabre 19189 suffered engine failure at 40,000ft. This aeroplane was one of four flying in close formation when the engine flamed out. Unable to re-light, he made a controlled gliding descent and a good approach to an open field where, just before touch down with the undercarriage retracted, he dumped the under-wing drop tanks and pulled off a very creditable 'landing', narrowly missing one very startled farmworker as the Sabre careered across the field. Squadron Leader Mackenzie was credited with shooting down eight enemy aircraft in the Second World War, and six months after this mishap he had the opportunity to go to war once again. Posted to Korea in December 1952 as a wing commander, Andy Mackenzie was himself shot down in an F-86 on his fifth operational sortie without being able to add to his score. He also survived that incident, but had to endure severe privations during the next two years as a prisoner of the North Koreans, before being released from captivity in December 1954.

A year later though, Flying Officer Joseph Jean Raymond Bédard – usually known as Ray – also from 439 Squadron, was not so fortunate. Ray had led a bit of a charmed life on the squadron so far. The squadron diary recorded that while taking off on 27 March 1953, in Sabre 19191, he was involved in a collision with 19196 flown by Flying Officer Wilkinson. There were no injuries to either pilot on this occasion, but '191 suffered extensive damage and '196 was slightly damaged in the incident on Luffenham's runway. Three months later in another runway incident, Ray blew the tyres on 19196 while aborting his take-off run after finding he could not persuade the Sabre to leave the ground. He emerged unscathed from that incident, too, but his luck finally ran out in Sabre 19193 during a training sortie over The Wash on 23 June 1953.

Flying Officer Ray Bedard RCAF, who died when Sabre 19193 crashed at Fosdyke on 23 June 1953. (Via Dave Stubley)

There was no flying scheduled for that morning, but after lunch a busy programme included practice interceptions, camera-gun attacks on target drogues and practice formation flying for the RAF Review or Great Coronation Fly-past, due to take place at RAF Odiham on 15 July. Ray was rostered for interceptions and was flying in company with Flying Officers Fowler and Wilkinson when he became separated from the formation and, with no warning, crashed on farmland near Algarkirk, south of Boston.

As always, these tragedies leave behind someone to grieve. In this case, it was Mizpah Emond who, in 2003, made an emotional journey from Canada to rural Lincolnshire to say goodbye to her first husband who died fifty years earlier. Mizpah was twenty-one years old and expecting their child when the news of husband Joseph Bédard's death was broken to her at their home in Melton Mowbray. She left England just four days afterwards and their son, who was unable to attend this ceremony, was born three months later. Now, fifty years on and remarried, Mizpah and members of her family came to White House Farm, near Fosdyke, to unveil a plaque dedicated to her pilot husband. The memorial is fixed to the roadside wall of the stable block whose roof was damaged by flying debris when the Sabre crashed in an adjoining field, and it was fitting that a strong breeze carried the stirring sound of bagpipes – played by niece Sylvie Bédard – across the fields where Ray died. The Lincolnshire Aviation Recovery Group, which had carried out a 'dig' at the crash site, was responsible for tracking down Ray's wife, erecting the plaque and organising the remembrance ceremony.

The Canadians lost another pilot, Flying Officer David Tracey, who died on 16 December 1953 when his Sabre 19137 ran out of fuel and crashed near Loughborough. Then came the mysterious loss of Wing Commander Walter Parks DFC★ in Sabre 19163 on 17 May 1954. 'Mystery Explosion off Lincolnshire Coast', ran the headline in the *Lincolnshire Echo*:

A loud explosion was heard at Skegness yesterday and it was thought to have originated over the sea about ten miles north of the town. Later it was stated that a Sabre jet fighter of the RCAF, engaged on a routine training flight was overdue at North Luffenham air station. Air-sea rescue aircraft from RAF Hemswell and RAF Topcliffe took part in the search. A spokesman for the RCAF said: 'The missing Sabre is now well overdue and must be presumed lost together with its pilot.'

At the time of the accident, Wing Commander Parks had only recently been appointed as Chief Operations Officer of No.1 Wing.

The RAF also operated the Canadair Sabre, initially with 2TAF in Germany, before No.66 Squadron at Linton-On-Ouse became the first unit in Fighter Command to be equipped with this jet. On 27 August 1954, during a routine formation sortie with two other Sabres, 66 Squadron lost XD776 (ex-RCAF 19797) when a fire started in the port ammunition bay. With the cockpit filling with smoke, Flight Lieutenant Gerald Gray opened the canopy but still found his forward vision impaired. When flames started to lick round him he ejected at 2,000ft. The Sabre F4 crashed at Home Farm, a mile from Blatherwyke, Northants. Flight Lieutenant Gray's safe exit added to his already eventful RAF career. Posted to North Africa during the Second World War he swam to safety when his ship was torpedoed then, flying Spitfires over Europe in 1945, he had to force-land behind enemy lines and was a Prisoner of War for three months. In December 1953 he crash-landed a badly damaged Meteor, receiving a Queen's Commendation for his actions, and in May 1954, when the Sabre he was flying suffered a flameout over the sea, he glided the aircraft down on to dry land. Lady Luck was certainly smiling on him. Handled well, the Sabre was good in a glide, as evidenced by an example in Korea that covered 100 miles from 45,000ft. During its three years in RAF service, fifty-nine Sabres (14 per cent of those delivered) were lost in accidents, in which twenty-two RAF pilots died.

'I think as long as there are aeroplanes, there will be accidents.' Thus declared the district coroner while returning a verdict of accidental death on Flight Lieutenant Ian Hart and Mr Cyril Brown, both of whom died when Meteor T7, WF823, in which they were flying, crashed in Grimsthorpe Park on 7 November 1952. At RAF Wymeswold on the morning of the accident there was no portent of the disaster to come. WF823 was wheeled out from No.504 Squadron hangar and Flight Lieutenant Hart flew it to RAF West Raynham with Flight Lieutenant Ronald Powling as passenger. According to an account in the *Lincolnshire Free Press,* Flight Lieutenant Powling said, 'They had found no fault in the aircraft. Mr Hart had left him and the Meteor was refuelled.'

The aircraft subsequently crashed on the outskirts of Little Bytham with two people on board: Flight Lieutenant Hart and a Mr Cyril Brown. Press reports are unclear as to the sequence of events, but it seems likely that Mr Brown, who was a civilian employee of the Air Ministry, may have asked for a lift to Wymeswold for official business reasons. The aeroplane was seen by two eyewitnesses flying low – at 200–300ft – and heading directly towards the wooded Park, where it was seen to explode among the trees. The T7 had a tandem cockpit enclosed by a long, heavily-framed canopy hinged to open to the starboard side. One of the essential pre take-off checks was to ensure the canopy locks were properly secured because if the canopy opened in flight, control of the aircraft became extremely difficult. As usual in such incidents, there was no clear explanation for the accident, although some reports have suggested that the cockpit canopy may have come open in flight and lodged inside the aeroplane.

At RAF Waterbeach, 1954 saw the start of a re-equipment programme to replace Meteor F8s with the new Supermarine Swift F1. For No.56 Squadron, this was not a happy process and it became not only the first, but also the last user of the Swift in the interceptor role. WK209 was the first aircraft to join the squadron on 20 February, but was lost when Squadron Leader Gordon Storey had to eject from it on 7 May. On charge by the end of February, WK208 followed it into the ground on 13 May, this time with fatal consequences. On 4 May, Waterbeach's OC Flying Wing, Wing Commander Michael Giddings OBE DFC AFC (later Air Marshal, KCB, AFC★) was lining up WK208 to land when the ailerons locked up. Unable to move the stick laterally and with little fuel left, he had to use all his flying skill to bring the Swift in safely. Subsequent inspection revealed no apparent fault and after an uneventful air test, WK208 was cleared to fly. On 13 May it was Flying Officer Neil Thornton's turn to take it into the air on what was only his second familiarisation sortie. Shortly after take-off, during a gentle turn to climb away, he reported that the aircraft was uncontrollable and that he was baling out. At 600ft the canopy was jettisoned but the Swift went into a dive and crashed two miles north-east of the airfield before Flying Officer Thornton could get out. As a result of this and other similar incidents, all Swifts were grounded pending investigation of their aileron control systems. Later, a modification was also made to lower the position of the face curtain firing handle on the ejector seat, which had been found difficult to grasp in the airflow rush encountered when the canopy was jettisoned.

During 1953, control of RAF Wittering passed from Fighter Command to Bomber Command. In December of that year, No.76 Squadron re-formed as a light bomber unit with the Canberra B2, one of three Canberra squadrons that in 1954 made up the Wittering Wing. A Canberra of No.76 Squadron and its crew of three was lost on 16 August when WH873 crashed into woodland on the nearby Burghley Estate that lay under the flight path just outside Stamford. Flight Lieutenant Kenneth Taylor (pilot), Flight Lieutenant John Marsden (navigator/observer) and Sergeant Alan Addy (navigator) were making a night landing approach under radar control (GCA) when the bomber flew into the ground a mile from touchdown.

Burghley Park, being under Wittering approach path, was no stranger to aero accidents over the years and collected another on 29 July 1955. Captain of Vickers Valiant B1, WP222 that day was Squadron Leader Eric Chalk AFC, holder of the London to Rome record (101 minutes in a Canberra) at the time. This No.138 Squadron bomber seems to have been the victim of mechanical failure, as an aileron trim tab was later found in a 'fully up' position, possibly the result of a runaway actuator mechanism.

WP222 lifted majestically from the Wittering runway and began a normal climb out. From the ground the Valiant was seen to reach about 6,000ft before starting a gentle turn to port instead of making the expected starboard turn onto its cross-country exercise track. When the

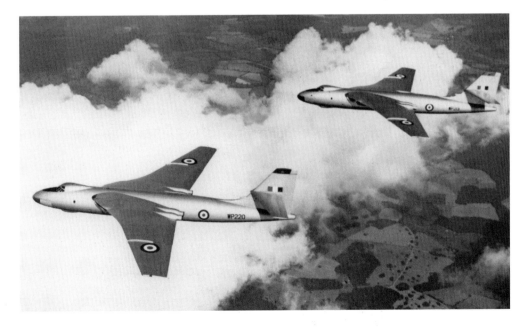

Vickers Valiant B1, WP220 and WP213 of No.138 Squadron.

nose began to drop and the bank increased dangerously, the crew entry door suddenly flew off and someone, later found to be the signaller Pilot Officer Arthur Lyons, baled out, but he died while doing so, possibly due to striking some part of the aircraft. Now the angle of bank became so steep that the huge bomber was side-slipping inexorably towards the ground. In the subsequent explosion, debris was strewn across the area known as Hills and Holes between Stamford and the village of Barnack. Other members of the crew, all of whom died, were Flight Lieutenant Andrew Allen, an engineering officer occupying the co-pilot's seat, and Flying Officer Theodore Corkin, navigator. The crew is buried side by side in Wittering village churchyard.

The arrival of the DH Vampire T11, complete with ejector seats, marked the beginning of a new concept for RAF Flying Training Command and also heralded the gradual closure of Advanced Flying Squadrons such as 206 AFS. The T11 was the first jet aircraft on which RAF trainee pilots would qualify for their wings during their time at Flying Training Schools.

Typical of the incidents involving this aircraft is one that occurred to XE961 of 8 FTS on 1 November 1955. The instructor, Master Pilot Francis Evans, and pupil, Acting Pilot Officer Robert Jago, were on what should have been a routine training flight from RAF Swinderby when problems occurred over The Wash. During a stall turn to starboard the Vampire rolled into a vicious spin to port. The instructor initiated normal recovery action but the rate of spin actually increased and when there seemed no possibility of recovery, the crew ejected at 15,000ft. According to the official report, the accident was attributed to incorrect recovery action being taken when, due to disorientation, the direction of the spin was not recognised.

In what was the first double ejection from a Vampire, both airmen baled out successfully and landed not far from the wreckage on Pocklington's farmland in Red Cow Drove, Holbeach Marsh. Holbeach fire brigade was quickly on the scene and fought the blazing aeroplane, travelling several miles to keep refilling their water-tender. Just over a year later, the matter of incorrect recognition of spin direction and attitude was also commented upon in the accident investigator's report into the loss of another Vampire T11, WZ429, from RAF College Cranwell, on 10 January 1957. On this occasion the pupil, Under Officer Martin Hicks, ejected safely, but for reasons not established, his instructor, Flight Lieutenant William Worsley, did not eject and died when the jet crashed at Sutterton Dowdyke, near Spalding.

Created in 1943 by the amalgamation of a number of independent units such as the Fighter Interception Unit, Air Fighting Development Unit and Fighter Leaders School, the original objective of the Central Fighter Establishment (CFE) was to increase the efficiency of fighter

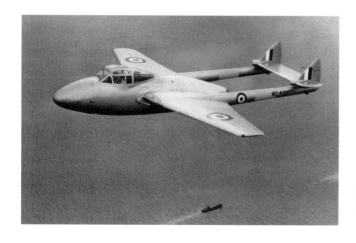

DH Vampire, WZ429, RAF College Cranwell crashed on 10 January 1957.

aircraft and crews in the many roles in which they were called upon to operate under war-time conditions. It also intended to create a link between those who used fighters and those who designed and made them. Clearly, at the end of the war, the pace of change – scientific, technological, strategic, tactical, etc. – continued into the new jet and atomic age. Naturally, too, new equipment in the form of aircraft, armament, radar, instruments and physiological aids would be designed, produced and tested during the manufacturing process. However, until the tactical and/or operational employment of all such devices is studied and tried, the powers that be will not know for certain whether they have achieved their original aim. This is where the CFE comes in.

The Establishment moved to RAF West Raynham after the war where it became an umbrella organisation for several specialist development units. It constantly evolved to take account, not only of changing RAF aeroplanes, but also the many different roles that went with that evolution. Aviation author Michael J.F. Bowyer summarised very succinctly the plethora of units and acronyms associated with CFE:

> The Air Fighting Development Squadron [AFDS] watched over the tactical development of the Meteor, Vampire, Venom, Swift and finally the Lightning, although AFDS flew the latter at Coltishall. The Day Fighter Leader School [DFLS] used Meteor 4s then 8s and evolved into the Day Fighter Combat School [DFCS] and later the Fighter Leader School [FLS]. The Night Fighter Leader School [NFLS] initially flew Mosquito 36s and later Meteor NF11s and NF14s and subsequently became the All Weather Wing [AWW, comprising AWDS and AWFCS] of CFE in 1951.
>
> These changes of names really meant very little but at least reflected tactical alterations from night fighting to all-weather operations. Fighter Command Instrument Training Squadron … became part of CFE in December 1952 and also working alongside CFE was the Naval AFDU, which conducted trials with the Wyvern, Attacker and Sea Venom from West Raynham.
>
> Gradually the CFE reduced its size [until] in 1959 the AFDS and AWDS moved out to Coltishall, leaving the Hunters of DFCS and AWFCS at West Raynham. These latter closed in 1962 leaving the two elements at Coltishall to proceed to RAF Binbrook in October 1962.

This, then, provides a background for some of the mishaps involving aircraft from West Raynham at this time. The All Weather Wing's inventory included Meteor NF14, WS784, an example of the final version of the Armstrong Whitworth night fighter fitted with the American APS-57 airborne radar – designated AI Mk 21 in RAF service.

With a full fuel load, including external ventral and wing tanks, sortie lengths with the NF14 could be stretched to just over an hour, depending of course on the altitude and speed profile of any particular flight. In the middle of 1955, trials began with a new version of the reliable *Gee* navigational system that it was hoped would enable pilots to quickly position their aircraft for a bad-weather Ground Controlled Approach, or even a visual approach, from about thirty miles out from an airfield, with the aim of wasting as little time as possible at the closing stage of a sortie when the fuel state might be critical.

Up at high altitude over The Wash, even as darkness fell on 24 January 1956, the weather was still quite bright and clear. Keeping a wary eye on the fuel gauges, Flight Lieutenant R.L. Bennett decided he was getting a bit low and brought a practice night interception exercise in WS784 to a close and headed for home. Bennett estimated he had sufficient fuel remaining to get him back to RAF West Raynham but as a precaution he decided to get his navigator, Flight Lieutenant A. Tanner, to bring them in on a direct approach using the *Gee* system. Approaching base and descending through cloud, Bennett called up Raynham tower only to find out that there was bad visibility and snow over the airfield. At 200ft altitude the *Gee* signals faded and Flight Lieutenant Bennett overshot the airfield. Carrying out a missed approach routine he climbed back up to 6,000ft where a fuel check showed he had just twenty gallons left. With no prospect of reaching the airfield before the tanks ran dry, Flight Lieutenant Bennett gave the order to bale out and they both abandoned the aircraft. Without the benefit of ejector seats both airmen had some difficulty in clearing the cockpit and Flight Lieutenant Tanner was struck a glancing blow by the tailplane as he broke clear of the cockpit. The crew landed safely near East Dereham while WS784 crashed at Gayton Thorpe near King's Lynn.

Around the same time, in addition to the aircraft mentioned above, CFE also had examples of the Canberra on its inventory. A PR7 photo-reconnaissance version of this versatile aircraft, WT529, came to grief five miles north of Grantham on 16 January 1956, together with a very experienced crew: Wing Commander Robert Cole DFC★ AFC★ (pilot), with 3,500 hours to his name, and Squadron Leader Peter Needham AFC (co-pilot), with 2,600 hours. Wing Commander Cole had been awarded both his DFCs in the Second World War, and his AFCs – and that of Peter Needham – post-war.

The crew took off from West Raynham, but after only fifteen minutes in the air returned to base to have some electrical faults rectified. When the work had been completed, the aircraft was declared serviceable and the crew took off again and left the circuit. A quarter of an hour later, WT529 was seen in level flight at about 3,000ft altitude. At this point it began to dive at an angle of 45°, but this increased quickly to a near vertical dive, leading to it hitting the ground and killing both airmen. Subsequent investigations suggested that a runaway trim motor may have produced a sudden nose down attitude from which, at that height and speed, no recovery could be made.

Coincidentally, a few weeks later, another Canberra, this time a T4 from No.231 OCU at Bassingbourn, crashed two miles west of Stilton in somewhat similar circumstances. Crewed by Flying Officer Jason Spokes and his navigator Flight Lieutenant Herbert Brice, it was carrying out a routine training flight on 24 February to practise asymmetric stalls and standard let downs. WJ871 was seen flying at 7,000ft by the OCU commander who was also in radio contact with it from his own aircraft nearby. Without warning, rapid and

Canberra PR7, WT504, of No.58 Squadron crashed near Chatteris on 24 October 1960.
(M. Retallack via R.C.B. Ashworth)

uncontrollable movement of the tailplane actuator to a fully nose-down trim position caused the jet to 'bunt' into a steep dive from which it did not recover. Both airmen died in the crash. The subsequent investigation report on the accident suggested that the actuator fault may have been caused by a short circuit between the pilot's press-to-talk radio button and the trim switch, both of which were located on the control column. It also noted that modified actuators were now being fitted.

Based at RAF Waterbeach, No.253 Squadron operated the Venom NF2 night fighter and on 27 September 1956, was one of many squadrons taking part in the year's first major air exercise, codenamed *Stronghold*. Fighter Command's task over a period of about one week was simply to intercept as great a proportion as possible of the raids mounted by various RAF Commands and NATO air forces.

At 10.52p.m., Flying Officer Terence O'Hare and his navigator Sergeant John O'Brien in WL832 were scrambled to intercept a target. Five minutes later both men were dead. The only eyewitnesses to the accident were two civilians who said they saw the aircraft for the brief space of time that its navigation lights were visible in a vertical path between the cloud base of 1,000ft and the ground. Their attention was attracted by the sound of an aircraft diving and it hit the ground and exploded half a mile from them at Sutton, near Ely. Accident investigators found an unusually large crater forty feet in diameter and in the near vertical dive, the engine had penetrated into the heavy blue clay to a depth of twenty-five feet. Each tip tank formed an adjoining subsidiary crater of ten feet across and nearly as deep. There were few clues as to the cause, and although the air brakes were found in the 'out' position, technical failure was felt to be an unlikely cause. An indication of the difficulties facing investigators at such times and the thoroughness with which they carried out their grim duties, can be seen from part of one of the reports on this incident:

> The indications are that the misfortune which overtook the aircraft was not the result of a technical failure in the airframe or the engine.
>
> It can be assumed that the pilot's and navigator's watches stopped on impact but as they were not apparently synchronised, neither can be accepted as showing the correct time of the accident. If either watch was correct, the aircraft struck the ground between two and five minutes after take-off. The distance in a straight line from Waterbeach to Sutton is seven and a half miles and allowing for the turn involved in reaching Sutton after a westerly take-off, the track of the aircraft would cover about ten miles. If the time elapsed were two minutes, this represents a ground speed of 300 mph or 260 knots.
>
> Alternatively, five minutes would allow for a climb on a track of about twenty miles to 17,000 feet or more, followed by a dive of increasing steepness. Unfortunately the track of the aircraft is not known. Sutton is NNW of Waterbeach and the aircraft was headed NNW when it hit but it was in a very steep dive. It may well have climbed in a spiral and finished NNW by coincidence.
>
> The case for two minutes is unlikely unless a sudden dive occurred from low altitude due to an inadvertent and very strong forward pressure on the control column such as might be the case with an inflated dinghy.
>
> The case for five minutes allows for the possibility of anoxia and the air brakes being out is suggestive of a last minute effort by the pilot to recover from a predicament of which he is suddenly aware.

But for all the painstaking investigation, no definite conclusion as to the cause could be reached.

One of the most exciting shapes to grace the sky during the 1950s was the delta wing Gloster Javelin, an interceptor fighter with all-weather capability. The fuel capacity of early models gave an unimpressive operational range of action, but the Javelin F(AW) Mk 5 redressed this with increased internal fuel capacity that allowed sortie times of sixty-five to seventy-five minutes. The resulting radius of action of about 230 miles could be further increased to about 400 miles when the aircraft was fitted with two under-belly fuel tanks.

In 1957 CFE West Raynham's All Weather Development Squadron (AWDS) was issued initially with two examples of the Mk 5 for trial purposes, both of which were lost in accidents but subsequently replaced. One of the new aircraft, Javelin XA642 'H', had undergone an engine change and on 6 December 1957, its two-man crew, Flight Lieutenants Arthur Wright and Reginald Ashworth, were briefed to carry out an air test on the new Sapphires. If this was successful, they were to link up with XA648 for some practice interceptions. Over The Wash, XA642 had been airborne for thirty minutes when Wright called up the second Javelin to arrange a rendezvous over West Raynham. Just one minute later, Flight Lieutenant Wright called again to report a double flameout. Calmly, Wright repeated this first on West Raynham approach frequency then on the distress frequency. After those transmissions, nothing more was heard from them again.

Seven naval vessels systematically searched the cold grey waters of The Wash, but all they came up with were the two ventral fuel tanks and the radome. The bodies of the crew were never found. Subsequently an investigation board, with conjecture being all it could offer, decided that both engines had flamed out above 30,000ft altitude and the pilot had been unable to re-light either of them. Because one of the recovered ventral tanks contained a turbine blade, it was considered the most likely cause of the flameout was due to an inboard

Gloster Javelin F(AW) Mk 5.

breakout of a turbine blade. This in turn probably punctured a fuel tank or pipeline setting off a chain of events leading to the total loss of the aircraft. Evidence of fire was also found in one of the ventral tanks. Torching of the main flame through the hole in the turbine may then have ignited escaping fuel that burnt cables to the VHF aerials, thus cutting off R/T communication. With this catastrophic chain of events, it was believed neither of the crew was able to eject, probably due to violent loss of stability because the fire may have weakened the tail assembly enough for it to break away.

While for their wives and six children, the loss of two husbands and fathers left an indelible mark on the families, it must have been particularly devastating for Flight Lieutenant Wright's American wife, who had lost her first husband during the Korean war only for her second to be taken from her in yet another air crash.

In 1956, still based at RAF Waterbeach, No.56 Squadron traded in its Meteors for the sleek swept-wing Hawker Hunter Mk 5. It is sometimes only a tiny component or omission that sets off a catastrophic chain of events. On the morning of 4 February 1957, Flight Lieutenant David Jones was bringing in Hunter WP115 on the final stages of a Ground Controlled Approach (GCA) exercise when the engine flamed out at 1,500ft altitude about seven miles from touchdown. The aircraft descended fairly steeply at this point and crashed into a ploughed field about five miles from the airfield. It was thought that Jones may have tried to re-light the engine and delayed his ejection for too long, or perhaps he stayed to try to avoid a village in his line of flight. Whatever the reason, Flight Lieutenant Jones ejected at very low altitude and died of injuries received when he struck the ground just as his parachute canopy deployed.

Although US bombers had been based in England since the early 1950s, it was not until the late '50s that the enforced removal of foreign aircraft from French soil meant more US fighter types would once again grace English skies. Thereafter The Wash air weapons ranges

Republic F-84F Thunderstreak of 55th FBS, 20th FBW USAF based at Woodbridge. (C.F.E. Smedley)

witnessed a procession of United States Air Force fast jets, beginning, for example, with Republic F84F Thunderstreak aircraft of 20th Fighter-bomber Wing based at Woodbridge. The 79th Fighter-bomber Squadron sustained a fatal casualty on 16 November 1955 when 52-6686 developed engine trouble. When it started a rolling motion, pilot First Lieutenant Edwin A. Kelly appeared unable to retain control at low altitude and died as the aircraft dived into the trees of Bedford Purlieu Wood, Wansford near Peterborough and exploded.

A routine low-level bombing practice went badly wrong for First Lieutenant Jack G. Rankin on 13 May 1957. In company with another Thunderstreak from 78 FBS, 81 FBW at Shepherds Grove, Rankin had just completed a bombing run on RAF Holbeach range when his aircraft, 52-7103, inexplicably dived into the marshland about a mile offshore and exploded. A rising tide prevented rescuers from reaching the crater on foot, and even though a helicopter was quickly on the scene, they had to wait until the tide receded before the grim recovery task could begin.

As has been made abundantly clear in the author's earlier book, *Combat Ready!*, air weapons training on The Wash ranges exacted a high toll of military aircrew and hardware in its first twenty years of operation up to the end of the Second World War. Furthermore, although well and truly established by the end of the 1950s, the development of jet age military technology had itself been achieved at a similarly high cost. The next five decades would witness an even greater leap forward in jet aircraft capabilities that in turn had its price, but despite this, served equally to re-emphasise the immense value of The Wash live firing ranges to the Royal Air Force and its NATO allies.

The 1960s got off shakily with the loss of English Electric Lightning F1, XG334 on 5 March 1960. Based at RAF Coltishall, aircraft 'A' of the Central Fighter Establishment's (CFE) Air Fighting Development Squadron (AFDS) was one of a development batch of Lightnings

English Electric Lightning F1A, XG334 of the Air Fighting Development Squadron, RAF West Raynham. Lost in The Wash on 5 March 1960.

used for a variety of flying experiments under simulated operational conditions. XG334 suffered hydraulic failure high over Norfolk, and with the complete loss of control-surface power, Squadron Leader R. Harding had no chance of landing his aircraft. So, trimming the aircraft in the direction of the sea, he ejected, parachuting to earth safely near the village of Syderstone in north Norfolk. Particularly anxious to recover this new-generation fighter, an Air Ministry salvage vessel, *Airmoor 2*, under the command of Captain K. Abbey, was rapidly despatched to The Wash where, despite assistance by an RAF Air Sea Rescue pinnace and several local fishing boats, an intense sea search of the area around Roaring Middle Light failed to find any trace of the missing aircraft.

With a spectacular advance in performance and designed from the outset as an integrated weapons system, the Lightning established a firm place in RAF history as its first truly supersonic fighter, entering squadron service with No.74 squadron in June 1960. Some years elapsed before the first fatality involving a Lightning occurred, but this was under slightly more unusual circumstances than an average squadron sortie. On 18 July 1963, Flight Lieutenant Alan Garside from No.111 Squadron at RAF Wattisham was detailed to take Lightning 1A, XM186, 'B' over to RAF Wittering and put on an aerobatics demonstration for students of the Imperial Defence College. Taking off at 3.30p.m., Garside pulled the fighter into the sort of steep climb that became a Lightning trademark. Climbing like a rocket to 4,000ft it banked into a horizontal turn to fly back towards the crowd. During this turn it entered a small patch of cloud and when the aeroplane emerged, it appeared to be in an uncontrolled spin and dived into the ground about 200yds from Collyweston water tower. Flight Lieutenant Garside died in the accident, the cause of which was unclear.

Speaking of firsts, it was 4 April 1960 when the first USAF F-100 Super Sabre went down on RAF Holbeach range. The sortie was meant to be just a routine training flight with some live firing passes for the jet-jockeys from 77th Tactical Fighter Squadron of 20th Tactical Fighter Wing (77TFS, 20 TFW) based at RAF Wethersfield. The 77th was no stranger to these skies, having been based, along with the 55th and 79th Squadrons comprising 20th Fighter Wing, at RAF Kings Cliffe during the Second World War and returning in 1952 to England, where it operated first with F-84G and then F-100D jets. Sadly it turned out to be the last flight for First Lieutenant Thomas R. Winsford when F-100D, 56-2994 dived into the mud flats for reasons that were, once again, never clearly established.

By this time, 81 TFW had been operating the McDonnell F-101A Voodoo fighter-bomber since 1958 from RAF Bentwaters, a USAF fighter base on the coast of Suffolk. Veteran Second World War ace Colonel Robin Olds – later to demonstrate in Vietnam that he had lost none of his old air-fighting skill – was commander of the 81st between 1963 and 1965.

In the single-seat F-101A he had a twin-engine and a tactical nuclear strike jet capable of over 1,000mph in level flight. This fighter-bomber was armed with four internal 20mm cannon but curiously, even though the 'A' model could carry a single 1,620lb or a 3,271lb tactical nuclear bomb on a centre-line pylon, it could not carry or deliver conventional bombs. It was intended to deliver the nuclear ordnance by means of avionics known as the Low Altitude Bombing System (LABS) and a technique known as 'toss-bombing', but although *The Weapon* – as it was euphemistically referred to – was said to have been carried on long distance training sorties over the Continent, there is no official evidence to suggest the F-101A carried it on practice sorties over The Wash ranges.

It is interesting to note that the emotive issue of *The Weapon* being in England and the danger it was perceived to pose, even while in storage, blew up (no pun intended!) as early as 1956. On 27 July a B-47 bomber from 307 BW, one of several operating from the base on a ninety-day rotation scheme from Lincoln (Nebraska) AFB, with no weapons on board, went out of control during a touch-and-go landing at Lakenheath airbase. It careered off the runway, crashed into a storage bunker containing three nuclear weapons

McDonnell Douglas F-101A Voodoo, 54-1444, 81st TFW USAF Bentwaters.

and exploded, killing its four-man crew. Each of the bombs in the store contained about 8,000lb of TNT as part of the trigger charge, which itself would have made a very nasty hole in the countryside had it gone up, but it was claimed that no nuclear material was actually in those weapons or the building in which they were stored. Fortunately, the blazing aircraft did not ignite the TNT so, apart from the localised devastation caused by the demise of the aeroplane, there was no nuclear contamination problem. This incident did not come to the general attention of the British public until late 1979, when the British press picked up the information from American sources discussing side issues in relation to the 'Three Mile Island' incident.

Returning to the F-101 now. On 5 August 1964, a Tactical Evaluation mission involving LABS bombing runs on Holbeach Range was being carried out by a flight of Voodoos from the 81st led by Captain Dee McCarter in 54-1446. In low visibility conditions, each aircraft made a couple of 'dry' runs across the target area then McCarter called the range control tower that he was starting 'hot' passes. Lining up 1446 he made the first run, simulated bomb release and pulled up in a climbing turn to starboard, heading out to sea. But instead of levelling out, the Voodoo's bank tightened inexorably until it crashed into the sea with a column of smoke marking the spot. Range control immediately aborted the exercise and set emergency procedures in train. Skegness lifeboat was launched and an RAF rescue helicopter scrambled to the scene, together searching an area of The Wash about three miles off the range, where Captain McCarter's body was recovered later that day. Next day, during salvage operations to recover wreckage from the Voodoo, an RAF helicopter had to make a forced landing on the river bank at the mouth of the Nene due to engine failure, but no one was hurt in that incident. Somewhat subdued by the loss of their buddy, the returning pilots were given this advice by Colonel 'Chappie' James, the 81 TFW director of operations at the time: 'Don't fly scared; fly smart.'

Although no exact cause was determined, two possible reasons might account for the accident. One is that the F-101 occasionally suffered from a nose-high, pitch-up problem that was never fully solved, even after an inhibitor was retro-fitted by McDonnell Douglas during 1956. Colonel Olds himself is said to have expressed the opinion that 'it did not take much to make the F-101 pitch-up suddenly and without warning.' Apparently this attitude change was caused by the way air flowed over its mainplanes and under its high-set tail. The other – and maybe more likely – possibility is that, at low altitude over the sea, given the reported low visibility at the time, the pilot may have 'lost' his horizon and become disoriented, a situation that would be neither the first nor last such occurrence over The Wash.

Including prototypes, eighty-six Handley Page Victors, last of the three famous V-bombers, were built for the RAF. Entering service in 1957, seventeen of these were lost in accidents of varying degrees of severity around the globe, with six occurring in this region between 1960 and 1982. During that period, this aesthetically pleasing aircraft could be seen at RAF Cottesmore, Marham, Wittering and Wyton, as well as further afield at Gaydon and Honington, and three examples of mishaps now follow.

XL159, a B2, was allocated to the A&AEE at Boscombe Down for, among other things, tests on whether to fit automatic leading edge flaps or fixed 'droop' leading edges. Having been fitted with the fixed droop – which became the accepted configuration – during a low-speed handling trial flight from Radlett on 23 March 1962, the experimental life of XL159 came to an abrupt end. Handley Page test pilot Paddy Murphy carried out some tests at 16,000ft altitude, including setting up a landing configuration that somehow resulted in the bomber entering a stable stall. This developed into a flat spin that, due to impaired airflow around the high-set tail in this condition, could not be recovered. Now losing altitude very fast, at 10,000ft altitude Murphy ordered the three civilian flight test crew in the back to bale out; then he and co-pilot Flight Lieutenant J. Waterton ejected. The occupants of the rear compartment did not have ejector seats and only one, navigator Mr J. Tank, was able, with extreme difficulty, to overcome the g-force and bale out. His two colleagues, Mr M. Evans and Mr P. Elwood, died in the crash that followed. The Victor came down on a house at Stubton (Lincolnshire), between Newark and Sleaford, killing two occupants: Mrs Annie Gibson and her niece Miss Cecily Gibson, and injuring Mr and Mrs Denis Burtt.

1963 saw the Victor B2 in service with No.100 Squadron at Wittering, and it was XM714 that came to grief on 20 March, three miles north-east of the station, while participating in a night bombing exercise with a supernumery exercise-umpire on board. New from the factory the previous November, XM714 made a normal take-off but, passing 800ft, a fire warning light appeared on No.2 engine. Co-pilot Flight Lieutenant B. Jackson warned the aircraft captain, Flight Lieutenant Alexander Galbraith, who told him to advise Wittering ATC before telling the rear crew to check their parachutes. As the captain began to claw for height, the speed fell away and the aircraft began juddering severely until, at about 5,000ft, it flicked over to port and fell away in a partially inverted spin. Flight Lieutenant Galbraith ordered the crew to abandon the aircraft but due once again to the high 'g' forces in the spin, only Flight Lieutenant Jackson escaped in his ejector seat. The other crew members who died were: Flight Lieutenant Edward Vernon, navigator; Flight Lieutenant James Churchill, navigator/plotter; Flying Officer Terence Sandford, AEO and Master Navigator Albert Stringer, an 'umpire' from 139 Squadron. The aircraft crashed near Barnack, three miles north of Wittering.

It was during another demonstration flight, this time for the benefit of the press, that Handley Page Victor, XM716, was lost together with its crew. XM716 was the first of the SR2 version to go into service with No.543 Squadron, a photo-reconnaissance unit based at Wyton. On 29 June 1966, its crew were briefed to show off this new PR aircraft and

Handley Page Victor SR2, XM716, moments before it disintegrated and crashed near RAF Warboys on 29 June 1966. (Courtesy of Handley Page Association)

the squadron's return to operational status at a demonstration for the press over the nearby former wartime bomber airfield of Warboys. All went well until the pilot pulled the aircraft into a high speed, high-G, turn at low level and the bomber broke up under the stress. All on board died: Squadron Leader John 'Dutch' Holland, aircraft captain; Flying Officer Harry Walsh, co-pilot; Flight Lieutenant Roy Norman, navigator; and Flight Lieutenant Kenneth Smith, air electronics officer.

Having had to leave its base at Chaumont, France as a result of a change in the French government's view of its membership of NATO, 15 January 1960 saw the first twenty-two F-100s of 48 TFW land at RAF Lakenheath. The remaining thirty aircraft flew in over the next ten days, marking the beginning of a long association of the Wing with this region.

Lieutenant Colonel Winfield W. Scott, the CO of 492 TFS, had a lucky escape from F-100D 56-2996, when its engine flamed out on 23 May 1966, but equally lucky were three young women chopping sugar beet on a farm near Metheringham. Just minutes before his jet crashed into their field, spraying cannon shells and debris in all directions, they had gone into a house fifty yards from the impact point to have their breakfast. Lieutenant Colonel Scott ejected safely but suffered injuries to both legs when he landed by parachute at Timberland. Flaring magnesium and exploding ammunition prevented the fire brigade from tackling the blazing wreckage for some time, but once it was under control, the ladies were quite nonplussed about their narrow escape and returned to work, 'just as if nothing had happened.'

Fortunately almost five years elapsed before another accident occurred in the vicinity of Holbeach range. 48 TFW was still resident at Lakenheath with the F-100D Super Sabre when the 452 TFS lost an aircraft on 5 May 1969. Two F-100s, 55-2846 and 56-3214, were tasked for a formation exercise rounding off with live firing on Holbeach Range. Both aircraft

North American F-100D, 56-2996, 492 TFS USAF, came down near Metheringham, Lincs on 23 May 1966.

were flying towards the range from the Wisbech direction when 3214 suffered engine failure. Captain Robert E. Riggs ejected safely while his jet crashed into farmland half a mile south of Thorney Toll, just 400yds from a group of agricultural workers who dived for cover as the aircraft plunged towards them. The F-100 disintegrated in an explosion that left the wreckage barely recognisable as an aeroplane, except for the fin and rudder assembly. Captain Riggs floated down to earth near March.

Later the same year, on 18 December, 20 TFW at Wethersfield lost an F-100D when 56-3001 from 55 TFS crashed into The Wash, two miles off Leverton sea bank while using Wainfleet Range. Its pilot, Captain J.M. Skiff, also ejected safely, parachuting into the village of Old Leake from where he was airlifted by a helicopter based at Coltishall and taken to Coningsby for a medical check-up before returning to his unit.

Meanwhile, from the mid-1960s, Douglas RB-66 Destroyer aircraft of 10 Tactical Reconnaissance Wing at Alconbury, its long-term resident unit, gave way to the ubiquitous McDonnell Douglas F-4 Phantom, and the RF-4C model would become a regular sight and sound in Fenland skies almost twenty-four hours a day, Monday to Friday. The 24th day in February 1970, though, was not a good day for the Wing. That was the day they lost RF-4C Phantom 64-1015 and its pilot through a series of 'Murphy's Law' events.

Lieutenant Colonel Richard F. Murray, 30 TRS operations officer, was airborne for a routine training flight with his navigator, Major Ronald J. McEwan when their RF-4C Phantom, 64-1015, suffered a major systems failure and the resultant fire spread to the cockpit. Major McEwan got clear of the aircraft safely, but Lieutenant Colonel Murray was unable to exit the aircraft and died when the Phantom plunged into farmland at Baldwin's Drove, Outwell near Wisbech.

In those days, former Sergeant Paul Whitman USAF was a technician with 10 TRW, specialising in autopilot avionics on the RF-4C. He remembered this tragedy clearly enough still to get upset by the sadness of it when he recalled his version of the events of that day.

McDonnell Douglas RF-4C Phantom, 64-1015, 10th TRW, Alconbury was lost in a crash at Baldwin's Drove, Outwell near Wisbech on 24 February 1970. (Pete Esposito)

Just as 1015 was getting close to Alconbury, the first event in the chain happened. Sergeant Whitman explained:

> USAF Command called a surprise ORI [Operational Readiness Inspection] for the base. An unexpected and unannounced inspection aircraft landed, the alarm went up and this meant that we had to launch every airplane as soon as humanly possible. Anything that was not 'RED-X grounded' lined up at the end of the runway for take-off. Excluding the ORI team's aircraft, if it looked like an aircraft it had to fly immediately – and they timed us!
>
> So, as 1015 started into the pattern and radioed for landing clearance, the crew was notified that the base had just gone into an ORI-state and they could not land. The crew was instructed to fly over to a nearby RAF base and kill time by doing some touch-and-go's to show off the Phantom; the RAF having just ordered its own first F-4s from McDonnell Douglas.
>
> The pilot, who was operations officer of 30 TRS, lived on base with his family and he was known by all the ground crew to be a regular guy and a good pilot. The story was that this aircraft was alone on a flight returning from a US base in Germany where the pilot and navigator had gone for annual altitude chamber qualification or something like that. Because the RF-4C was classed as being on a ferrying mission, all the camera gear had been removed from the nose compartment, as was the custom whenever the aircraft were not on a routine reconn mission. As was also the custom whenever this occurred, the crew would bring back souvenirs from Germany for themselves and whatever their friends had ordered. All quite common practice by the way and this particular sortie was no different, so the nose compartment of 1015 was full of all sorts of things.
>
> Anyway, off they went and did several low passes and touch-and-go's, showing off the aircraft to use up time. At some point – whether during the touch-and-go's or heading back to Alconbury is not clear – the crew realised the aircraft was on fire and it is thought this

had started in the nose compartment. They climbed to a safe altitude and both wanted to bring it in but with flames advancing into the front cockpit, the pilot decided to eject the navigator [a late model gave the pilot this control].

The story goes that the pilot had recently returned from [Viet] Nam where he regularly flew the Thud [F-105 Thunderchief] or F-102. It is speculated that as he went to eject from the F-4, he instinctively grabbed the side handle and pulled it instead of either the between-the-legs or face-curtain handle. On his other fighters [the side handle] was the ejection handle but on the F-4 it is the ground emergency eject system that fires the canopy and cuts ALL of the restraining belts holding the crewman in the ejection seat. In addition, with the restraining belts cut, the ejector seat will not fire so he was screwed; flying a burning ship with no way out. He died while trying to crash-land the burning aeroplane.

While patiently awaiting re-equipment with the F-111 and having relocated to RAF Upper Heyford in Oxfordshire, F-100s of 20 TFW still made the cross-country journey to conduct live firing practice on Holbeach range. The day of 28 May 1970 saw the loss of Super Sabre 55-3655 from 77 TFS when it went down in The Wash between the range and Hunstanton. Captain Guy F. Baker ejected successfully from his stricken aircraft, but was slightly hurt in the process. He was picked up from his survival dinghy by the coastal survey vessel HMS *Enterprise*, then airlifted by helicopter to RAF Lakenheath base hospital.

RAF Honington in Suffolk was principal UK land base for the RAF Buccaneer in its anti-shipping role, although in those days the Royal Navy also operated the S2 version from its fleet carriers. Occasionally Royal Navy squadrons were deployed to RAF Honington and it was from there that Buccaneer S2, XV351, R/030 of 809 Squadron (HMS Ark Royal) met a sudden end on 11 November 1974. Carrying eight 4lb (2kg) practice bombs, the crew of XV351, Lieutenant Stephen Kershaw RN (pilot) and Lieutenant David Thompson RN (observer), were tasked to drop these bombs one by one from low level on the bombing target at RAF Wainfleet range, which covered a 42km² area between Boston and Skegness.

North American F-100D, 55-3655, 77th TFS, 20th TFW USAF, lost in The Wash, 28 May 1970.

Hawker Siddeley Buccaneer S2, XV351, 'R 030' No.809 Sqn, Royal Navy. This aircraft crashed into The Wash on 11 November 1974.

As daylight began to fade, the Buccaneer was seen starting its second pass across the range when, suddenly, the sky was lit up by a brilliant flash. XV351 had ploughed into the mud flats and exploded. Both airmen managed to eject and with darkness falling, the crew of a dredger, the *Jean Ingelow*, who had spotted a little white flashing light that was believed to be one of the airmen, went to investigate but ran aground on the ebb tide. The light was on Lieutenant Thompson's equipment and he was quickly rescued by the crew of the Boston Pilot cutter *Arthur Lealand*, also fortuitously close by as it returned from a pilotage job. The accident occurred in the area known as Clay Hole, just after high tide, but the *Arthur Lealand*, being shallower draft, could get near enough to pick up the floating observer. It was still touch and go though because the pilot boat's screw fouled Thompson's parachute lines, threatening to drag the injured airman under the water, until two seamen jumped in and cut him free. When the tide had finally gone right out, the crew of the stranded *Jean Ingelow* left their ship and began searching the sands where, shortly afterwards, the body of Lieutenant Kershaw was found. He had suffered injuries during ejection and drowned before he could be rescued.

Significant changes were underway as USAF Tactical Fighter Wings in England began to receive the General Dynamics F-111 fighter-bomber during 1970. Having now given up its F-100s, 20 TFW at Upper Heyford operated the F-111E version and this soon became a familiar sight and sound at low level all over the region and The Wash ranges.

The first F-111 to be lost by 20 TFW in a training accident over the ranges was 68–0060 from 77 TFS on 5 November 1975. While running in to the Wainfleet range at low level, a bird struck and penetrated the right-hand cockpit windscreen. Captain James E. Stieber called an eject and he, with his WSO (weapons systems operator) Captain Robert L. Gregory,

General Dynamics F-111 E, 68-0060, as 'JT' 77 TFS, 20 TFW Upper Heyford, lost in The Wash on 5 November 1975.

The F-111 crew escape module recovered after the accident to 68-0060. (67 ARRS, USAF Woodbridge)

Phantom FGR2, XV405 of 228 OCU RAF Coningsby. (C.F.E. Smedley)

parted company from '0060 in the cockpit escape capsule peculiar to the F-111. Although Gregory was injured when the windshield burst, both airmen survived the ditching of the capsule in the cold waters of The Wash just off Freiston Shore. Eventually that escape capsule itself was recovered by 67 Air Refuelling & Rescue Squadron from RAF Woodbridge and it is believed to have languished at that base until acquired from the USAF by Dumfries & Galloway Aviation Museum in 1986, ending up on display a long way from the scene where it fulfilled its purpose most effectively.

A few weeks after this incident, RAF Coningsby lost Phantom FGR 2, XV405, this time from No.228 Operational Conversion Unit, when a control systems failure forced pilot Flight Lieutenant M. Smith and his navigator Flight Lieutenant R. Lunn to abandon the aircraft. As it crashed into the sea off Skegness pier – missing the roof of the coastguard hut by inches – Mr B. O'Reilly, remaining steadfastly at his post in the hut, spotted the airmen descending by parachute and promptly called out the lifeboat. Both airmen were fished safely from the water, landed on the beach and soon whisked back to Coningsby by helicopter. In a ceremony later to mark its gratitude, a grateful 228 OCU presented the RNLI crew with a squadron plaque that is proudly displayed in the new lifeboat station to this day.

The worst air accident in this region since the Second World War also involved a US aircraft and occurred on 28 August 1976. The Lockheed C-141A Starlifter was a regular sight in the sky, climbing out or letting down as they made their way between various bases in the USA and RAF Mildenhall in England. Carrying 27,000lb of cargo, a normal crew of six, plus eight members of a reserve crew and four other passengers, this day should have been just another one of these routine transport flights – except that a string of 'sod's law' events came together once again to precipitate a major air catastrophe.

Departure point for C-141A, 67-0006, from 438MAW, was McGuire AFB, New Jersey, and it had almost completed its 3,648-mile flight when it ran into the forces of nature that were to destroy it. Since being built, 67-0006 had accumulated 15,000 hours in the air and

Lockheed C-141 A Starlifter, 67-0006, 438 MAW, McGuire AFB.

subsequent official investigations into the accident identified that it had a history of problems with its APN-59 weather radar equipment – alleged to have been faulty on eight occasions prior to this flight.

The weather radar was declared operational but shortly after take-off the set went faulty once again. The flight-deck crew, led by Captain John R. McNally and co-pilot First Lieutenant David A. Lynch, did not feel this was worthy of an abort as severe weather was not forecast. A couple of hours into the flight, UK weather sources issued a warning of moderate to severe clear air turbulence from 24,000ft up to 40,000ft altitude. The crew of 67-0006 did not get this report. Four hours into the flight and the crew received a weather report that informed them of cloud at low level, winds gusting from 12 to 22 knots, and visibility of five miles in thunderstorms. One hour out, they tried to get an update from Mildenhall but could not make contact, although another station responded and advised thunderstorms up to 26,000ft. Beginning the descent, the C-141 entered clouds and at 15,000ft the crew, now in contact with Mildenhall air-traffic control, asked for a route around the bad weather. Mildenhall control informed the aircraft that, due to its own primary radar being u/s, it would be difficult to provide the necessary vectors to do so. The aircraft then entered the front of a very strong line of thunderstorms encountering at some point what a later estimate suggested might have been a vertical 100mph down draught with catastrophic results.

The starboard wing was ripped away from the fuselage and the upper half of the vertical stabiliser broke off. It was seen to emerge from clouds at about 2,000ft, in flames and with the major missing components fluttering down with it to explode on farmland in Old Knarr Fen Road, near Thorney. There was no way the eighteen people on board could survive such a crash. A memorial stone and plaque near the site mark the passing of these unfortunate airmen.

Coincidentally, the USAF lost a second C-141A, 67-0008, the very same day. That crash, which occurred in Iceland, also cost the lives of those on board, but was not caused by weather conditions.

MD F-4 D Phantom, 66-8781, as 'HB' of 389 TFS, 12 TFW in 1971, crashed in The Wash on 6 July 1977 while serving with 23 TFS, 51 TFW, Spangdahlem AFB.

In the 1970s, RAF and USAF Phantoms were a common sight around The Wash area and occasionally, Continental-based units, as well as those in the UK, used the ranges. For example, 52 TFW operated the F-4D model at Spangdahlem airbase in what was then West Germany.

It is believed an engine flameout was responsible for the loss of 66-8781 from 23 TFS, 52 TFW in The Wash on 6 July 1977. Pilot, Captain K.R. Dolan, died in the crash, but his WEO, Captain R.L. Logan, ejected and although slightly injured, was eventually rescued from The Wash by an RAF Whirlwind HAR 10 helicopter scrambled from RAF Leconfield.

Come rain or shine, night bombing practice on RAF Wainfleet range has been a regular part of Fenland life for decades. RAF and USAF jets thunder at low level – above minimums of course! – across towns like Spalding following course of the River Welland to the target area. The day of 12 December 1979, though, was a wild weather night for Heyford's F-111s and well dark by 6.30p.m. as 68-0045, of 79 TFS, 20 TFW began its bombing run. But it never completed the mission. Wainfleet range staff saw it go into a dive and hit the sea before the crew could eject, killing Captain Randolph P. Gaspard (pilot) and Major Frank B. Slusher (WSO). Despite an intensive air and sea search in gale force conditions, it was only after two days that some wreckage of the aircraft was found. At the time of his death, Captain Gaspard was on an exchange posting to the 79th from 380 BW at Plattsburgh AFB.

RAF Wittering soon became known as the 'Home of the Harrier', and the 1970s saw the GR3 version of the remarkable BAe Harrier being operated by No.1 Squadron and No.233 OCU. Ever since, there are few days when Harriers are not seen transiting the Fens to and from The Wash ranges, with a bit of aerobatics and dog-fighting thrown into the mix as well.

XV756, '26', was on a routine flight to the bombing area on 8 November 1979 when it suffered an engine fire and was destroyed in a crash on Holbeach range. It caught fire and came down about two miles out from the shore, but the pilot, Falklands combat veteran and former Red Arrow, New Zealander Flight Lieutenant Ross Boyens, ejected safely and landed close to the sea bank, where his erstwhile rescuers caught up with him as he walked along the

Harrier XV756 as a GR1 with early nose configuration at No.233 OCU. Modified to GR3 standard at the time of its crash on 8 November 1979. (Tony Hancock)

bank towards the range camp. Eyewitnesses in Hunstanton saw 'a triangle of flames' fall from the sky and crash into the marsh. Another oft-quoted reason for the cause of this particular accident was that a ricochet from one of its own cannon shells had hit the Harrier, but this theory was never proven.

Not so fortunate was Flying Officer John Sewell from 233 OCU at Wittering, who died when his GR 3, XV742, crashed on Holbeach range on 28 October 1983. The Harrier was seen to pull out of a shallow dive after making a firing pass at the ground targets. It was in a tightly banked turn from which it dived into the mudflats and completely disintegrated on impact. Recovery of the debris was severely hampered by the tidal flow and took several days to complete. At the inquest into Flying Officer Sewell's death, it was stated that the board of enquiry considered it a possibility that this Harrier may also have been struck by a ricochet 30mm shell that may even have hit the pilot. However, despite this speculation and an extensive investigation, no positive cause for the accident could be established.

The shattered engine from Harrier XV742.(*Lincolnshire Free Press*)

Sepecat Jaguar GR1, XX122, seen here with No.54 Squadron at RAF Luqa in 1978. (F. Coleman via R.C.B. Ashworth)

The Wash ranges played host to many foreign aeroplanes visiting the region to participate in the ever-growing number of NATO air exercises and, of course, many foreign pilots had exchange postings with the RAF. One such pilot was Captain Tore Bjornstad, a Norwegian AF pilot stationed at RAF Coltishall with No.54 Squadron. The squadron operated Jaguar GR1 aircraft and it was in one of these, XX122 'GA', that Captain Bjornstad met with a fatal accident over Holbeach range on 2 April 1982.

This aircraft was No.3 in a formation awaiting the arrival of a fourth Jaguar before beginning weapons training runs over the range. The weather was hazy, so the leader cautioned the pilots that conditions would be conducive to disorientation and reminded them to keep checking attitude instruments. It was decided that the fourth aircraft would fly to the range alone to carry out a weather check while the others remained at 1,000ft in a holding formation. As No.4 Jaguar passed beneath the holding formation at 450ft, its pilot noticed No.3 bank away from the formation and head towards him, at the same time being called on the radio by Captain Bjornstad to say he was in visual contact with No.3 and would follow him through the range. The No.4 Jaguar continued through the range area but Captain Bjornstad did not, and when he could not be contacted by radio, the alarm was raised. Captain Bjornstad's aircraft was later found to have crashed into the sea half a mile off Heacham. A reconstruction of the final flight path of XX122 suggested that in the descending and accelerating turn towards No.4, its pilot may have become disoriented due to the haze and unaware of his closeness to the sea. Wreckage of XX122, containing the body of the pilot, was recovered by HMS *Kinloss*.

The Royal Netherlands Air Force No.311 Squadron lost F-16 Fighting Falcon, J626, on 13 June 1986, believed to be the only one of this type ever lost in the region. One of four F-16s on a NATO exchange attachment to RAF Coningsby, it suffered an engine flameout during a training sortie over The Wash. The pilot was unable to relight the burner and had to eject over the sea. He came down safely while his jet joined the long line of aeroplanes hidden beneath the waves of The Wash.

GD F-16 A, J-626, No.211 Squadron, Royal Netherlands Air Force. (John Woodrow)

There had been a series of unit changes at Alconbury since May 1976, when Northrop F-5E Tiger IIs of the 527th Tactical Fighter Training 'Aggressor' Squadron replaced one of the 10th TRW RF-4 Phantom squadrons and again in 1982 when USAF SAC deployed the 17th Reconnaissance Wing with Lockheed TR-1 and U-2 reconnaissance aeroplanes. In August 1987, 10 TRW was redesignated as 10 TFW and re-equipped with the last American type to grace the skies before the USAF finally pulled resident aircraft out of Alconbury in 1992. This was the formidable Fairchild Republic A-10A Thunderbolt II ground attack fighter of which, in addition to those at Alconbury, 108 aircraft also operated with the huge, six-squadron 81 TFW based at Bentwaters/Woodbridge, the first overseas unit of the USAF to receive the A-10 in 1978.

The first A-10A to be lost in the region was 79-0083 from the 81st at Bentwaters on 8 May 1981. First Lieutenant Henry L. Gagne was No.2 in a pair of A-10s that departed Bentwaters for a training mission to RAF Wainfleet air weapons range. After two 'dry' and three 'hot' low-angle strafe passes using the huge, nose-mounted GAU-8A 30mm, multi-barrel gun, First Lieutenant Gagne called the tower and at 2.45p.m. came in for his first low-angle bomb delivery run. Without warning, 79-0083 flew into the ground on The Wash shore near Friskney and disintegrated. First Lieutenant Gagne attempted to eject, but sustained severe injuries from which he died later that evening in RAF Nocton Hall hospital.

In the years that followed, few days passed when the A-10 was not seen in these skies. Jinking around at what seemed like rooftop height in groups of two, three or four, it was a standing joke around the Fens that if you spotted three close by then you could be sure the fourth would creep up on you and buzz you even lower! They did, however, roam far and wide across the UK. On 22 December 1988, for example, 81-0986 from 511 TFS was returning to Alconbury from Pembrey air weapons range in West Wales when the pilot, First Lieutenant Frank M. Cavuoti, declared an emergency because his fuel system packed up. Both engines flamed out and the pilot ejected safely, ten miles east of his base. The aircraft was destroyed when it fell into open farmland.

Fairchild Republic A-10 A, 80-0183, 81st TFW, that crashed at Benwick.

Panavia Tornado GR1s, upper: ZA591 'F', and ZA592 'G', from No.9 Squadron. (BAe)

Not so lucky was Captain Donald R. Roberts from 510 TFS, 81 TFW who, flying 80-0183 as No.1 of a pair, was airborne on a Flight Lead Upgrade mission on 17 April 1989. While simulating a 'dry' close air-support manoeuvre at low level, his aircraft flew into the ground around Benwick, near Chatteris (Cambridgeshire) and he was killed. A small wooden cross has been erected at the site in his memory.

Equally prolific over the area were the new Panavia Tornado GR1s of the RAF, and it was not long before these entered the accident statistics. First to go, on 27 September 1983, was ZA586 'A' from No.9 Squadron based at RAF Honington. The bomber was on its way back to base from a training sortie over the North Sea when it suffered a complete loss of electrical power to the instruments and engine controls. The pilot, Squadron Leader Michael Stephens, ordered his navigator, Flight Lieutenant N. Nickles, to eject, which he did successfully, but Squadron Leader Stephens was himself unable to eject before the aircraft crashed on Wolferton Marsh, not far from Sandringham. All Tornados were grounded for a week while an investigation took place, and it was later reported that modifications were made to all similar aircraft in service. A memorial plinth has been erected at this site.

Just one month later on 28 October – the same day as the Harrier accident mentioned above – a second Tornado, this time GR1, ZA558, from 617 Squadron at Marham, was lost at the eastern end of The Wash. This set off much speculation in the press and among the local Members of Parliament about safety issues with the new aeroplane. This Tornado was returning to base after a sortie over the North Sea when the accident happened. The navigator, Squadron Leader G. Thurston, also survived and reported that the aeroplane had inexplicably begun rolling and losing height. He was unable to get any response from the pilot Flight Lieutenant Ian Dixon and, thinking he may have been incapacitated in some way, Thurston operated both ejector seats just before the aircraft reached fully inverted, close to the surface of the sea. Squadron Leader Thurston was slightly injured during the ejection and was rescued from his survival dinghy by the crew of the German ship *Lynn*. The pilot's seat is believed to have fired fractionally after the navigator's, just as the aircraft became fully inverted, and would have been directed into the sea. Flight Lieutenant Dixon was posted as missing. This was indeed a grim day for the RAF.

Ten years were to elapse before 20 TFG sustained another F-111 loss in this region, but when F-111E, 68-0001 erupted into a thousand pieces on 5 February 1990, it was as if the clock had been turned back to 1917 in the flash of the explosion. After turning over the preliminary orange range marker near Fishtoft Cut End, the fighter-bomber, one of a pair tasked to drop six small practice bombs each, appeared not to level off at the usual 200ft before running on to a target on the RAF Wainfleet range.

Located just yards from the site of the First World War airfield at Freiston Shore is the Plummers Hotel, watering hole for many RNAS pilots all those years ago. Although pretty used to the low level antics of aeroplanes using the range, that night pub landlady Norma Kavanagh thought she and her pub were 'goners' when an F-111 screamed over the rooftop before hitting the sea a mile and a half away. Interviewed by the *Boston Citizen*, she said:

We were so lucky that it didn't crash here. Just a few seconds earlier and it would have landed on top of us. I've been told it was like a ball of fire as it passed over the pub – my God we were so lucky! I was in my lounge when I saw a massive explosion, one moment the sky was flames and then it was all smoke. They didn't have a chance to get out. They fly really low over here, sometimes the place shakes, but we have got quite used to it.

As soon as the alarm was raised, civilian authorities were quickly on hand to search for survivors. At first it was believed the aircraft had crashed near Wrangle, but as a result of prompt action by Boston harbourmaster, Captain Graham Hulland, pilot Trevor Woods and coxswain Alan Cox, the scene of the crash was found to be in the area of Clay Hole (again). Within fifteen minutes of the alarm being given, these three had jumped aboard the pilot cutter *Lyn Ellis* and sped to the area. Having found the impact area, mainly by the strong smell of aviation fuel and from the presence of floating debris, they were able to co-ordinate various rescue parties to the scene. Wearing a dry suit, Alan Cox dived three times into the icy water to recover wreckage and twice he led shore groups to investigate other pieces. To do this he had to drop into the water in the darkness and then walk up to his chest in water, while dragging himself 300–400yds through mud to reach the shoreline. Captain Woods said they were unable to recover debris, the largest of which was about three feet wide, with a boat hook because it was blowing hard and the falling tide was running too swiftly to keep the boat steady alongside the pieces. This was when Alan Cox went in to drag some of them inboard. Directed by radio from the *Lyn Ellis*, Skegness and Hunstanton lifeboats joined in the search and were soon augmented by three helicopters from RAF Leconfield, RAF Coltishall and the USAF. Later, Skegness lifeboat picked up the largest floating piece of wreckage – an eight-foot length believed to be from the tail section.

Meanwhile, the grim discovery of the first body, that of WSO First Lieutenant Thomas G. Dorsett, fell to Captain Hulland and his crew. He told a reporter from the *Boston Standard* later:

> At about 7pm just off Freiston Low, in the light of the searchlight we saw a red float, so went towards it and promptly ran ashore because there was so little water. We got the boathook in around the harness of what proved to be a life jacket and when we lifted it up, a body became visible. We had five foot of freeboard on the boat and we could not pull him up, so we called the Hunstanton lifeboat over and we passed the airman over to them and they took him in to Boston.

Fire engines from Boston, Kirton, Leverton and Skegness converged on Freiston Shore where their crews began a search for the airmen and wreckage. When news broke that one body had been found, this became a search for the missing pilot, Captain Clifford W. Massengill, but by 10.30p.m. darkness made it impossible to continue and it was resumed at first light the next morning.

Daylight and the receding tide showed the full extent of the wreckage field, with a myriad of small pieces of charred debris scattered across the marsh, each to be marked simply when found, with a stick topped with such everyday items as a brightly coloured beer mat or a piece of red ribbon. The stench of the explosion that had ripped the aeroplane apart hung in the air and in places even the mud was blackened. USAF crash investigators and local coastguard volunteers waited for low tide before venturing onto the marsh to continue the search for the missing man, but sadly he was still unaccounted for by the end of that week.

In 1993 (Heckington), 1996 (Southorpe), 1999 (Surfleet) and 2008 (Ashwell), four more Harriers, all GR7s, were lost in 'off-airfield' incidents in the region, but thankfully all pilots ejected successfully, escaping unharmed and without incurring civilian casualties.

An incident that might quite easily be regarded as bringing this story 'full circle' is one that occurred on 24 October 2006. It will be recalled that the first story in this book involved Lieutenant Leonard Dawes, a founder member of No.2 Squadron who experienced engine failure with his BE2 aeroplane at Long Sutton in 1912. This more recent incident also involved an aircraft from No.2 Squadron, still very much in business, but now operating the Tornado GR4 from RAF Marham.

Once again it was during a 'routine' weapons training sortie to the Holbeach air weapons range that the accident occurred. Running in for a low-level 'hot' pass, ZG711 'O' is believed to have taken a major bird strike causing rapid and total loss of power to both engines. The crew ejected safely and the Tornado slithered to a halt on its belly on the shallow tidal mud flats, leaving a trail of debris but ending right-way up, reasonably intact, below the high water line. Skegness and Hunstanton lifeboats were launched, but the airmen were quickly rescued from the sea by the crew of a Sea King helicopter and flown to hospital for treatment to back injuries consistent with their ejection. It is interesting to note that, on 18 June 2006, ZG711 experienced an engine problem that caused its pilot to abort his take-off run for a display routine at Kemble Airshow.

Full circle. Tornado GR4 ZG711 'O' of No.2 Squadron crashed due to a bird strike during run-in to Holbeach range, 24 October 2006. (Courtesy Howard Cargill)

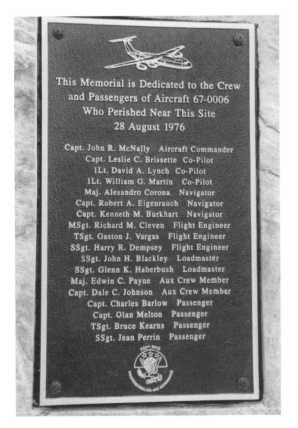

This Memorial is Dedicated to the Crew and Passengers of Aircraft 67-0006 Who Perished Near This Site 28 August 1976

Capt. John R. McNally   Aircraft Commander
Capt. Leslie C. Brissette Co-Pilot
1Lt. David A. Lynch Co-Pilot
1Lt. William G. Martin   Co-Pilot
Maj. Alesandro Corona Navigator
Capt. Robert A. Eigenrauch Navigator
Capt. Kenneth M. Burkhart Navigator
MSgt. Richard M. Cleven   Flight Engineer
TSgt. Gaston J. Vargas   Flight Engineer
SSgt. Harry R. Dempsey   Flight Engineer
SSgt. John H. Blackley   Loadmaster
SSgt. Glenn K. Haberbush   Loadmaster
Maj. Edwin C. Payne   Aux Crew Member
Capt. Dale C. Johnson   Aux Crew Member
Capt. Charles Barlow   Passenger
Capt. Olan Melton   Passenger
TSgt. Bruce Kearns   Passenger
SSgt. Jean Perrin   Passenger

Memorial to the crew of C-141 that crashed near Thorney.

Chapter 5

COLLISION!
RAF, RCAF & USAF Mid-Air Accidents

Part 1: First World War & Inter-War

Collision! That rare but devastating occurrence is the theme of this final chapter, one in which all those well-known astrological forces – fate, chance, luck, the roll of the dice, etc. – may be thought to play their part in deciding whether men live or die. Considering the innate frailty of flight, often heightened by an enemy striving to upset that tenuous equilibrium still further, the possibility of collision in the air, while always present, was and is probably regarded by airmen as 'an occupational hazard'. Mention was made in an earlier chapter of the relatively high volume of flying training conducted in the area around The Wash during the First World War – Cranwell and Freiston Airfields, for example, being the focus of much of this activity. In those days, however, there was by no means the same quantity of flying conducted overall – compared, that is, to later decades.

The first mid-air collision in the region occurred as far back as 8 September 1916 close to the newly opened Royal Naval Air Station at Cranwell, Lincolnshire. It was most unfortunate too that it should involve the senior officer in charge of flying operations at Cranwell, Squadron Commander Ian Hew Dalrymple-Clark and one of his flight commanders Lieutenant Hinshelwood. Both were piloting single-seat Bristol Scout D biplanes to Cranwell when they collided in cloud not far from the airfield. The undercarriage of Hinshelwoods'

Sopwith Pup B6062 awaiting recovery to Freiston.

aircraft was torn off by the impact and Dalrymple-Clark died when his aircraft, 8975, crashed to the ground. Hinshelwood, flying 5564, somehow managed to retain control of his aircraft and landed at Cranwell without injury. After this inauspicious start it was nearly two years before another collision occurred, but by that time, under the demands of war, the aeroplane and pilot population and the quantity of flying hours in the region around The Wash had increased dramatically. As the majority of flying training now involved quite intensive final stages at Cranwell sadly it was almost inevitable that any collisions might involve airmen from that station.

A satellite of RNAS Cranwell, Freiston Airfield became a 'finishing school' for aircrew due for posting to 'The Front' – wherever that might be. Aircrew went to this airfield on the edge of The Wash for about two weeks of final gunnery and bombing practice prior to joining their operational units. Flight Sub-Lieutenants Owen Dampier Bennett and Norman Grimsditch RNAS are typical examples of such airmen undergoing that final stage of flying training at No.4 School of Aerial Fighting and Gunnery (No.4 SAFG) at Freiston Airfield, just a few miles up The Wash coast from Boston. Aeroplanes in current use at the school were also typical of the times, with the well-known Avro 504, BE2e and Sopwith's One-and-a-half Strutter, Pup, Camel and Triplane making up the majority of the inventory in 1917.

Airborne in the morning sunlight of 26 April 1918, both pilots were practising combat manoeuvres 7,000ft up in the sky above the River Witham outfall, just a few miles from the airfield. Round and round they flew, each twisting and turning to gain an edge on the other. Inevitably, the position of the biplane wings in relation to the pilot's position would mean they could quite easily lose sight of one another momentarily. Suddenly the pair collided. There was no immediate explosion or disintegration; instead they simply locked together in a deadly embrace, the wings and wheels of one punching holes in the flimsy wings of the other. Down they went. Grimsditch's Pup, B6021, was least damaged by the impact and when the two aeroplanes drifted apart again at 1,300ft, regaining sufficient control he landed safely back at Freiston. Sub-Lieutenant Bennett in BE2e, B3716 was beyond help though, his broken machine continuing its plummet to earth, taking him to his death.

It was only three weeks later, on 18 May, when the second incident occurred, also involving two aeroplanes from No.4 SAFG. Canadian Second Lieutenant James Johnston, RFC, a native of Athens, Ontario was flying Avro 504G, N5803 when he collided with Sopwith Pup,

Sopwith Pup, N6160, after its collision with an Avro 504G, N5803 near Freiston on 18 May 1918.

N6160 whose unknown pilot was lucky to escape with his life. Struck off charge as a result of the accident, this Sopwith Pup – in common with other aircraft relegated to training duties at Freiston – is worthy of a closer look, since it had led an eventful life prior to its demise.

Built at Kingston on Thames, N6160 first went to war on 1 February 1917 when it was allocated to No.3 (Naval) Squadron. In February and March, flying this aeroplane, famous fighter ace Flight Sub-Lieutenant Raymond Collishaw was credited with shooting down two German Halberstadt DIIs near Bapaume, his only victories flying that type of fighter. When Collishaw left 'Naval Three' to take command of 'Naval Ten', N6160 passed to Flight Sub-Lieutenant Alfred Carter DSC who brought down a Halberstadt DIII with this nippy Pup on 6 April. Another budding ace, Flight Sub-Lieutenant Harold Kerby then made excellent use of N6160 by shooting down one enemy Albatros and causing two others to collide and crash, all in one day (23 April). Coincidentally, both Carter and Kerby each went on to be appointed officer commanding Freiston Gunnery School during 1918.

In combat day after day, sometimes on several offensive patrols in a day, it is understandable that aeroplanes deteriorate quickly – that is, if they survive combat at all. Airframes become overstressed and engines wear out. N6160 was no exception and was sent back to England for overhaul on 21 August, after just six months of hard combat work. Front-line service over, it was re-engined with an 80hp Gnome replacing the original 80hp Le Rhone and then issued to Freiston in April 1918 where it survived for a month before Johnston's accident.

In addition to showing that the new RAF was in all respects a multi-national service, there were sadly no survivors from the next collision on 19 August 1918 involving a DH6, B2787, with flying instructor Lieutenant Norman Campbell, a South African and his eighteen-year-old pupil Flight Cadet Charles Wiltshire on board. Their aircraft collided with an Avro 504K, E2929, flown by Canadian, Second Lieutenant Clarence Sherlock and another eighteen-year-old, NCO Cadet Snowden Scott close to Cranwell Airfield, and all four young men died. At this particular time, Cranwell was operating three heavier-than-air Flights – designated as Nos 56, 57 and 58 Training Depot Stations – with Scott and Sherlock attached to 57 TDS and Wiltshire to 58 TDS. Lieutenant Campbell was a staff pilot. Thankfully there was only one more collision in Lincolnshire during the First World War, but it claimed the lives of two more young Cranwell airmen. On 4 November 1918 Captain Hugh Sutherland, aged twenty-one, and his pupil Cadet J. Hofs in BE2c 8409, both attached to 58 TDS, collided with the Avro 504K, D8916, being flown solo by Lieutenant Henry de Bathe from 56 TDS. Sutherland and de Bathe died that day, but although badly injured, Cadet Hofs lived to tell the tale.

Even with the end of the shooting war, there was to be no sudden halt to flying training – indeed, it would take time to demobilise anyway – while in the meantime, the armistice was not ratified until 1919 and there was an air component in the occupying force in Germany. Even the Russian revolution drew in RAF fighters. And while there was flying training, accidents and collisions were ever-present hazards.

Captain Philip Marsh, aged twenty-three, was awarded the Military Cross for his exploits above the Western Front, and then found himself posted as a flying instructor to No.7 Training Depot Station at Feltwell Airfield, to pass on his hard-earned experience. Fate decreed, however, that his experience would count for nothing when he collided with an aeroplane flown by Lieutenant Caryl Jacobs on 20 December 1918.

Giving evidence at the inquest Henry Galloway, a carpenter working on a nearby estate, told the coroner:

The aeroplane seemed to be in trouble and I said to my mate, William Pearson, that it looked as though it was coming down. With that, I saw it coming down the drive of the house with its left wing downwards. It carried on for about seventeen chains [*sic*, 375yds or 340m] before it crashed down onto its left wing. We ran to the machine and found it smashed with the two airmen dead inside.

Captain Marsh was flying with Air Mechanic Third Class Dudley Brown in the back seat of an Avro 504, believed to be E7705. Lieutenant Jacobs, who had just completed his flying training course, took off to carry out some local aerial photography in Avro 504K, E3540. Lieutenant Jacobs gave his account of the incident to the coroner:

I left Feltwell aerodrome at 12:35 to take some aerial pictures and Capt Marsh took off in company with me. Both machines climbed to 1,000 feet with the Captain's aircraft about 50 to 100 feet in front and above. I took my pictures and then did a left turn which brought my machine at right angles to Capt Marsh's, with my back to him. I did not see Capt Marsh's aeroplane again until I felt a jolt on the rear of my machine. On looking round I saw that half my tailplane had been taken away. I switched off my engine immediately and went into a side-slip. Capt Marsh seemed to be gliding down in the opposite direction. I hit a tree during my own landing and ran back to the aerodrome to report the accident and have an ambulance sent out to the other machine.

Since no explanation could be found for the accident, the verdict 'accidentally killed' was returned on the two victims.

At the age of thirty-one, Alfred Pitkin would be considered quite old to be undertaking flying training. However, this married man from Letchworth was a Sergeant undergoing pilot training with No.47 Training Squadron at RAF Waddington when he died in a mid-air collision on 7 June 1919, near Lincoln. His DH 6 trainer was in collision with a DH 9, flown by Second Lieutenant Roy E. Heater, aged twenty, from Iowa USA, who also died in the accident.

In the period between the wars, operational flying training was generally carried out by the units to which aircrew were posted after leaving a Flying Training School (FTS). At these FTSs, pilots were given basic instruction on such types as the Avro 504 or Tiger Moth, before graduating to more powerful aircraft like the Hawker Hart or Audax. Later on in the FTS courses, for example during the period leading up to the Second World War, depending on the role to which they might be allocated, aircrew would receive tuition on single-engine Masters or Harvards or the twin-engine Oxford. Set-piece formation flying, with an emphasis on station keeping, became a prominent feature of the RAF inter-war training programme in the belief that mutual aid from rear guns would overcome an attacker.

These rigid tactics called for concentration and accurate flying on the part of a pilot and were deemed an essential part of flying training. Furthermore, when developed to include aerobatic manoeuvres, perfected for example by the famous teams that thrilled crowds at Hendon, they were a delight to behold. However, during the earlier stages of learning formation-flying discipline the close proximity of those aeroplanes themselves presented pilots with the possibility of collision. After the incident in 1919 mentioned above, there was a long gap before a similar military event occurred.

Based at RAF Grantham, No.39 Squadron was designated as a day bomber unit equipped with the ubiquitous DH9A. It was a bad day for the station when two of these biplanes collided in the air on 10 June 1924, causing the loss of both machines and four airmen, during what was described as 'a routine formation practice'. The aircraft flown by Flying Officer L.G. Lucas with his observer, AC1 L. Coppleston, hit the underside of the aircraft flown by Flying Officer Rowan Heywood Daly DSC DFC and Sergeant W.H. Brewer.

A flight of DH 9A aircraft from No.39 Squadron at RAF Grantham (Spitalgate).

The undercarriage of Daly's machine became embedded in Lucas's top wing and, locked together, both aircraft dived to the ground.

This incident is a prime example of how luck can carry an airman through everything the enemy can throw at him, only to perish in a peacetime accident probably not of his own making. Rowan Daly was one such man. As a Flight Sub-Lieutenant in the RNAS he built an impeccable reputation as an air fighter in the First World War. Mentioned in despatches in July 1917, he won the DSC, gazetted in August, for action against German Gotha bombers attacking south-east England in daylight. Daly also won a DFC for gallantry displayed while flying operationally during the British military campaign in South Russia in 1919/20. All in all, a brave airman, whose death was a sad loss to the RAF.

A similar incident occurred on Cranwell Airfield on 6 June 1930, but on this occasion, although inexperienced pupil pilots were involved, the hand of fate decreed that one would live to tell the tale to the Sleaford coroner. The scene was set when Flight Lieutenant Henry Drake, a flying instructor and commander of 'A' Flight at the College, took off in an Avro 504 to give dual instruction to Flight Cadet Francis Beresford-Pearce, who was occupying the back seat. Other Avros were out in the air and on the ground but this was quite normal on any good flying day such as this. In one of the other aircraft was Flight Cadet George Montague, who had received thirteen hours' dual instruction and done three hours solo flying up to the day of the accident. Asked by the coroner to recall the events of the previous morning, as reported in the *Lincolnshire Standard*, he said:

> I was flying solo in an Avro [504] and was going to land. I noticed another machine taxying where I wanted to land so I put on the engine and turned to the right and then to the left again. I did this to avoid the aeroplane on the ground. Another machine seemed to come from above me, from left to right and I think it was rather in front of me – that was my

impression but I can't be certain. Then I noticed the other machine falling out of control and found my ailerons would not work. When the machine above flashed over me, it hit my top left wing and that is what put the ailerons out of order. My machine lost speed and nearly stalled, so I landed and broke my undercarriage as I did so.

Sergeant Lionel Spier, a flying instructor, was standing outside the hangars and witnessed the whole event. He told the coroner:

The first thing I noticed was that two machines were going to land. One [Drake] was about 200 feet up, gliding to land in a straight approach from west to east. On the left of this machine, about 80 to 100 yards away from it, I saw a second machine [Montague] that was fifty feet from the ground. Cadet Montague put his engine on and from flying straight, turned about forty degrees to the right and started to climb, while the first machine continued in its straight glide. The lower machine climbed up into the path of the machine that was coming down and they collided. I saw them touch then Flight Lieutenant Drake's machine nose dived and crashed. Cadet Montague's machine continued for some distance then landed.

Flight Lieutenant Drake was fatally injured and died shortly after reaching hospital, while Cadet Beresford-Pearce sustained severe injuries from which he subsequently recovered. Cadet Montague emerged unscathed, but the memory of that day would undoubtedly stay with him for a lifetime. The officer who gave evidence of identification was none other than Flight Lieutenant Dermot Boyle who, by 1956, had risen to command the RAF itself. He was the first ex-Cranwell cadet to do so.

The Munich Crisis of 1938 brought an increase in flying training activity in its wake. In turn this led to a corresponding rise in the air accident rate. There was and always remains the further risk that in any air accident, civilian life and property might be endangered in addition to the military personnel and material involved. It must be pointed out, though, that as far as the result of air collisions in this region are concerned, there have been miraculously few civilian tragedies. The first such civilian casualty, however, occurred on 15 September 1938.

It was on that day, simulating wartime conditions, that five Gloster Gauntlets of 213 Squadron formed up in the sky near Wittering, and set off to take up various individual patrol lines fanning out to the east of their base. Flying K7840, Pilot Officer Brian van Mentz, a South African, was detailed to leave the group and patrol a line north-east towards Spalding. At 700ft over Ketton he broke away, starting a climbing turn that would take him over Stamford and on to his patrol course. Meanwhile, Pilot Officer John Sing, another member of 213 Squadron, had taken off a little earlier on a local flight in Miles Magister L2863, with Aircraftman F. Humphries in the back seat. The Magister was heading back to base, descending on an opposite course to the Gauntlets, when it was in collision with van Mentz's aircraft as the latter was still climbing. It seems likely that each pilot had his view of the other aeroplane obscured by the main plane, the Magister hitting the Gauntlet's top wing, losing one of its own in the process. With both aeroplanes doomed to crash, all three airmen baled out and were fortunate to land without injury. Van Mentz came down on Northfield recreation ground while Humphries landed in a tree in The Meadows, with Flying Officer Sing nearby. The remains of the Magister fell in the gardens of 6 and 7 Freemans Cottages, fortunately without causing damage to life or limb.

Not so fortunate was a young lady in Stamford below. Miss Mary Russell, aged twenty-two, died as she ran from her home in Lancaster Road when the shattering noise of the Gauntlet plunging onto its roof drove her to run out in panic. Not realising she was running into danger, the young lady was crushed by falling masonry and wreckage from the aeroplane as the house collapsed around her. She was the only occupant of the house at the time.

Both van Mentz and Sing continued their service with 213 Squadron into the war, taking part in the Battle of Britain and each winning a DFC as fighter pilots. The former was killed, not in battle but in a cruel twist of fate while off duty when a German bomb hit the public house he was in near his fighter station. After the Battle, John Sing became an instructor on the staff of 56 OTU Sutton Bridge in November 1940. He survived the war and retired with the rank of Wing Commander.

It was the summer of 1939 and war clouds were already gathering when Sergeant John Bullard gave his life to save schoolboy Denis Nahum from certain death in a doomed Blenheim fighter. Denis, a pupil at Oundle School, was just sixteen, but no stranger to this aeroplane, having already had four other flights under the auspices of the Public Schools Air Liason Scheme. This, his fifth trip, was as a passenger in L8368, flown by Sergeant Bullard, one of three Blenheim Mk 1s detailed for local formation practice. RAF Wittering's No.23 Squadron was playing host to a number of these lads who enjoyed the thrill of flying and aspired to a service career. Take-off was to be at 2.30p.m. on 20 July and together with some of his pals, Denis waited eagerly at the dispersal area.

Within minutes of clearing the runway L8368 joined L1448, flown by Pilot Officer A. T. Williams, the formation leader, and a third Blenheim with Sergeant Charles Young in the pilot's seat. Sergeant Bullard eased his aeroplane into position on the left of the 'vee' formation. Over in L1448 Denis could just make out his pal Arthur Whitten-Brown (whose famous father was navigator on the first non-stop Atlantic flight in 1919), while in the third aircraft was another friend, Herbert Ellis. To complete the crew, each aeroplane carried an aircraftman air-gunner in its turret. Denis sat to the right and slightly behind Sergeant Bullard in the position normally occupied by the observer/navigator. For fifteen minutes the formation circled Wittering at 2,000ft then, climbing gently to 3,500ft, left the circuit heading towards Peterborough.

Passing through a layer of cloud Sergeant Bullard momentarily lost contact with his leader and upon being buffeted by someone's propeller-wash, he sheered away to port. The leader radioed for him to rejoin but the next thing Pilot Officer Williams saw was L8368 overshooting the formation a mere ten yards away from him. Instinctively Williams threw the yoke forward in an effort to dive out of danger. It was effective, but Bullard's aircraft drifted into Sergeant Young's path, with dire consequences. Writing from his home in Bogota, Colombia in 1990, Denis Nahum recalled what happened next:

There was a loud bang as a prop sliced into the tail. Our aeroplane just slopped about, swooping around in a very unstable way – not really in a dive. Sergeant Bullard reached up and jettisoned the escape hatch above my head. When I was ordered out of the hatch (the gunner having already abandoned through the rear escape hatch) I climbed onto my seat but suddenly realised I had not clipped on my parachute. Outwardly calm and trying to keep the Blenheim steady, Sergeant Bullard found the pack and passed it up to me to secure to my chest harness-clips. He put my hand on the rip-cord D-ring, shouted 'Count five and pull the handle!' then gave me an enormous heave upwards out of the hatch. I fell clear and have little recollection of the fall except for pulling the rip-cord almost immediately.

It was only then, floating safely but lop-sided beneath the canopy, that I discovered my parachute pack was held on by only one of the two harness clips. In my haste I had not secured it properly to both!

Blenheim L8368 crashed near Sacrewell Lodge, to the east of the Great North Road near Peterborough. Denis landed about a mile away, sporting a black eye, cut lip and numerous bruises to mark an ordeal that made him the youngest person to bale out of an aeroplane in difficulty. In those final moments of the Blenheim's plunge to earth, Sergeant Bullard had little time left to save himself. He cleared the hatch but may have hit some part of the aeroplane, for he was found dead with the parachute canopy damaged and torn as if it had come into contact with a propeller. As Denis observed:

> I had been told the 'short-nose' Blenheim was notorious for getting out of, as one tended either to be blown back against the fin or into the propellers.

It was only a year later that No.23 Squadron's own CO, Squadron Leader Joseph 'Spike' O'Brien, had cause to remember that notoriety when he had to bale out of his Blenheim during a night combat with a Heinkel. One of O'Brien's colleagues recalled what happened:

> At that time popular opinion was that no pilot had ever got out of a spinning Blenheim alive. This was because the only way out was through the top sliding hatch, so you were most likely to fall through one or other of the airscrews. Our 'new boy' [a passenger with O'Brien] probably didn't know about that when Spike had to help him out. He undid his seat belt, unplugged his oxygen and pushed him up out of the top hatch while holding his rip-cord. He [Spike] told me afterwards that he felt sick when the lad fell through the airscrew. Spike then had to get out himself. He leaned out and grasping the wireless aerial behind the hatch, pulled himself up to it; turned himself round so that his feet were on the side of the fuselage; then pushed outwards as hard as he could. He felt what he thought was the tip of an airscrew blade tap on the earpiece of his helmet – but luck was with him that night and he got away with it!

But for Sergeant Bullard's calmness and devotion to his duty – seeing to the safety of his young passenger – Denis Nahum might well have become a victim of the crash too. Later, the *Stamford Mercury* reported that Wittering's Station Commander sent a letter to HQ No.12 Group requesting consideration be given to a posthumous bravery award for Sergeant Bullard, but no such award materialised. Herbert Ellis, in his autobiography *Hippocrates, RN*, recalled the incident vividly:

> After take-off we were soon in cloud and whilst my pilot [Young] concentrated on his instruments, I nervously peered outside at the fog, for I knew we had followed another Blenheim [Bullard] into the cloud and this had another boy, Denis Nahum, as a passenger. Almost imperceptibly at first, I made out the gloomy shape of the other aircraft and its tail just above our starboard propeller but getting rapidly closer. I tapped my pilot on the shoulder and in looking up he pulled the control column slightly back, sufficient to get our propeller into the tail of the other aircraft. I remember every detail of the next few minutes, even though fifty years have passed. The tail of the other aircraft was sliced clean through and disappeared, swept away in the slipstream. I next heard a klaxon horn (the undercarriage warning) as my pilot closed the throttles and went into a steep dive, soon emerging from cloud. I could see the green grass of RAF Wittering below and our starboard propeller stopped, the blades twisted. I momentarily saw an open parachute beneath us and a developing plume of smoke rising from the ground before we landed with one engine out of action.

And what of Denis Nahum? He wrote:

I didn't (what, after that experience!!) join the RAF. When my time came to help the war effort I went into the Royal Navy as a Sub-Lieutenant on High Frequency Direction Finding equipment (HF/DF), hanging around [*sic*] the Atlantic and sometimes venturing into the Med to sink U-boats.

Modestly he omitted to mention that he was twice awarded a Mention in Despatches.

Herbert Ellis carved a distinguished career as a doctor in the Fleet Air Arm, serving until 1959 and receiving the Air Force Cross for his work. He assisted the US Navy with its pre-man-in-space experiments and worked in the field of industrial medicine for a further twenty years. Arthur Whitten-Brown joined the RAFVR in 1939 and served in his father's old squadron, but later, having transferred to night intruder flying, was killed in action over Holland on D-Day 1944.

There is a further twist to this tale, though. The incident on 20 July was not Sergeant Bullard's first experience of a mid-air collision. In 1938, 23 Squadron was equipped with the Hawker Demon two-seat fighter. On 3 November that year, Sergeant Bullard was airborne from RAF Wittering in K5730 with his air-gunner, AC1 Harold Lee, when they were involved in a collision with K5712 flown by Pilot Officer A.E. Slocombe.

It was while practising battle formations that these two aircraft struck each other, Slocombe, on this occasion, being the one who overshot the formation. Both Bullard and Slocombe – who was flying solo – baled out safely, but Aircraftman Lee was not so fortunate. Possibly encumbered by heavy flying clothing and weaponry in the cramped rear cockpit, Lee failed to get clear before the aeroplanes crashed, one on each side of the railway line, between Barholm and Casewick estate, near Stamford and was killed. After landing by parachute, the two survivors surveyed the wreckage and chatting to Sergeant Bullard, Pilot Officer Slocombe was overheard to say he felt sure he had 'had it' when he 'hit the silk',

Hawker Demon two-seat fighter. This example is K4499 from No.604 Squadron but No.23 Squadron lost K5730 and K5712 in a collision near Stamford on 3 November 1938.

because the aeroplane turned over on top of him and he was struck a heavy blow by the top wing as he fell through the air. It can only be imagined, therefore, as to the thoughts racing through Sergeant John Bullard's mind as he struggled to help Denis Nahum clear of that doomed Blenheim – but there is no doubt at all that he did his duty in a brave and selfless way.

Part 2: Second World War

One of the most well-known collision incidents in this region during the Second World War involved Pilot Officer John Gillespie Magee Jr, famous the world over for his inspirational poem *High Flight*. Over the years, much has been written about Magee's life, but we will confine ourselves here to the background and circumstances of the collision itself. The son of an American father and English mother and with an affinity to the plight of England, John Magee did what many of his countrymen did and joined the RCAF. He was nineteen years of age when he was posted in September 1941 to No.412 (Canadian) Squadron based at RAF Digby in Lincolnshire.

Since its formation that July, No.412 Squadron had carried out convoy patrols with its Spitfire II fighters off the Lincolnshire coast, but the majority of its time in the air was spent practicing dog-fighting and formation-keeping to build up experience for more challenging operations. In September, the squadron took part in sweeps over northern France, operating from forward bases at RAF West Malling and RAF Manston, but Pilot Officer Magee did not fly on the first few of these operations. In late October 1941, though, the squadron re-equipped with the Spitfire V and moved from Digby to its Wellingore satellite field. Then, on 8 November, John Magee took part in his only cross-Channel sweep, which developed into a frantic aerial battle over Dunkirk, in which he acquitted himself well and emerged unscathed. This was the last sweep for No.412 for several months, although the convoy patrols and endless practice continued.

The morning of 11 December 1941 dawned fine but with an overcast cloud layer, and Canadian Pilot Officer Rod Smith, who flew with John Magee that fateful day, recalled what happened:

> The squadron was ordered to take part in a wing formation exercise with a squadron from RAF Kirton in Lindsey. The weather was fairly good with an overcast starting at 1,500 feet and going up for several thousand feet. We were to join the other squadron above the cloud layer. We took off from Wellingore in a long wavy line abreast, led by Jack Morrison. As soon as I got airborne I noticed some white smoke coming back from the top of my engine cowling near the propeller and I realised my coolant filler cap had not been fully screwed down. I left the squadron just before it entered the cloud and turned back and landed. It only took a minute to get the coolant cap screwed down but it was then too late to go looking for the squadron.
>
> After about an hour and a quarter the squadron approached Wellingore from the south, under the cloud, at about 1,000 feet altitude and made a circuit for landing. At that moment Operations rang to inform us that a Spitfire had crashed between Wellingore and RAF Cranwell. When I got the word, I took off immediately to look for it and soon spotted a crashed aeroplane burning in a field, near a wood, about a mile or so north of Cranwell. I returned to Wellingore where, after landing, I found out that John Magee had not come back with the squadron. Some of us jumped into a car and drove to the scene. An ambulance was just leaving the site, heading towards Cranwell and we could not approach the aircraft

because cannon ammunition was still exploding in the fire. We then walked over to the Airspeed Oxford that had crashed about a third of a mile away, just to the east of Roxholm Hall, which it narrowly missed.

That evening, the circumstances of the accident emerged when the CO, Squadron Leader Jack Morrison, had to acquaint a local police constable of his side of the story. Rod Smith remembers the account as follows:

When the wing formation practice ended, Jack was instructed by the wing leader to take his squadron home. Coming within a few miles of Wellingore, still above the cloud, Jack noticed a small hole going right down through the cloud. As was normal in those days he preferred to lead the squadron down a hole rather than do a slower and more stately let-down through the cloud. When sweeps or exercises were over, squadrons often only had five or six minutes of fuel left and were anxious to get their wheels on the ground. So Jack ordered the squadron into line astern and dived almost vertically down through the hole, with the others in a long line behind him, each about a hundred yards apart.

Unfortunately, the hole happened to be in Cranwell's northerly circuit and an Oxford happened to pass under the bottom of the hole just as the eleven-strong line of Spitfires was coming out of it. Their speed had built up to nearly 450 mph in this steep dive so it is little wonder, therefore, that the slow-moving trainer could not be avoided. That was when John Magee's Spitfire Vb, AD291, hit the Oxford, T1052, flown by Pilot/UT LAC Ernest Griffin with disastrous consequences for both airmen. Pilot Officer Magee was seen to jump clear of his aircraft but he was too low for his parachute to deploy, while LAC Griffin had no chance of escaping from his cockpit.

Said to be 'shortly afterwards', but believed to be on 9 January 1942, there was an almost exact replica of this collision in similar circumstances and in a similar location. Detailed for a wing formation exercise, No.412 Squadron was descending to base through a hole in the cloud cover when Sergeant Charlesworth's Spitfire (believed to be AD426) and another Oxford (believed to be X6661) from Cranwell collided wing to wing. The wing of the Oxford came off and the instructor, Sergeant Reginald McCoy and his pupil, AC2 Thomas Hart, died in the crash. By some miracle the wing of the Spitfire, though sliced back to the main spar, did not break off and Sergeant Charlesworth was able to pull off a belly landing in a field not far from Magee's crash site. It is also recorded that No.412 Squadron lost another pilot in a mid-air collision on 31 August 1941 when a Spitfire flown by Pilot Officer William Hughes was in collision, in daylight, with Hampden AD939 from No.44 Squadron over RAF Waddington. The Hampden crew also died.

Adverse weather conditions also had a significant effect on the training accident rate, proving particularly hazardous during mock combat practice. In those days, enthusiasm rather than caution was more likely to be applied (refer to the author's earlier book, *Combat Ready!*). Mix an aerial 'cocktail' of pilots in powerful Hurricanes, keen to get into combat and determined perhaps to steal a march on their quarry, concentrating thought and vision on that juicy target of a bomber, growing rapidly in their gun-sight. Let said pilots misjudge the closing speed on a lumbering Stirling, add a touch of haze, and what might have been a close pass becomes a one-way track to oblivion. Such were the ingredients of a training sortie involving Pilot Officer Derek Browne, from RAF Sutton Bridge, on 17 January 1942. Arrangements had been by No.7 Squadron at RAF Oakington, some thirty miles distant, to call upon the services of a No.56 OTU Hurricane for an affiliation exercise with one of their Stirlings that morning. Browne would practice attacks using the Stirling as his target while the Stirling crew were to brush up their fighter evasion tactics. It would also provide an opportunity for Squadron Leader John Mahler DFC, newly arrived from No.15 Squadron, to put in some cockpit time with an experienced crew.

Once again, who or what caused the collision will never be known. Pilot Officer Browne, in Hurricane V6865, and all the crew of Stirling W7467, led by Australian Pilot Officer Ronald Taylor DFM, were killed when both aircraft plummeted to the ground just north of Earith Bridge in Cambridgeshire.

Not all collisions involved fighter boys, although it would be the end of 1943 before that emphasis began to change. Plans to step up the bomber offensive were taking shape in 1942 and as has been outlined in an earlier chapter, OTUs were to play a part in this rather earlier than their crews might have expected. When, on 30/31 May 1942, over 1,000 bombers of all types took off for the famous attack on Cologne, many of that number were drawn from bomber OTUs. Just prior to the raid, toiling ground crews brought ageing aeroplanes as close as possible to operational standard and motley crews of instructors and pupils were briefed for the momentous trip. Overall RAF losses that night, including the intruder sorties, totalled forty-four aircraft, considered 'acceptable in the circumstances' by top brass (Hastings, *Bomber Command* and Middlebrook *Bomber Command War Diaries*), but despite the fear of collisions, the 'boffins' predicted a collision rate of just one per hour over the target. They were proved spot on, with two in two hours over enemy territory and just the following one among the hundreds of returning aircraft over England.

No.14 OTU, a bomber-training unit based at RAF Cottesmore in Rutland, lost three Hampdens on the raid. One, P5321, was almost within sight of home when it was in collision with Halifax W1013 from No.78 Squadron based at RAF Croft, Yorkshire, which was well off course. Having bombed Cologne successfully the No.14 OTU Hampden pilot, Squadron Leader Donald Falconer DFC, started down through cloud at 2,000ft over Norfolk, breaking through the thin layer at about 1,000ft in the vicinity of March (Cambridgeshire). At 4.00a.m., right above him, Pilot Officer Geoffrey Foers in a Halifax from No.78 Squadron was doing exactly the same thing. The starboard propellors of the Halifax chopped into Falconers cockpit, mangling it, but by some miracle, missing him and throwing him clear out of his seat. Fortunately, as was usual for a Hampden pilot, he was wearing a seat-type parachute, which undoubtedly saved his life. Being so low when they cleared the cloud, his crew, however, had no chance to escape from their cramped positions. Warrant Officer Cecil Hobbs, observer/navigator Pilot Officer John Knowling (WOp/AG), and Pilot Officer Harvey Little (WOp/AG), rear gunner, all died when the bomber plunged onto Plantation Farm, Whitemoor, near March.

Chaos also reigned aboard the Halifax. The impact broke off the starboard outer engine and the starboard inner was on fire. With the aircraft shaking violently and in a dive, Pilot Officer Foers gave the order to bale out as he fought to retain a measure of control with precious little altitude in hand. Flight engineer, Sergeant Harold Curtis clipped on his parachute, ran to the rear door and jumped. With just seconds to spare, his canopy blossomed and he hit the ground unscathed. With great skill – or great luck – Pilot Officer Foers brought the Halifax down for a mighty crash-landing that caused such disintegration that it threw the rest of the crew out of the aircraft as it slithered along the ground. Foers survived with serious head injuries, but the wireless operator Sergeant George Bolton and rear gunner Sergeant Andrew Cale died.

By August, Foers was back on operational flying duties, but his luck finally ran out on 10 October when the Halifax he was flying, W1275, was shot down during a raid on Krefeld, killing him and five of his crew. Donald Falconer eventually left 14 OTU and returned to operational flying. During 1944 he was posted to the Pathfinder Force with which he completed his second tour. Promoted Wing Commander of No.156 Squadron at RAF

Upwood, with the DFC and AFC and a tally of fifty-five operations to his name, on 30/31 December 1944 he volunteered for 'just one more' – coincidentally to Cologne. Both he and his crew failed to return.

A month later No.14 OTU lost another Hampden in a non-operational collision, this time with less damage to the crew, but still with fatal consequences. It was July 1942 and Spitfires from the Central Gunnery School at Sutton Bridge were now a familiar sight in the Fenland sky. On 2 July, Sergeant Charles Scott, a pilot on attachment to CGS from No.137 Squadron RAF Matlaske, was airborne in P8583 carrying out a tactical air combat exercise in company with a CGS Wellington. Flying in the vicinity, the Hampden went apparently unnoticed until the Spitfire flew head on into it. In the impact the Spitfire lost a wing and dived vertically into the ground on Holme's Farm, Cloot Drove, Cowbit, about five miles south of Spalding, killing Sergeant Scott instantly. Losing height and with smoke pouring from the gap where its starboard engine was knocked askew, Hampden P2067 staggered eastwards over the River Welland before Flight Sergeant F. Hill brought it down for a crash-landing at Four Mile Bar, Deeping St Nicholas, with the crew shaken but unharmed. Witness to this tragedy was Percy Chapman, carting hay that fine evening – it was 6.00p.m. – not far from his cottage at Brotherhouse Bar and just a quarter mile from where the Spitfire made its final dive. Stunned by what he saw, he watched the Hampden disappear from view and the Wellington circle the hole made by the Spitfire before it, too, flew off in the general direction of Sutton Bridge.

Recovery of Sergeant Scott's body was an arduous task for the men of No.58 Maintenance Unit due to the depth of the hole and having to battle against water seepage giving the blue clay the consistency of porridge. Interviewed many years later, Jim Grommet, then a corporal crane driver in the recovery team, recalled: 'we finally removed the pilot at a depth of about twelve feet with what was left of the aeroplane sinking almost as fast as we could pull the wreckage out.'

Flying training was still moving apace at Peterborough (Westwood) Airfield, the home since June 1942 of No.7 (Pilot) Advanced Flying Unit (7 PAFU). Equipped with the Miles Master, it was this unit's objective to 'polish up' the skills of pilots from various flying backgrounds, and to satisfy the ever-growing operational demand for more pilots with single-engine aeroplane experience. With an original pupil population of ninety, 7 (P)AFU grew rapidly over the next year to around 200 trainees, operating up to 130 Masters from Westwood and its satellite airfield at Sibson. Inevitably, it was not long before tragedy stamped its mark on the school, formation flying once again being at the root of this collision.

Scheduled as a dual formation exercise, Master II, DL849, flown by Sergeant Donald Knott with Sergeant Frederick Andrew (a Canadian) in the back seat, headed towards Wisbech on the morning of 7 September, in company with DL838 flown by Sergeant Keith Letch and Pilot Officer Noel Bailey (a New Zealander). They never returned. All four airmen died when the two aeroplanes collided – allegedly while indulging in 'unauthorised low flying and fighter tactics' – and crashed at West Walton, just to the east of the town.

In the words of No.167 Squadron (RAF Ludham, Norfolk) Operational Record Book (form 540), 1 January 1943 marked 'an unhappy end to the Old Year.' Behind that gloomy entry was the sad loss of two of its pilots in a collision during an exercise with American bombers over The Wash the previous day.

Situated to the south of Cambridge, Bassingbourn was home to B17 Flying Fortresses of 91st Bomb Group (91 BG) USAAF, which had been in residence since mid-October 1942. Operational missions began in November, but there was still a long way to go before Eighth Air Force bomber crews learned, through bitter experience, the most effective defensive tactics to be employed against Luftwaffe fighters. With aircraft and crew losses bringing home the harsh reality of the daylight bomber campaign, individual Groups, anxious to accumulate as much fighter-defence practice as possible for their combat crews, set up exercises with any RAF fighter squadrons willing to co-operate. It was just such an exercise that saw the demise of Flying Officer James Pickering in Spitfire Vb EP289 and Pilot Officer Peter Franklin in EP235. Continuing, the form 540 stated:

> They collided carrying out 'attacks' on the Americans from Bassingbourn. One pilot was seen to bale out over The Wash but no trace of either pilots or their aircraft could be found.

In the absence of the squadron intelligence officer, who was on leave, the adjutant went over to Bassingbourn to get their side of the story. All the American pilots who participated in the exercise were most sympathetic and courteous, but could throw little light on the tragedy. Both pilots are classified as missing.

Constantly in use as a bombing and firing range, an assembly area for daylight bombers, and a prominent navigation aid by day and night, the skies above The Wash became a veritable 'Piccadilly Circus' during the war. Hardly a day passed by without an assortment of aeroplanes wheeling and cavorting about the aerial and ground targets, loosing off equally assorted ordnance in all directions. On one such sparkling, sunny day, 21 January 1943, Lysander III, V9797, attached to No.3 OTU at RAF Cranwell, was making its stately passage across the range area towing a banner target.

Banking into a slow turn up-sun, which took them out into The Wash, was a formation of seven Spitfire Vb fighters from 'B' flight No.411 (Canadian) Squadron based at RAF Digby, airborne on a practice 'sweep'. During the sortie it was planned that all pilots should have the

In the distinctive yellow and black diagonal markings of a target-tug, Westland Lysander T1444 flying over The Wash in 1942.

opportunity to test-fire their cannon armament over the sea. Crossing the coast at Skegness, the flight commander gave an order to break formation according to a pre-arranged plan. In turn, each Spitfire was put into a dive towards the sea, its pilot firing a burst of cannon fire into the water near the Wainfleet range, before pulling out to rejoin the formation. Warrant Officer John MacMillan's turn came and he pushed the nose of AA754 down … and flew straight into the Lysander! Neither he nor the two-man crew of the target-tug, flown by Warrant Officer William Atkins, stood a chance of survival as both aeroplanes plummeted into the icy waters of The Wash. As MacMillan's colleagues circled to mark the spot, an air-sea rescue launch was quickly on hand, but no survivors could be seen. Some time later, however, Skegness lifeboat crew recovered the bodies of two airmen, believed to be those of the Lysander crew, from the vicinity of the crash.

When No.56 OTU left RAF Sutton Bridge in March 1942, it was replaced by the Central Gunnery School, which brought with it Spitfires, Hampdens and Wellingtons. The type of flying done at CGS made it particularly vulnerable to collisions, starting with the loss of Spitfire II P7677 and Wellington Ia N2865 on 10 April 1943.

The early evening sortie was to be a camera gun exercise for both aircraft, with full evasion manoeuvres thrown in. It was during a quarter attack by the Spitfire that things went wrong. The Spitfire pilot, Flying Officer E. Griffiths (an Australian), bore in on the Wellington but left his break too late and hit the rear turret of the bomber. Both aircraft fell out of control, but Griffiths managed to bale out in time. The crew of the Wellington were less fortunate

Wellington IA, N2887, of the Central Gunnery School, RAF Sutton Bridge in its role of turret gunnery instruction seen with a CGS Spitfire breaking away after making a simulated stern attack.

and staff pilot Flight Lieutenant Terence Stanbury, staff gunnery instructor Flight Sergeant Eric Cooke, and four gunnery school pupils died when the bomber crashed two miles west of Huntingdon. The subsequent inquiry found that the mishap was 'an accident – neither pilot to blame'. Seven more GCS lives were lost in identical circumstances on 13 August, when spitfire P7530 (Flight Lieutenant H.C. Bennett) collided with Wellington P9228 (Flight Lieutenant E.M. Shannon and five crew) over Stallode Wash near Lakenheath – a piece of fen that has also 'collected' a Ventura, a Lancaster and a B-50 in crashes.

In its role of evaluating fighter tactics, the Air Fighting Development Unit (AFDU) could boast examples of most RAF types. Taking up residence at RAF Wittering in mid-July 1943, it numbered a few Hurricane IVs in its inventory. Since AFDU's purpose was to conduct tactical combat exercises, who better to practise on in the daylight hours than spare 'bods' from an operational bomber squadron? This, then, was the scenario on 9 November 1943, when Hurricane IV, KW800 flown by Flight Sergeant R.H. Brown, met up over Ely with Stirling III, LK380 from 90 Squadron based at RAF Tuddenham in Norfolk.

In a swooping dive upon the Stirling from the rear, Brown, probably misjudging his speed, suddenly found himself very close to the bomber. Buffeted to such an extent by turbulence from its four engines, KW800 was thrown into contact with the bomber. With its rear fuselage and tailplane smashed by the collision the pilot Flight Lieutenant Robert Rodger and his crew plunged to their deaths at Sedge Fen. Acting as co-pilot for the sortie, taking an opportunity to gain experience, was Flight Sergeant Lees Smith, who also had two air-gunners, Flight Sergeant Morley Loyst and Sergeant Gordon Batten, from his own crew on board, bringing the total fatalities to nine airmen. Having been involved in such a collision, Flight Sergeant Brown – exceptionally – managed to bale out of the stricken Hurricane to escape safely with only minor injuries. Another of the region's recovery groups, from the Norfolk & Suffolk Aviation Museum, excavated this site in 1975.

The Nene Valley countryside to the west of Peterborough was littered with USAAF airfields whose circuits were perilously close together. USAAF daylight missions involved take-off times early in the day but sometimes, when weather forecasts suggested that returning aircraft might encounter bad weather in the base area, mission take-off times were brought forward into the pre-dawn darkness. Take-off in darkness and with other aircraft doing the same thing at airfields nearby increased the collision hazard. Molesworth (303 BG) and Kimbolton (379 BG) Airfields shared some circuit airspace and it was this sort of situation that caused the loss of a B-17 from each station on 5 January 1944. Both Groups were assigned a mission to bomb Kiel. Due to an adverse weather forecast for the afternoon, it was decided to bring forward the departure time so that the bombers would return to base before the arrival of the weather front. Being mid-winter, this meant that take-off time and the formation assembly would be in darkness, which put quite a strain on the pilots and navigators.

For Second Lieutenant Benajah Burkitt's crew, this would be its seventh mission. Their earlier missions included the one seeking out the blockade runner *Osorno*, mentioned in a previous chapter. For that mission and a couple of others, they used B-17F 42-5054 *Belle of San Joaquin*, but this latest would be flown in an unnamed B-17G replacement aircraft, delivered to base just four days before. Taking off on a southerly heading, the flight path of B-17G, 42-31441, PU-E of 360 BS, 303 BG, with Second Lieutenant Benajah G. Burkitt in command, took it across that of a B-17G, 42-37887 from 379 BG and the two collided with disastrous results. Burkitt's crew all died when it crashed two miles west of Catworth, a few miles south of the airfield, while seven airmen died in the other aircraft that came down at Covington, north-west of Kimbolton. That day Catworth was also the scene of a second crash when 42-29747 from the 379th crashed on take-off with the loss of another seven lives.

Plans for the aerial part of the invasion of France in mid-1944 began to take shape in the early months of that year. Transport aeroplanes and gliders would form a veritable armada in the sky above Normandy and the Cotentin peninsular. Practice in formation keeping for aircrew, together with tactical co-ordination for airborne troops, was therefore a vital component of that planning. But the 'Grim Reaper' joined these formations, too.

From mid-February 1944, the 316th Troop Carrier Group (316 TCG) of the US 9th Air Force took up residence at RAF Cottesmore, Rutland. Its four Troop Carrier Squadrons, 36 TCS ('4C'), 37 TCS ('W7'), 44 TCS (6E') and 45 TCS ('T3'), were equipped with C-47 Skytrain transports, plus American WACO CG4A and some British Airspeed Horsa gliders, all under the command of Lieutenant Colonel Burton R. Fleet. By the time D-Day arrived, 316 TCG was able to put seventy-two C-47s into the sky over the drop zone.

The last major practice drop of paratroops prior to the actual invasion was code-named *Operation Eagle* and scheduled for the night of 11/12 May 1944. *Eagle* called for a maximum effort from each US Troop Carrier Group in eastern England to assemble at night, navigate a course equivalent to the D-Day route to a drop zone, drop a stick of paratroops, then return to base via a dispersal beacon. No less than 800 aeroplanes from the four TC Wings took part that night, with nearly 7,000 men of the US Army's 82nd and 101st Airborne Divisions on board. On D-Day, the 316th would carry paratroopers of the 82nd Airborne Division and since this Division contained many veterans of the Sicily airborne invasion, its top brass chose to have only a token quantity of paratroops jump on this exercise, with each aircraft carrying a jumpmaster/observer who would remain on board. As this was the last dry-run opportunity for his men, Lieutenant Colonel Fleet took personal command of the 316th, going along as Air Commander in C-47A, 42-92679, flown by Major James R. Farris. Even the Group Chaplin, Captain Floyd N. Richert, got in on the act by hitching a ride in this lead aircraft, the only other passengers on board each C-47 being a US Army officer and two paratroopers.

Under a three-quarter moon, all went smoothly and according to plan on the outward journey, which took the 316th to a drop zone near Devizes in Wiltshire where each small group of soldiers was disgorged. The next stage of the exercise required those aeroplanes from units based in the Stamford and Grantham area, such as 316 TCG, to fly to a dispersion point centred on a radio beacon known as a 'buncher', in this case located at March in Cambridgeshire. This phase, too, was accomplished uneventfully, but disaster struck at 03.00 on 12 May as a melee of C-47s circled the town of March before heading home. Major Farris's Skytrain was in collision with 42-10887, flown by First Lieutenant Joseph L. Sharber Jr, and both crashed. Everyone on board both aeroplanes, a total of fourteen airmen and soldiers, was killed:

Role	36 TCS C-47 42-92679	44 TCS C-47 42-10887
Pilot	Maj James R. Farris	1/Lt Joseph L. Sharber Jr
Co-pilot	2/Lt Dickson H. Spencer	Flight/Off Hubert M. Bayless
Navigator	1/Lt Glenn R Still	1/Lt Harry Gallack
Engineer	S/Sgt Thaddeus T. Tomchek	S/Sgt Floyd V. Asleson
Radio operator	T/Sgt John M. Elliott	S/Sgt Harlan C. Sandlin
Group Commander	Lt Col Burton R. Fleet	–
Group Chaplin	Capt Floyd N. Richert	–
Officers i/c paratroops	Capt John D. Rice	2/Lt William A. Gullick, 82nd Airborne Division

Regardless of this blow, 316's preparation for the big day carried on under a new Commander, culminating in the Group dropping 1,300 paratroops, gliders and heavy equipment near Ste-Mere-Eglise in the predawn of D-Day itself. Their next big test would be over Arnhem, but fortunately without the accompaniment of further tragedy.

By far the worst air accident in terms of loss of life ever to occur in the region dealt with in this book involved two more American C-47s, this time from 315 TCG based at Spanhoe, Northants. Having been fully committed on D-Day the 315th returned to re-supply work and more training. On the evening of 8 July, thirty-three Skytrains took off from Spanhoe. On board were 369 paratroops of the 1st Independent Polish Parachute Brigade, scheduled to be dropped over RAF Wittering as part of an exercise code-named *Operation Burden*.

Now assembled in formation, the olive-green C-47s flew in a column of three squadrons, five minutes apart, with each squadron in flights of three aircraft in a 'Vee' with 200–500yds between each section of three. They made a splendid, stately sight against a backdrop of sunset as they headed for Wittering at 1,300ft. The 309th was lead squadron, with Lieutenant Colonel Smylie C. Stark at its head. According to USAAF accident investigation documentation, First Lieutenant James G. Leonard in '341 led the third element of 309 TCS, with Second Lieutenant Leo L. Byrne in '873 on his left wing and First Lieutenant Tudor in '833 on his right.

It was all over in an instant: 43-15341 (element leader) and 42-108873 (on leader's left) touched and locked together, diving to the ground on the banks of the River Welland, near

Douglas C-47 Skytrains of 309th TCS ('M6') 315th TCG showing the tight formations these troop carriers flew. (Dave Benfield)

the village of Tinwell. From a position looking back from a Skytrain in the next element ahead, former Polish company commander, Lieutenant Albert Smaczny, claimed to have seen an unexpected turning manoeuvre and the subsequent impact. Some years ago he wrote an account that was published in the Peterborough *Evening Telegraph*:

> Suddenly something horrible is happening. The aircraft on the left is making a tight turn to the right, careering on the starboard wing [*sic*] and making a circle on to the middle aircraft. The pilot of the middle aircraft, retaining his cold blood and senses, suddenly pulls up thus avoiding a collision and missing the other by inches. For the aircraft on the right this is a complete surprise. I can see as both aircraft are plummeting down shedding debris as they go down to crash.

When the detail of that account is compared to the official USAAF drawing of the formation positions of each aircraft, it should be borne in mind that the eyewitness is looking *back* at the three aircraft behind him. Lieutenant Smaczny's account suggests that Lieutenant Tudor's aircraft turned towards that of Lieutenant Leonard, and the latter took avoiding action and missed Tudor by a whisker, with that same action unfortunately taking him into the path of Lieutenant Byrne's aircraft.

Radio operator Corporal Thomas Chambers USAAF, acting as dispatcher, was wearing a parachute and standing in the open doorway as the drop zone approached. Immediately the collision occurred he baled out and was lucky enough to escape unhurt. He was found dazed and shaking with his feet embedded in the mud at the edge of the River Welland. It is believed some Polish paratroops from one aircraft attempted to jump, but the few who did so were too low to survive. Corporal Chambers' record of events – if one exists – has not been found.

Tragic though this event was, it became swallowed up by the tide of war – except, of course, for the villagers of Tinwell. In their mind's-eye would remain forever the heart-rending sight of those tattered bodies and torn aeroplanes. So that those men from faraway lands would never be forgotten, the villagers hung a framed parchment memorial in their tiny Norman church. It recorded for posterity the names of all thirty-four men who died: twenty-six from the Polish 3rd Battalion's 8th Company and eight US aircrew. This parchment has, in more recent times, been replaced by a similar brass plaque.

Troop Carrier Groups were scattered across airfields all around the Grantham district, each playing a vital role in the invasion plan. Over at RAF Barkston Heath, between Grantham and Sleaford, 61 TCG had also been operating in the same part of Normandy as the 316th. Training did not stop after D-Day itself but continued apace, for there were now resupply drops to organise and even the prospect of more para-drops should the allied bridgehead be contained by the enemy.

It was on 28 July, during a routine local area supply-drop practice in good visibility, that two C-47s from 59 TCS/61 TCG came to grief a couple of miles to the west of Sleaford. As in the earlier accident, it was not an error caused by inexperience, since both pilots had over 1,000 hours' flying on this type. But tight formations required concentrated, accurate supply drops under combat conditions, and it needed only seconds to transform order into chaos. Flying at a height of 1,500ft, there was little time for recovery action if the aeroplanes sustained damage that affected their flying capability. Thus it was that Skytrain 42-23334, flown by First Lieutenant Thomas A. Gall and a crew of four (Second Lieutenant John L. Craven, co-pilot; First Lieutenant Robert E. James, navigator; Technical Sergeant Max E. Turner, engineer; and Sergeant Robert R. Meyers, radio), was in collision with 43-15097 from the same unit, crewed by First Lieutenant George B. Hartzell and his crew of three (Second Lieutenant Arthur F. Gruel, co-pilot; Staff Sergeant M.S. Lujan, engineer; and Staff

Sergeant Harold E. West, radio). Nine more airmen perished when these C-47s crashed near South Rauceby and Broadwater.

Each passing year saw more new airfields being constructed at such a rate in eastern England that the Fenland area was virtually outlined by an almost unbroken 'circle of runways'. Four-engine bombers, for whom many of these airfields were built, had been operational in growing numbers themselves since 1942. Not only were greater numbers of aircraft needed to pound the Third Reich more heavily, but also to release aircraft for training and to replace both operational and accidental losses. Although the roles of the region's airfields included single- and multi-engine training, transport and operational bombing, it is the latter which now captures the spotlight in the context of collisions.

In the middle of 1944, following hard on the heels of the invasion, RAF Bomber Command directed that daylight sorties, which had been abandoned a year earlier, were to be resumed. These sorties would be in support of the advancing allied armies, against enemy lines of communication or specific targets such as the V-weapon sites. 'Bomber' Harris was not too keen, in view of the high losses on daylight raids earlier in the war, but as long as the bombers operated within the cover afforded by the superior allied fighter escort capability, it was possible to avoid losses on the earlier scale. The result of this resumption was to place RAF bomber pilots in the unaccustomed position of having to polish up their formation flying ability. Many simply had no experience, as this was a skill rarely called upon in the night bomber 'streams'. A sad consequence of this occurred on the morning of 23 June 1944 at RAF Coningsby.

Aircrews of No.97 Squadron were in high spirits as they waited to be driven to their aeroplanes. As a prank they all descended upon a small Fiat car owned by Flight Lieutenant

Perkins' crew in the winter of 1943. Back row from left: Sergeant Coxhead, Flight Lieutenant Perkins, Flying Officer Hunt, Flight Sergeant Fairbairn. Front: Sergeant Coman, Flight Sergeant McBride, Sergeant Russell. No.97 Squadron Lancaster ND981. McBride and Russell were replaced by WO Partos and Flying Officer Ward by the collision date. (R. Perkins)

Edward Perkins and heaved it onto the top of an air-raid shelter. Perched precariously, it remained there as they all took off for an unaccustomed daylight practice formation flight over south Lincolnshire.

Starting a gentle turn to port just south of Spalding, the Lancaster of Flight Lieutenant Henry Van Raalte, ME625, drifted above the formation leader, Bill Gee. As he slid back to regain position ME625 was tossed about by engine turbulence, smashing into Flight Lieutenant Perkins' aircraft, ND981, and breaking off its tail unit. Both aeroplanes spun out of control and crashed. Much subdued, the squadron returned to base, where Perkins' little car was lifted down gently from atop the shelter. Of the fourteen airmen on board these two aeroplanes, only one, Wireless Operator/Air-Gunner Sergeant Coman, the rear gunner in Perkins' crew, survived. Interviewed in 1980, local resident Percy Chapman, who lived in a cottage not far from the scene at Four Mile Bar, said he witnessed the incident and gave a vivid account of the collision:

> They collided high over the River Welland and I watched one come down on Atkinson's Farm at Four Mile Bar, Deeping High Bank, wreckage straddling the farm roadway. This aeroplane spun round and round and seemed to have its tail cut off. A parachute opened just at the last moment before the bomber hit the ground and exploded in a ball of fire. Smoke and flames shot a hundred feet in the air and bullets soon began to crackle and shoot off in all directions.

From this description and the information that follows, it is certain the Lancaster which fell to the east of the river on Atkinson's Farm was Perkins' ND981.

This incident was also seen by Peter Sanderson, then an apprentice electrician and a keen-eyed aeroplane enthusiast, as he walked along Cowbit Road. He watched one of the machines fall to the west side of the river, in the area near what is now known as Postland Airfield and Cloot Drove. This was confirmed later for him by his uncle, Stan Sanderson, a resident of Cowbit who was working in fields near the crash site at the time. He remembered some wing wreckage and an engine buried itself in a dyke, recalling seeing large quantities of oil floating on the water. His information was verified in 1979 when an engine, undercarriage legs and fuselage components from ME625 were excavated from that very dyke by the Lincolnshire Aircraft Preservation Society. More engines and wreckage were recovered from the same area in 1983.

Six weeks after the accident, Sergeant Coman took to the air again on a training flight with a new crew. The horror of the crash, however, still lingered in his mind and proved too much of a burden for him to bear. He never flew again.

In stark contrast to the resource-starved early days, the later stages of the war saw vast numbers of Lancasters in service, with a plentiful supply of aircrew available. Special units were therefore established to handle more thoroughly the final stages of pre-operational training on this type of aeroplane.

Known as Lancaster Finishing Schools (LFS), one such unit, No.3 LFS, formed at RAF Feltwell in December 1943. Remaining there until January 1945, it was then disbanded as the RAF had, by that time, reached a state of over-supply of aircrew. The price of training, though, still ran high. Daylight or darkness, in formation or alone – it seemed to matter little to the possibility of collision. Fourteen men from the School, the complete crews of Lancaster W4851, flown by New Zealander Pilot Officer Rex Newman and ED376, flown by Canadian Flying Officer Richard Whitby, died on 17 June 1944 when each was returning from an independent cross-country flight. Accident investigators were unable to determine the cause of either of the two crashes, but the close proximity of the two crash sites and the similar time at which they occurred (2.00a.m.) were factors that suggested two aeroplanes had strayed into the other's path and collided. ED376 fell on farmland near Southery, five miles south south-east of Downham Market, and W4851 dived into the ground at Shallock Farm, Lakenheath.

Another fourteen airmen from the same unit died in similar circumstances on 18 December. Two aircraft, Lancasters R5674, A5-K and R5846, A5-H, each having completed a 'Bullseye' bombing and navigation exercise, were in the Feltwell circuit when the accident occurred. Led by Flight Sergeant Horace Harler (Australia) and Flight Sergeant Thomas Jacobs (New Zealand), both crews perished when the Lancasters crashed near Hockwold cum Wilton, south-west of the airfield. The site of R5674 was excavated by FAWNAPS in July 1980. When it crashed, the aircraft ran up against a chalk layer and penetrated only to a depth of ten feet. It appeared, too, that the wartime salvage team recovered the engines and then threw much of the other wreckage into the holes from which the engines were taken. After much work, a bomb door ram, parachute release and buckles, an escape hatch, two ASIs, a propellor boss and fire extinguisher were recovered from the site.

With airspace in Lincolnshire always at a premium, the wonder is that even more collisions than those recorded here did not occur. Probably the most persistent feature of such accidents was when two or more aeroplanes manoeuvring in close proximity, although aware of each other's presence, focused so intently on 'the game in hand' that they strayed unwittingly into the path of another aeroplane with dire results. This scenario fitted the circumstances of a crash at Ruskington Fen in the heart of 'bomber country'.

In what was described as excellent visibility, Lancaster ND572 from No.57 Squadron, East Kirkby and ME473 from No.207 Squadron at Spilsby were lost in a training accident when they collided on 2 March 1945. At the start of a fighter affiliation exercise with a Hurricane, the pilot of ND572 had just begun to throw his Lancaster around the sky when ME473, on its way back to base – after completing a quite separate fighter affiliation exercise of its own – flew into it. The Hurricane escaped any involvement in the collision. On board ND572 was twenty-year-old AC2 Hunter Aitken, a navigator under training with No.57 Squadron, who died alongside aircraft captain Pilot Officer Robert Anscomb and the remaining six members of his crew. The collision also caused ME473 to crash with the loss of all eight airmen on board Australian Flight Lieutenant Edward Lawson's bomber. His crew that day included LAC John Morrison, who was Lawson's batman, and had simply been invited along for the ride.

ME473 came down on Ruskington Fen Farm and ND572 onto White House Farm, North Kyme Pitts near Billinghay. In the absence of any survivors among the sixteen airmen, the subsequent investigation made the rather obvious recommendation that two fighter affiliation exercises should not be allowed to take place at the same height, time and area. Only fifteen bodies were recovered from the wreckage of the two aeroplanes. All eight airmen on board ND572 were identified but only six of the eight in ME473 could be named for certain. Of the remaining two men, one could not be found and was posted as 'missing', and another body that was found could not be identified. These two men were Flight Sergeant Arthur Henderson and Sergeant Robert Banks. At the time, for reasons that are not clear now, the inquest coroner thought the unidentified body was most likely that of air-gunner Sergeant Robert Banks, but since he could not be absolutely certain, when the remains were buried the headstone simply read 'An Unknown Airman'. As a result of the coroner's assumption, the missing airman was recorded as being the bomb aimer, Flight Sergeant Henderson.

For fifty-one years, this is the way things remained until, in 1995, the mystery of who was who was finally resolved with something of an unusual twist. The dedicated aircraft archaeologists of Lincolnshire Aircraft Recovery Group obtained a licence to dig the site of ND572, but such was the closeness of the two locations that, after they began to uncover wreckage, they discovered they were actually on the site of ME473. Question marks began to appear when amongst the wreckage they found evidence of human remains, something that should not have been the case if the site was indeed that of ND572. Conscious of the ethical and emotional delicacy of their find, they probed further and this was when personal effects were found that subsequently proved invaluable in solving the mystery. In accordance with official guidelines, work was halted and the MOD was advised of the situation. RAF experts launched an investigation and, with the help of the personal effects, were able to confirm the remains found in the wreckage at the site were those of Sergeant Robert Banks. An RAF spokesman said: 'We have no doubt now that it is Flight Sergeant Henderson who is buried in the Unknown Airman's grave.'

The final act in this long-running story came on 25 October 1996 when Sergeant Robert Banks was laid to rest in Cambridge City Cemetery, with full military honours. A fly-past by the BBMF Dakota was a link with the past together with some former airmen from 207 Squadron, but sadly, no family members could be traced. However, the discovery of course enabled Flight Sergeant Henderson's family to know that the fate of their relative had been accounted for and his sister watched as a new headstone, complete with his name, was placed on the grave of the brother she last saw when she was seventeen.

Very similar circumstances on 20 March brought a premature end to the lives of Flight Sergeant Charles Jones and an unknown number of airmen he was carrying in DH Dominie NF889. Trundling along at 5,000ft in the vicinity of Bourne, on what should have been just an innocuous wireless instruction flight, this Dominie from No.1 Radio School at RAF College Cranwell was rammed by Spitfire Vb AR395 from 1653 Conversion Unit as the latter broke away from a simulated attack on a Lancaster. Questioned later, eyewitnesses stated that the Dominie's track was unlikely to have constituted a danger to the other two aeroplanes involved in the fighter affiliation exercise. But in the blink of an eye, tragedy struck. Writing in 1978, Mr Anthony Turner of Little Bytham remembered these aeroplanes crashing near Witham-on-the-Hill, in a field that, in the 1970s, was used by a gliding club.

A small glimpse of a somewhat obscure unit operating in Fenland skies, is provided by way of a collision between Stirling IV PW391 from RAF Matching in Essex and Master II DM336 from 7 SFTS, now the latest unit resident at RAF Sutton Bridge. Towards the end of 1944, the Operational and Refresher Training Unit (ORTU) of No.38 (Airborne Forces) Group moved to RAF Matching. Equipped with Stirling IVs and later Halifaxes, ORTU was tasked to provide flying practice for crews being held in reserve as replacements for those lost hauling gliders into action. Even the ORTU itself was required on some occasions to contribute directly to airborne operations, such as the Rhine crossing. Meanwhile, No.7 SFTS Sutton Bridge – now a satellite of RAF Peterborough and still in the business of training newly qualified pilots – provided the second player in this scenario. The unfortunate pilot was Corporal R. Debienkiewicz, a Frenchman drawn from the ranks of one of several batches of his countrymen processed by 7 SFTS and its predecessor 7 (P)AFU, at Peterborough and Sutton Bridge since September 1944. Thus the aerial scene was set, but there is another aspect to this incident to be considered.

In 1945 Mrs Betty Spridgeon was a young Land Army girl, working on farms in the Thorney area. She remembered the collision vividly, not as an eyewitness, but as one who may have escaped injury from its fall-out. Betty takes up the story:

I was working with other Land Army girls in the pea field on Knarr Cross Farm, Thorney, into which the Lancaster [sic] fell. It was near Whitsun holiday and being allowed a three-day break, we asked our foreman if he would let us finish work a little earlier than usual. This would enable us to go back to our hostel, get changed and hopefully catch an earlier train to go home to see our Mums. Mr Gilbert, no doubt with a twinkle in his eye, said that IF we worked VERY hard, he might agree – which he did.

It was not until we returned to the farm after the holiday that we found out about the aeroplane crashing into that very field shortly after we had left it to go home. I remember seeing four craters in the field where the engines had buried themselves and felt sadness for those poor airmen but relief for myself.

The official view of the accident states the Stirling, with Flight Lieutenant Walter Howes in command, was on a cross-country training flight in good weather. All seven members of the crew were killed when, on 29 March 1945, it was in collision with a Master, the pilot of which also died.

Considering the close proximity of many of the American airfield circuits to each other and factors such as the complex bomber formations employed by the Americans sometimes requiring an hour or two to assemble, often under the most taxing of weather conditions, there are surprisingly few collisions recorded – at least in the East Midlands region. Generally the only personnel involved were airmen serving their country, and while such incidents are regrettable, it has to be said that they represented an occupational hazard to such men. The same cannot be said, however, for civilians caught by a deluge of wreckage from the sky, of which there are, again, surprisingly few.

One of the most poignant stories in this region emerged from an account of a collision between B17Gs 43-37806 and 43-37894, researched in detail by author and air historian Ian Maclachlan.

The date was 6 February 1945. In the village of Prickwillow, farmhand Syd Leonard sat in his yard, hands clasped tightly round his early morning 'cuppa' when a loud noise made him look up. His jaw dropped in amazement as there, heading straight towards him, was the huge form of a four-engine bomber! This was no illusion, though. Before any sound forewarned the sleeping village, B-17, 43-37894, smashed the Legge family bungalow into near oblivion, flipped over a high drainage bank where the remnants smashed into Gladys Howe's 'Lilecote Cottage' on the other side, turning it into a fireball of blazing petrol. Miraculously, most of the drowsy inhabitants of these homes escaped death due to the bravery of villagers who rushed to the scene within minutes of hearing the explosions. Despite this prompt action, however, Mrs Edith Legge sustained severe injuries from which she never really recovered. Dazed, confused and suffering cuts and burns, Gladys, her mother and her daughter managed to scramble their way out through rubble and flames to where willing hands helped them to safety.

Bearing the brunt of the impact, the Legge bungalow was completely demolished. With little thought for his own safety, Syd Leonard, helped by men from the village, hacked his way inside to rescue Edith. But her baby daughter, Josephine and a ten-year-old evacuee girl, Pamela Turner, were beyond help, and both perished in the conflagration.

The cause of the crash was a collision between two B-17s, from different units, climbing through thumping propellor-wash, fog and partial darkness while assembling for a raid on German synthetic oil plants. B-17, 37894, *Big Poison*, flown by Lieutenant John W. Hedgcock, was from 849 BS, 490 BG based at Eye in Suffolk, from where it had taken off at 5.45a.m. When the collision occurred, amazingly Lieutenant Al Elias (bombardier) managed to replace the arming pins on eight 500lb bombs before baling out. All ten crewmen jumped clear, but a couple sustained fractured bones on landing. Tail gunner Sergeant Ed Tijan was not so fortunate, and died when his parachute failed to open.

The scene of devastation after the impact of B-17G 43-37894 on the Legge bungalow (on left) in Prickwillow. The wrecked tail of B-17G 43-37894, with these numbers just visible above the aircraft identification letter 'R', can be seen in the garden against the drainage bank. (Russell Zorn via Ian Maclachlan)

Minus her nose, *Miss B. Havin* makes it back to base after the collision on 26 April 1945. (Stuart Evans)

Abandoned by its crew, the second B–17, 37806, piloted by Lieutenant George F. Thompson Jr from 561 BS, 388 BG, aptly named *Miss Fortune*, crashed in open farmland on Brack's Farm, Soham. Its load of ten 500lb bombs exploded, creating an enormous crater, but causing only light damage to a few buildings in the area. Sadly another airman, co-pilot Lieutenant Robert A. Wettersten, died as the result of his parachute failing to open. Gradually the devastation was cleared up. New dwellings were built and others repaired, but nothing would erase the scars of that day for the Legge and Howe families, nor wipe the sights and sounds of that day from the minds of the villagers of Prickwillow.

In this region, the last American collision of the European war occurred on 26 April and involved two B–17Gs from another Suffolk-based Group, the 486th at Sudbury. The 486th flew its last combat mission over Europe on 21 April, but since there was a possibility of being posted to the Pacific theatre, training had to continue. Poor formation-keeping during one such training exercise was alleged to be the reason for an 834 BS Fortress, 44-8687, flown by First Lieutenant Clyde E. Simmonds, being in collision with 43-38859, flown by First Lieutenant William D. Dobbins from 835 BS. By 26 April, Simmonds had completed three combat missions and on this particular day was not flying with his own crew. He had just been re-assigned as a 'lead pilot' and was getting in some practice with an experienced crew when the accident happened.

A three-squadron formation was practising turns to right and left at about 12,000ft and flying through thin cloud when 38859 (No.9 of the lead Squadron) collided with 8687 (No.2 of the low squadron). B–17G, 38859's propellor blades chewed into the rear section of 8687 from above, cutting off the tail assembly. B–17G, 8687 fell out of control and crashed into a potato field at Lutton Marsh near Long Sutton. Lieutenant Simmonds died along with five of his crew: First Lieutenant Donald L. Williamson, co-pilot; First Lieutenant James G. Olson, observer; Sergeant Robert L. West, radio; Sergeant Edward G. Geron, gunner; and Sergeant John J. Hill, flight engineer, who baled out but was too low for his parachute to open. Two more – Second Lieutenant Vincent T. Colletti, navigator, and Second Lieutenant Robert F. Bradley, bombardier – baled out and sustained minor injuries. Breaking away from the formation on impact, the second machine, 43-38859 *Miss B. Havin'*, lost its plexiglass nose, suffered numerous dents in the port wing and the blades of the port inner were bent at the tips, but she managed to stay in the air and none of the crew was injured. Lieutenant Dobbins struggled back to base on three engines and made a relatively 'normal' landing.

The final collision of the war period in this region is perhaps the one that represents most graphically all the freak elements of chance in such an incident. Almost all of the foregoing are what might be described as 'close-proximity' collisions, where at least there was a general awareness of the danger and the other party. This one, however, had a slow, inexorable build-up to a catastrophe of which none of those involved could have had the slightest inkling of its approach. 'It was a chance in a million', said one Peterborough newspaper. 'Rain of fire from the sky', wrote another. A chance in a million, indeed.

Confirmation that ORTU, the refresher unit mentioned earlier, changed to Halifaxes is given by the involvement of NA702, a Mark III, in a night collision with Wellington X, LP906 during the early hours of 3 June 1945. The war in Europe was over, but keeping crews trained to tow glider-borne forces in support of the Far East campaign against Japan was felt to remain very much a necessity. ORTU therefore still had a role to play, and in the late evening of 6 June, Flight Sergeant Sydney Cook from that unit, with his crew of five, was airborne on a practice cross-country exercise. Flight Sergeant Albert Collins in the Wellington from No.81 OTU, also on a cross-country, had with him a crew of four. It is interesting to note how the crews of both these aircraft appear to have a slightly smaller complement than might have been the case only a month previously. The crewmen omitted may well have been the odd gunner or two, clearly not required in peacetime. Perhaps, though, those extra pairs of eyes were sorely missed when the tracks of the two aeroplanes converged over the Gunthorpe district of Peterborough.

Virtually all the collisions mentioned so far have involved aeroplanes travelling over relatively short distances prior to the particular incident. Just what are the odds, then, of such a three-dimensional intersection taking place a few thousand feet over Peterborough in pitch darkness, when one considers the Wellington was based at RAF Sleap near Shrewsbury (110 miles west) and the Halifax at Matching, near Harlow in Essex (sixty miles south)? But they did, with the result that eleven airmen died. So complete was the destruction that at first it was thought the Halifax had simply caught fire in the air and exploded. It was not until a wing of the distinctive construction of a Wellington was found that it dawned on the rescue services that two aeroplanes were involved. That wing was the only identifiable part of the Wellington to be found. By yet another twist of fate, the rain of destruction miraculously missed the city and wreckage, falling over an area of fifty acres, caused no damage to civilians or property.

Part 3: Post War

The arrival of peace brought no respite. There were three collisions in the region in 1946 near Cranwell, Spilsby and Digby, involving pairs of Harvards, Martinets and Spitfires respectively, and four airmen died in these. Two Wellington T10s collided on approach to RAF Swinderby on 15 October 1950 with the loss of eight from their crews. When flying embraced the jet age, coupled with an upsurge in the RAF's Cold War training activity at this time, there was little change in the incidence of this hazard – evidenced, for example, by the mid-air collision between two Meteor F8s, VZ569 and WA985 from No.65 Squadron, near RAF Strubby on 3 July 1951.

Glistening in sunlight reflecting from RAF North Luffenham's rain soaked apron are Canadair Sabres of No.1 Wing RCAF. In the foreground is 19181, one of a pair of Sabres destroyed in a mid-air collision over The Wash on 15 April 1952.

As mentioned earlier, the RCAF arrived at RAF North Luffenham and soon its intensive flying programme over the region brought the inevitable mishaps. Tragedy struck first at No.410 (Cougar) Squadron with the loss two pilots on 18 April 1952, when new boy Flying Officer Jerry Kerr in 19177 collided with Flying Officer A.E. Rayner in 19181. Both Sabres fell onto Wainfleet range and although one pilot managed to eject, both died as a result of the accident.

On 11 July 1952 the RCAF was fortunate not to be on the receiving end of more casualties. Canadian Sabres were filling the role of inbound targets on a practice interception exercise with DH Vampire FB5 aircraft from No.93 Squadron that were over in the UK on detachment from their 2nd Tactical Air Force (2TAF) base at Jever in Germany. Pilot Officer John Wood was leading a section of four Vampires from their temporary base at Duxford, detailed to intercept two Canadian Sabres over The Wash. The Vampires eventually found the Sabres and a dogfight developed at 20,000ft during which Pilot Officer Wood, in VV224, coded T-X, collided with his number four, WA189, T-T. The twin booms of VV224 broke away but Wood baled out safely before the jet exploded, scattering wreckage across a wide area on the south-east edge of The Wash. Much to the chagrin of a retired naval Commander, the plummeting engine made rather a mess of his garden in the village of Terrington St Clements, while part of the fuselage fell to earth nearby. One wing came down on the sea bank and Pilot Officer Woods himself parachuted onto a mudbank off North Wooton, dislocating his shoulder in the process. Lying helpless waist-deep in the mud, with his comrades circling overhead, he was in some pain and peril before local ferrymen came out to rescue him from the clutches of a rising tide. The rescuers had to leave their boat, run half a mile along a stone bank then wade a hundred yards in mud up to their thighs to reach the airman, who greeted them with: 'I'm *** *** glad to see you!' WA189, meanwhile, was able to limp back to Duxford.

RAF Oakington was home to No.206 Advanced Flying Squadron (206 AFS), essentially a Meteor OTU, which saw the loss two pairs of Meteors as a result of collisions. On 9 September 1952, Flying Officer P.G. Rowley in Meteor F3, EE401 was on a formation exercise with Flying Officer J.H. Lucop in Meteor F4, VZ405. Lucop was in the lead and signalled visually for Rowley to change from line astern to echelon port. During the change Rowley lost sight of his leader and the next he knew was that his aircraft had rammed EE401, breaking off its tail unit. Both aircraft spun in and crashed near the villages of Over and Swavesey (Cambridgeshire), but not before the pilots baled out safely.

Later that same year, two more Meteors from 206 AFS were lost when, on 16 December, F4, VT218 collided with T7, WG978. Flying in line astern at 9,000ft altitude, '978 struck the underside of '218 with such force that '218's fuselage broke off aft of the wing, while '978's broke forward of the wing. Flying Officer Dennis Dowell in '978 died when his cockpit canopy was shattered by the impact, but Flight Sergeant E.W. Ginger was able to bale out of the F4. Flying Officer Dowell and the wreckage of both aircraft fell to earth on arable land belonging to H.H. Bowser and H. Tunnard, at Leadenhall Farm, near RAF Holbeach range. Suffering from shock and bruising, Flight Sergeant Ginger was taken to Mr Lewis Johnson's house to await an ambulance from RAF Marham. Recounting his story to a local newspaper reporter, eyewitness George Leake said:

I was working in the yard of Leadenhall farm when the aircraft passed overhead at a great height. I heard a roar and looked up over the marshes and saw two pinpoints of light. They looked like flares falling to the ground. As they neared the ground they drew slowly apart. Then there was a terrific explosion and smoke shot upwards like a mushroom.

Changing formation position caused problems for Squadron Leader Gordon Storey (later Wing Commander OBE AFC) and Captain C.G. Gillespie USAF (an American officer on

The Forth railway bridge makes a fine backdrop for this formation of Gloster Meteor F4s of No.222 Squadron in 1950. Nearest the camera, VT218, ZD-R passed from frontline service to No.206 Advanced Flying School at RAF Oakington with whom it crashed on 16 December 1952.

an exchange posting), in Meteor F8s, WK726 and WH378 respectively, while they were on a camera gun and formation exercise on 19 April 1955, over the flat land around Peterborough. This pair was airborne from No.56 Squadron based at Waterbeach when they collided at 6,000ft and fell within a quarter mile of each other in Bukehorn Road, Thorney. One Meteor burst into flames as it plunged to earth and the other exploded on impact. Two tractor drivers out ploughing were showered with debris but escaped unharmed. Both pilots ejected and parachuted down safely.

This was 'Twinkle' Storey's second baleout, his first, also while he was with No.56 Squadron, gaining him the dubious honour of being the first to eject from a Supermarine Swift. His Swift F1, WK209, went into a spin and crashed four miles south of West Raynham on 7 May 1954. In February 1954, 56 Squadron began to re-equip with the troublesome Swift but after several accidents – including the one involving WK209 – it was decided to withdraw the aeroplane from the squadron in March 1955. This accounts for why Storey and Gillespie were flying relatively old Meteor 8 aircraft when they collided. The Meteors were stopgap aircraft pending the arrival of Hunter 5s with which 56 Squadron was due to re-equip in May of that year.

Airman Second Class Vernon Morgan always wanted to be a pilot. His lot in life, though, was to become a ground crew mechanic serving with the USAF at Alconbury airbase near Huntingdon. The saving grace for him was that at least he could be close to those whom he admired and be around aircraft that he loved. Life, though, can play cruel tricks, and on Friday 13 June 1958 – a fateful date if ever there was one – Vernon Lewis Morgan, aged twenty-one from Elizabeth, Indiana, simultaneously had his moment of glory and became one of its saddest victims.

By mid-1958, the USAF had all but withdrawn its fleet of ageing North American B-45A Tornado four-engine medium bombers from active service at Alconbury, replacing them with the Douglas B-66 Destroyer. There were, however, a couple of examples of the former still attached to the 86th Bomb Squadron which was detached from the 47th Bomb Wing's home base at Sculthorpe in Norfolk. Morgan worked on the B-45 on the flight line and he got to know them intimately, no doubt taking every opportunity to familiarise himself with engine start-up procedures and flying control functions during the course of his work.

Something of Morgan's Walter Mitty-like characteristics was brought to light in the aftermath of the story that now unfolds. It seems he was a married man but, in common with many young servicemen on unaccompanied overseas postings, liked to spend his time in the company of the local young ladies, in this case in nearby Peterborough. It was later reported in the local press that Vernon befriended a sixteen-year-old Peterborough girl who alleged he told her he was divorced and they dated each other regularly. During these meetings his ambition to become a pilot emerged and in her words, 'he was mad about flying planes', and boasted to her that, one day, he would show her just what he could do. It was said that Morgan was so taken with the girl that he bought her a ring as a token of his affection. No one will really know if the girl or her family may have felt the relationship was getting out of hand, but on 12 June a significant event occurred which could well have been the catalyst for the tragedy that followed. In the subsequent enquiry, USAF investigating officers discovered that, during the evening, the girl had tried to break off the relationship and had given back the ring to Morgan.

Fate then took a vicious hand in events. That most notorious of superstitious dates, Friday the 13th, was but ten minutes old when the night sky near the base was rent by the flash and explosion of a mid-air collision. Alconbury control tower was quickly aware of the accident,

North American B-45A Tornado, 47-0046, of 86 BS, 47 BW USAF involved in the events of 13 June 1958.

which occurred in its control zone, and within minutes rescue services went into action and the base was brought to a major alert state.

In the midst of all the confusion that accompanied these sort of events, Vernon Morgan seized the opportunity he had longed for. He would show everyone right now that he could be a pilot! With no previous flying experience whatsoever he calmly started up all four jet engines of B-45, serial number 47-046, and taxied the bomber onto the main runway. Before anyone could grasp what was happening or take preventative action, Morgan opened the throttles and according to eyewitnesses, the B-45 thundered down the runway into a perfect take-off!

Morgan's ambition was short lived, however, because the aircraft banked progressively and lost height until it crashed a scant three minutes later, killing him instantly. On first impact it scraped along the ground for 100yds, then hammered into the railway embankment at Green Lane Arch, Wood Walton, cart-wheeling and disintegrating across the main east coast railway lines, completely blocking the tracks. The alarming prospect of a further disaster was narrowly averted when an express train was stopped only minutes away from the wreckage. All trains were diverted for more than four hours until the lines could be sufficiently cleared and repaired.

The aircraft involved in the earlier collision were a USAF Lockheed T-33A, 56-1604 from the 20th Fighter-bomber Wing at Wethersfield and an RAF Canberra PR7, WJ823 from No.58 Squadron based at Wyton. Both were on quite independent routine night training flights and the T-33 was in contact with Alconbury tower only thirty seconds before the collision. The crews were, respectively, Captain David C. Evans, a flying instructor from Alconbury, and First Lieutenant Edgar L. Stephenson, his pupil from the 55 FBS, 20 FBW, Wethersfield. In the Canberra was Flying Officer Bryan Crocker, pilot, and Flight Lieutenant

English Electric Canberra PR7 similar to WJ823 that collided with T-33, 56-1604.

Lockheed T-33A, 56-1604 of 20 FBW USAF that collided with Canberra WJ820.

Walter Stevens, navigator. All four airmen died in the collision, which occurred over the village of Spaldwick, about six miles south of Alconbury.

Several former USAF servicemen who were based at Alconbury came forward with recollections of this incident, and Paul J. Parker recounted the following story, which offers a view of the incident that did not later make it into the newspapers:

> I had many memorable experiences as a controller but none quite like Friday 13 June 1958, which was a most memorable night for me. I was a young air traffic controller who had just arrived at RAF Alconbury that week. Lee Netzler, who had been an air traffic controller at the base for a year and I were detailed to relieve a three-man crew in the base Ground Controlled Approach (GCA) unit and work the midnight to 08.00 shift. We walked into the GCA unit and the young duty controller was talking to our AACS Squadron CO. The 'T-bird' [Lockheed T-33] had just made a touch-and-go and was climbing out towards RAF Wyton, which was about five miles off the end of Alconbury's runway. The controller said to the T-bird: 'You have a target dead ahead one or two miles, altitude unknown.' Then the targets converged and disappeared. He called the T-bird several more times but got no reply.
>
> It was 13 June 1958, just after midnight and the sky was clear. Unknown to the duty controller, RAF Wyton had a Canberra landing and in view of the overlapping circuits, it would have to cross the end of Alconbury's runway. Prior to that period in time there was no air traffic co-ordination between Wyton and Alconbury – a very dangerous situation. We all know what happened next – the two aircraft collided in mid-air. The on-duty GCA crew called Alconbury tower but got no response because after the collision, one of the aircraft hit a power line and knocked out all power to both Wyton and Alconbury towers. Fortunately Alconbury GCA unit was powered by a diesel generator and was still operating and on the air. After several minutes Alconbury tower got its own standby generator going and got back on air. We discussed amongst ourselves what had happened then, as there was not much room in the GCA unit and nowhere for me to sit, I stepped outside for a while. The GCA unit sat on an old abandoned runway and was about 400 feet from the main runway. As I was standing by the GCA unit, I heard the engines on a jet aircraft accelerating. Next thing I knew, a B-45 rolled down the runway, less than 400 feet from me, in the OPPOSITE direction to that being used by aircraft landing that night. I went back into the GCA unit and told the crew what I had just seen. The crew called the tower and we discussed what I saw. The tower crew said that it was probably the Canberra from RAF Wyton trying to land. I knew that the two aircraft looked similar but I was sure it was a B-45.

We watched the GCA search radar as this aircraft climbed out to about ten miles and then it made a right turn. I went back outside to look for it – remember it was around midnight and dark but the sky was clear and there was a bright moon. As I was looking for the B-45, I saw it off to my right. It was just off the end of the abandoned runway on which the GCA unit was sitting. I stepped up to go into the GCA unit to tell the crew to get out when the B-45 did a loop and crashed somewhere off the end of the runway.

Later we found out that a young USAF airman stole the B-45 and took it off. Some said he was heading for the USA, others said he was jilted by a young English girl and went crazy. The fact that he got the airplane into the air was an accomplishment in itself. Most USAF pilots couldn't even do that! The B-45 was the first USAF jet bomber and was very old and poorly designed. Almost everyone said that they were a piece of junk! At that time there were only six B-45s left in the USAF and they were all at Alconbury. When we had base 'Alerts' we usually could not get any of these planes in the air and even if one ever did manage to take off, you could bet it would always come back as an emergency.

Thus did Friday 13 June 1958 begin with the ending of five lives, the loss of three aircraft and who knows what impact on the life of one young woman.

As we saw in an earlier chapter, RAF Lakenheath had long been home to USAF fighters with 48 TFW in residence since the early 1960s. During what was described as 'a routine gunnery exercise', 492 TFS lost a pair of F-100D Super Sabres, 55-2792 and 55-2786, on Holbeach range on 15 July 1963. Their pilots were manoeuvring to start their 'hot' firing runs from the east, parallel with the shore, when the two jets collided and fell into the sea five miles off King's Lynn. One pilot, First Lieutenant L.C. Marshall, managed to eject from 2792 and was winched, unhurt, from his drifting dinghy by a rescue helicopter. First Lieutenant. D.F. Ware in 2786 failed to eject and died in his aircraft.

Piper Pawnee 235, G-ASVX, in collision with XV493. (Tony Hancock)

McDonnell Douglas Phantom FGR2, XV493, in collision with G-ASVX. (Tony Hancock)

Sometimes, sadly, it takes a disaster to bring into the open procedural weaknesses that these days might seem common sense issues. Such an event occurred on the afternoon of 9 August 1974.

Piper PA25 Pawnee, G-ASVK, a crop-sprayer, was returning to its Bexwell operations centre, on the old wartime airfield of Downham Market, having completed the day's task of spraying potato fields not many miles away at Denver. Around the same time, RAF Phantom FGR2, XV493 from No.41 Squadron at Coningsby was airborne on a routine low-level navigation exercise taking it over Holbeach Range, Downham Market and back to Coningsby. The authorised altitude was not less than 250ft AGL and its speed was to be maintained at 420 knots. Civilian authorities were advised of the Pawnee working in the area and as it was in a recognised military low-flying area, RAF Marham, the nearest RAF airfield, had been notified earlier in the year that aerial spraying would take place in the area from June to August. There was no requirement for either the military or the civil operators to notify each other of individual flights at specific times.

These two aeroplanes collided at 300ft over the Denver Sluice area and both were completely destroyed. The Phantom pilot, RAF Coningsby's station commander, Group Captain David Blucke, his navigator, Flight Lieutenant Terence Kirkland and Pawnee pilot, twenty-four-year-old New Zealander, Paul Hickmott, were all killed outright.

Put simply, the official cause of the crash was that neither pilot saw the other aircraft in time to avoid a collision, but the 'see and be seen' principle of airmanship was inadequate for the circumstances of this incident. A significant contributing factor was said to be the absence of any effective procedural system for co-ordinating military and civil low-flying activities in known low-flying areas and link routes. The Deptartment of Trade's report went on to make recommendations about high-visibility paint schemes and strobe anti-collision lights for civilian aeroplanes operating in such areas, but the main recommendation was for wider publication of military low-flying routes in the UK. Furthermore, closer liaison between

Tornado GR1, ZA321 'B-58' of the TTTE at RAF Cottesmore, similar to the aircraft that was in the collision over Mattersey in 1999.

military and civilian aviation authorities was considered essential if this type of accident was to be prevented in the future.

There were other incidents similar to this one, but perhaps it is a measure of the effectiveness of changes in procedure that it was not until the 1990s that such incidents again hit the headlines. Among these, single military/civil incidents occurred elsewhere in the UK in 1991 and 1993 while one example happened in this region on 21 January 1999. Cessna 152, G-BPZX and Tornado GR1, ZA330, coded B-08, collided over the village of Mattersey (Nottinghamshire) with the loss of all four occupants: James Robinson and Richard Bowskill in the Cessna and Flight Lieutenant Greg Hurst (RAF) and Tenente Mattio De Carlo (Italian AF) in the Tornado.

RAF Cottesmore had for some time been home to the Tri-national Tornado Training Establishment (TTTE) and similarly, the former wartime airfield at Gamston had for many years provided civilian flying training and facilities for business and private flying operations. At 11.25a.m. ZA330 took off from Cottesmore and began the low-level segment of a routine training sortie. The MoD investigation report stated:

> … and six minutes later the crew began a routine check of their cockpit instruments. Whilst they were conducting this check, at a speed of 435 knots and an altitude of 650 feet, ZA330 collided with the Cessna.

It was alleged that the Cessna pilot had not filed a flight plan with ATC nor used the Civil Aircraft Notification Procedure (CANP) before setting out at 11.00a.m. on what was believed to be an aerial photography sortie from Gamston Airfield. According to witnesses on the ground, the Cessna was seen circling the villages of Mattersey and Mattersey Thorpe for six to eight minutes prior to the collision.

The military investigation concluded that the accident was caused by the failure of both crews to see each other in time to take avoiding action, and it is interesting to note that 'the limitations of the "see and avoid" principle' were again listed as a factor. Among the recommendations made were that military and civil aircraft operating below 2,000ft should be fitted with a collision warning system 'with all possible haste', and that there should be a more effective system of exchanging information about military and civil low-flying operations. The information exchanges have been implemented but – probably due to the economic issues involved – there is no sign yet of collision warning systems in small civil aircraft of this type.

There were a number of military collisions after the 1974 incident, involving a variety of aircraft types, one of the most devastating of which was that over Wisbech in 1979. RAF Wittering is well known as the 'Home of the Harrier', and until recent years, was principal base for the RAF ground-attack and close support role, fulfilled by the BAe (formerly Hawker Siddeley) Harrier. The 1970s saw the GR3 version of this remarkable aeroplane being operated by No.1 Squadron and ever since, there are few days even now when Harriers are not seen transiting the Fens to and from The Wash ranges, with a nice little bit of aerobatics and dog-fighting thrown in for good measure!

Former Red Arrows leader Wing Commander Richard Duckett in XV757 and Flight Lieutenant C. Gowers in XZ128 were en route to the range at 8,000ft when their two aeroplanes collided over Wisbech on 9 September 1979. Both pilots ejected safely but unfortunately both Harriers then crashed into the populated area, one of them with devastating results. An aircraft fell on 5, 7 and 9 Ramnoth Road, demolishing three houses and causing the deaths of former mayor of Wisbech, Mr William Trumpess, Mr. Robert Bowers, and his two-year-old son Jonathan. Seven other civilians were injured.

BAe Harrier GR1, XV757 of the Harrier Operational Conversion Unit at RAF Wittering. Destroyed in a collision over Wisbech. (Tony Hancock)

Phantom FGR2, XT903 survived a collision near Billinghay on 14 April 1982. (Tony Hancock)

Phantom FGR2, XT912 destroyed in collision near Billinghay on 14 April 1982. (Tony Hancock)

The second Harrier fell in New Drove on the outskirts of the town, fortunately without causing further casualties.

It was shortly after the start of an air-defence training sortie that McDonnell Douglas Phantom FGR2, XT912 and XT903 clashed in mid-air between Walcott and Billinghay on 14 April 1982. The aircraft, from No.228 OCU at Coningsby, were crewed by Squadron Leader Guy Slocombe and his trainee navigator, Flight Lieutenant Richard George, while in XT903 were a trainee pilot and a staff navigator. Levelling out in a right hand turn at 1,000ft, Squadron Leader Slocombe, on the inside of the turn, dropped down and back to cross over to the left of XT903. As he accelerated to maintain contact XT912 pitched up of its own accord and hit the underside of the other aircraft. XT912s cockpit canopies shattered and the Phantom rolled to the left, vibrating violently. Slocombe and George ejected safely from XT912 before it nose dived and exploded in a ploughed field near the village of Walcott. They were soon packed off to RAF Hospital Nocton Hall with slight back injuries. Debris from the explosion rained down close to the village, smashing through a barn, damaging a car and some crops. Houses were shaken by the blast, but the only person to be hurt on the ground was Mrs Jenny Pearson who sustained bruising of the hip when she was hit by a piece of flying Perspex. XT903 suffered damage to the right wing and tailplane and lost its starboard drop tank. Nursing his aircraft upwards, the pilot jettisoned the other drop tank over the sea then made it back safely to Coningsby. He was awarded the Queens Commendation for Valuable Service In the Air in December 1982.

Flight Lieutenant John Leeming played an active part in the air fighting during the Falklands conflict only to lose his life in a routine training sortie when he returned to England. He began flying the Harrier in 1979 and it was due to his experience and flying ability that he was posted for combat duty.

On 21 May 1982, during the landings at San Carlos Bay, he was on loan to the task force from No.3 Squadron RAF and flying as wingman to Lieutenant Clive Morrell RN. During what later became known as the Battle of Falkland Sound, they were scrambled from HMS *Hermes* for a Combat Air Patrol (CAP) and tried, unsuccessfully, to contact the air controller on board HMS *Brilliant*. There was a lot of chatter on the radio but eventually Lieutenant Commander 'Sharkey' Ward, CO of No.801 Squadron, advised Morrell of the general situation.

Morrell, flying XZ457, could see the flash of bombs near the stricken HMS *Ardent*, then spotted three Argentinian Skyhawks flying at low level, conspicuous against the grey sea. He advised wingman John Leeming, in XZ500, about the Skyhawks and both Sea Harriers set off in pursuit at wave-top height. Flight Lieutenant Leeming tried to arm his Sidewinder missiles but, having only flown a Sea Harrier fitted with AIM 9 Sidewinders once before, he could not find the correct switches at this crucial moment. The switch positions were quite different to those with which he was familiar on the RAF Harriers so he decided to attack with his two 30mm Aden cannon. Leeming latched onto the tail of one of the A-4s and opening fire at 800yds firing short bursts all the time, he closed the range to 100yds and the Skyhawk exploded. Meantime, Morrell also downed one A-4 and damaged another so severely that it staggered only as far as Port Stanley before crashing. By the end of the conflict, John Leeming was also credited with the destruction of an Argentinian helicopter on the ground. It is believed his Skyhawk 'kill' was an AAF A-4C flown by Teniente Lopez, who ejected but subsequently died.

On his return to England, Flight Lieutenant Leeming was posted to No.233 OCU as an instructor, and for a sortie on morning of 23 February 1983, he was briefed to carry out combat manoeuvres with a student Harrier pilot. John Leeming took off with Flying Officer David Haigh in two-seat Harrier T4, XW926 and they met up with another instructor, Flight Lieutenant David Oakley, in Harrier GR3, XV795, high over the countryside near Peterborough.

Harrier GR3, XV795 in collision near Peterborough. (Tony Hancock)

At the commencement of their fourth simulated combat engagement, the two aircraft turned towards each other at 10,000ft. The T4 seemed to be going to cross the GR3 path to pass down its port side but in fact they ended up pointing at each other. Despite Flight Lieutenant Oakley taking rapid avoiding action, the aircraft collided. Leeming and Haigh died instantly but Oakley ejected with only minor injuries. The wreckage of XW926 came down in open land on Catwater Farm, Thorney and that of XV795 near Pioneer Garage on the outskirts of Eye, near Peterborough.

The Thorney area witnessed another collision when on 10 December 1986, two Tornado GR1s from No.617 Squadron at RAF Marham took off at 6.00p.m. on a night close-formation sortie to Scotland. The formation leader in ZA605 was settling onto a northerly heading at 6,500ft and instructed the number two, ZA611, 500ft below and two miles astern, to join him in close formation. It was during the close-up manoeuvre, about five miles from March (Cambridgeshire) that ZA611 hit the underside of ZA605 and sent it out of control. The crew of '605, Flight Lieutenants R.P. Lewis and A.M. Randall, ejected safely before the aircraft crashed onto farmland a mile and a half north of Thorney, while the crew of '611, steering well clear of built up areas, returned to base intact.

National and local press made quite a fuss about Tornado accidents and low flying in general, reporting, for example, that in the five years since its introduction in 1981, eleven Tornado aircraft had been lost in accidents. Ten years later, in 1996, the former Tornado navigator and author John Nichol, in a preface to one of his books, noted:

> In the five years between January 1991 and May 1996, eighty-three military aircraft were lost in crashes during training, resulting in the loss of over seventy lives. Eighteen of the aircraft were Tornados.

Harrier T4, XW926 in collision near Peterborough. (A. Pearcy)

As always with statistics, such figures need to be put into some kind of perspective. Throughout the twentieth century, British governments have declined to publish military accident information relating to hours flown on the – quite reasonable – grounds that such crude statistics mean very little and because every incident is thoroughly investigated and actioned upon in its own right. However, the following raw data about a small selection of RAF aircraft non-combat losses may be of interest:

Type	In service period	Years	Quantity in service	Destroyed	%
Tornado	1980 to present (2010)	29	401	55	14
Harrier/Sea	1969 to present	40	252	94	37
Phantom	1968 to 1992	24	180	54	30
Lightning	1960 to 1988	28	251	125	50
Hunter	1954 to 1995	41	977	277	29
Meteor (1-10)	1944 to 1982	36	2318	774	33

Data from *Directory of Britain's Military Aircraft*

The Tornado figure includes two F3s, ZE166 'AF' and ZE862 'AB', both from No.56 (R) Squadron at RAF Coningsby, which scattered wreckage over a ten-mile area of Digby Fen when they collided on 10 January 1996. ZE166 took off separately to take up a position acting as target aircraft for two more F3s, ZE862 and another that together would engage it in a co-ordinated interception. During the ensuing simulated missile attacks, the starboard wings of two of the F3s collided and substantial pieces of the wings broke away causing both aircraft to become uncontrollable. Despite one crew sustaining major injuries, once again the airmen's reactions and their escape systems worked magnificently to save their lives, and the aircraft came down in open ground at Rowston, near Metheringham and Ewerby, near Sleaford.

In the area covered by this book, seventy-four collision incidents have been traced since 1916, although not all have been examined. The numbers are as follows:

First World War:	5
Inter-war:	11
Second World War:	37
Post war:	21

It should never be forgotten, however, that they claimed the lives of 261 military personnel from among the crews and passengers on board the 148 aeroplanes involved. Six civilians also died on the ground as a direct result of these crashes – which in view of the odds, is a remarkably small number. Thankfully, in the context of the vast quantity of military air movements in modern times, mid-air collision remains a very rare occurance.

Tornado F3, ZE258 'AQ' of No.56 (R) Squadron, RAF Coningsby, the type involved in the collision on 10 January 1996.

Those involved in these events were just fallible human beings: airmen, soldiers and civilians going about their duty. In an instant they found themselves on a very fine line separating bad luck from good luck where, very often, just a few seconds here or a few feet one way or another made all the difference. Now their stories are no longer such a little-known part of the aeronautical history of this region.

BIBLIOGRAPHY

BOOKS

Allen, Michael (1999) *Pursuit Through Darkened Skies*, Airlife

Andrews, C.F. & Morgan E.B. (1989) *Vickers Aircraft Since 1908*, Putnam

Bagley, G.S. (1986) *Boston, Its Story and People*, Bagley

Bishop, Cliff T. (1986) *Fortresses Of The Big Triangle First*, East Anglia Books

Barnes, C.H. (1964) *Bristol Aircraft Since 1910*, Putnam

Blake R., Hodgson M. & Taylor W. (1984) *Airfields Of Lincolnshire Since 1912*, Midland Counties

Barker, Ralph (1965) *The Thousand Plan*, Chatto & Windus

Bennett, Tom (1986) *617 Squadron, The Dambusters At War*, Patrick Stephens

Bowman, Gerald (1955) *Jump For It, Stories of the Caterpillar Club*, Evans Bros

Bowman, Martin W. (1986) *Castles In The Air*, Patrick Stephens

Bowman, Martin (1989) *The Wellington*, Airlife

Bowman, Martin W. (2008) *RAF Marham, Bomber Station*, The History Press

Bowyer, Chaz (1985) *Tales From The Bombers*, W Kimber

Bowyer, Michael J.F. (1987) *Action Stations, Military Airfields of Cambridgeshire*, PSL

Bowyer, Michael J.F. (1987) *Action Stations, Vol 2*, PSL

Boyd, George (2002) *Boyd's War, Story of RNVR Fighter Pilot in WW2*, Colourprint Books

Boyle, Andrew (1955) *No Passing Glory, Biography of Leonard Cheshire*, Collins

Brett, R. Dallas (1928?) *History Of British Aviation, Vols 1&2*, Aviation Book Club

Brickhill, Paul (1951) *The Dam Busters*, Evans Bros

Brickhill, Paul (1954) *Reach For The Sky, Douglas Bader his life story*, Collins

Brookes, Andrew (1988) *Handley Page Victor*, Ian Allan Ltd

Bruce, J.M. (1987) *Britains First Warplanes*, Arms and Armour Press

Caine, Philip D. (1998) *American Pilots In The RAF*, Brassey's

Caygill, Peter (2002) *Jet Jockeys*, Airlife

Cole, Christopher & Cheesman, E.F. (1984) *Air Defence Of Britain 1914-1918*, Putnam

Cooper, Alan (1991) *Beyond The Dams To The Tirpitz, Later Ops Of 617 Sqn*, Goodhall

Cummings, Colin (1999) *Lost To Service, RAF Aircraft Losses 1959-1996*, Nimbus

Davies, Jim (1995) *Winged Victory*, R J Leach & Co

Douglas, Sholto (1966) *Years of Command*, Collins

Dye, Peter (1997) *RNAS Training Establishment Cranwell, Casualties 1916-1919*, Dye

Ellis, P.B. & Schofield J. (2003) *By Jove, Biggles! The Life of Captain W. E. Johns*, Norman Wright (limited reprint)

Falconer, Jonathan (1992) *RAF Bomber Airfields Of World War 2*, Ian Allan

Falconer, Jonathan (1995) *Stirling Wings*, Sutton Publishing

Finn, Sid (1973/1983) *Lincolnshire Air War, Books 1&2*, Aero Litho Co.

Franks, Norman (1978) *Fighter Leader, The Story of W/C I.R. Gleed DSO DFC*, Kimber

Franks, Norman (1988) *Valiant Wings*, William Kimber

Franks, N., Giblin, H. & McCrery, N. (1995) *Under The Guns Of The Red Baron*, Grub Street

Freeman, Roger (1970) *The Mighty Eighth*, MacDonald & Jane's

Gibson, Michael (1980) *Aviation In Northamptonshire*, Northamptonshire Libraries

Goodrum, Alastair (1997) *Combat Ready!*, GMS Enterprises

Goodrum, Alastair (2005) *No Place For Chivalry*, Grub Street

Halley, James J. (1980) *The Squadrons Of The Royal Air Force*, Air-Britain

Halpenny, Bruce Barrymore (1981) *Action Stations, Vol 1*, PSL

Hamilton, Alexander (1977) *Wings Of Night, Secret Missions of G/C Pickard DSO DFC*, William Kimber

Hancock, Terry (1978) *Bomber County*, Lincolnshire Library Service

Hancock, Terry (2008) *Directory Of Britain's Military Aircraft, vol 1*, The History Press

Harbour, Ken & Harris, Peter (2009) *The 351st BG In WWII*, 351 BG Association

Hastings, Max (1981) *Bomber Command*, Pan

Haugland, Vern (1980) *The Eagle Squadrons*, David and Charles

Hinrichs, Edward (1995/2004) *Missing Planes of the 452nd Bomb Group*, Trafford Publishing

Hoskins F., Robson R., & Meadley B. (2005) *From Blue To Grey; 54 Entry to RAFC*, Woodfield

Ingrisano, Michael N. (?) *Valor Without Arms, 316 TCG History 1942-1945*, Merriam Press

Jackson, A.J. (1990) *Avro Aircraft Since 1908*, Putnam

Jackson, A.J. (1962) *De Havilland Aircraft Since 1915*, Putnam

Jackson, Sqn Ldr K.R. (Jacko). (2006) *Fifty-Two Years In The Cockpit Vols 1&2*, Tucann

Jackson, Robert (1976) *Fighter Aces of World War 2*, Arthur Barker Ltd

Jackson, Robert (1980) *Bomber! Famous Bomber Missions of WW2*, Arthur Barker Ltd

James, Derek N. (1990) *Gloster Aircraft Since 1917*, Putnam

Johnson, AVM J.E. (1985) *The Story of Air Fighting*, Hutchinson

Johns, Capt W.E. (1935) *Biggles Learns To Fly*, Brockhampton Press Ltd

Jones, Geoffrey (1981) *Night Flight*, Kimber

Kelley, Maj David H. (2000) *They Too Served; Unit History 496FTG*, ACSC Marshall AFB.

King, H.F. (1990) *Sopwith Aircraft 1912-1920*, Putnam

Kuhl, George C. (1993) *Wrong Place! Wrong Time!*, Schiffer Publishing Ltd

Lincke, Jack *(1970) Jenny Was No Lady, Story of the JN-4D*, W.W. Norton

McLachlan, Ian (1989) *Final Flights*, Patrick Stephens

Mason, Francis K. (1969) *Battle Over Britain*, McWhirter

Mason, Francis K. (1991) *Hawker Aircraft Since 1920*, Putnam

Melrick, Michael T. *439 Tiger Squadron RCAF*, 1953 unpublished diary

Merrick, K.A. (1980) *Halifax, An Illustrated History of a Classic WW2 Bomber*, Ian Allen

Middlebrook, Martin (1980) *The Battle Of Hamburg*, Alan Lane

Middlebrook, Martin (1988) *The Berlin Raids*, Viking

Middlebrook M. & Everitt C. (1987) *The Bomber Command War Diaries*, Viking

Musgrove, Gordon (1976) *Pathfinder Force*, MacDonald & Jane's

Nichol, John (1996) *Point Of Impact*, Hodder & Stoughton

Noble, Marjorie (1987) *Thurlby, An Ordinary Village*, Noble

Oliver, David (1990) *British Military Aircraft Accidents, The Last 25 Years*, Ian Allan

Penrose, Harald (1969) *British Aviation, The Great War & Armistice 1915-1919*, Putnam

Pudney, John (1960) *A Pride Of Unicorns (David & Richard Atcherley of the RAF)*, Oldbourne

Ramsey, Winston, ed. (1987/1988) *The Blitz Then and Now, Vol 1, Vol 2*, After The Battle

Rennison, John (2003) *The Digby Diary*, Aspect Publishing

Richards, D. & Saunders, H. St G. (1974) *Royal Air Force 1939-1945, Vols 1-3*, HMSO

Robertson, Bruce (1964) *Lancaster, Story of a Famous Bomber*, Harleyford

Rochford, E.H. (1977) *I Chose The Sky*, Kimber

Sawyer, G/C Tom (1982) *Only Owls & Bloody Fools Fly At Night*, Kimber

Scutts, Jerry (1987) *Lion In The Sky, US 8AF Fighter Ops 1942-45*, Patrick Stephens

Searby, John (1991) *The Bomber Battle For Berlin*, Guild Publishing

Semple, Clive (2008) *Diary of a Night Bomber Pilot*, Spellmount

Shaw, Michael (1986) *No. 1 Squadron*, Ian Allan

Shores C., Franks, N. & Guest, R. (1990) *Above The Trenches*, Grub Street

Simpson, Flt Lt William (1942) *One of Our Pilots is Safe*, Hamish Hamilton

Smith, D.J. (1978) *Spitfire Crash Logs Vols 1 & 2*, Smith

Strong, Russell A. (1982) *First Over Germany, A History of the 306th Bomb Group*, Hunter Publishing Co.

Sturtivant, R. & Hamilton, J. (2007) *Flying Training & Support Units since 1912*, Air Britain

Sturtivant, R. & Page, G. (1992) *RN Aircraft Serials & Units, 1911-1919*, Air Britain

Terraine, John (1997) *The Right Of The Line*, Wordsworth Editions

Thetford, Owen (1957) *Aircraft Of The RAF Since 1918*, Putnam

Turnill, Reginald & Reed, Arthur (1980) *Farnborough, The Story of RAE*, Robert Hale

Wright, N.R. (1986) *The Book Of Boston*, Barracuda Books

Wynn, Kenneth G. (1989) *Men Of The Battle Of Britain*, Gliddon Books

JOURNALS AND NEWSPAPERS

Air Clues: RAF Flight Safety Journal

Air Link: Journal of the Lincolnshire Aviation Society

Bury Free Press

Cambridge Daily News

Cambridge Independent Press & Chronicle

Cambridgeshire Times

Daily Mail

Ely Standard

Flight magazine

King's Lynn Citizen

Lincolnshire Free Press

Lincolnshire Echo

London Gazette

Mildenhall Register, Newsletter of the 15, 149 & 622 Sqn Association

Peterborough Citizen

Piloteer: World War One magazine of RNAS Cranwell

REVI: bi-monthly Czech aviation magazine

Royal Observer Corps Magazine

Spalding & Lincolnshire Standard

Spalding Guardian

Stamford Mercury

Wisbech Advertiser

Wingspan magazine

INTERNET RESOURCES

Commonwealth War Graves Commission cwgc.org
Theaerodrome.com
RAFbombercommand.com
March Air Reserve Base web site
303 BG; 351 BG; 388 BG; 486 BG; 490 BG web sites
MoD Military Aircraft Accident Summaries
littlefriends.co.uk
warbirdsresourcegroup.org
armyairforces.com
ejection-history.org.uk
memories.384thbombgroup.com
92ndma.com
439 Sqn RCAF
polebrook.com
spaads.org (Canadian: Sabre Pilots Association Air Division Squadrons)

PUBLIC RECORDS

National Archives
MOD (Air Historical Branch), London
AIR class 27 for Squadron Operations Record books (ORB Form 540)
AIR class 28 for Station Operations Record books
AIR Class 50 for Combat Reports

NB. These have been consulted and Crown copyright material is drawn upon and/or reproduced with the permission of the Controller of HMSO and the Queen's Printer for Scotland.

INDEX

Visit our website and discover thousands of other History Press books.

www.thehistorypress.co.uk